DRAWING HORSES
SPECIAL EDITION

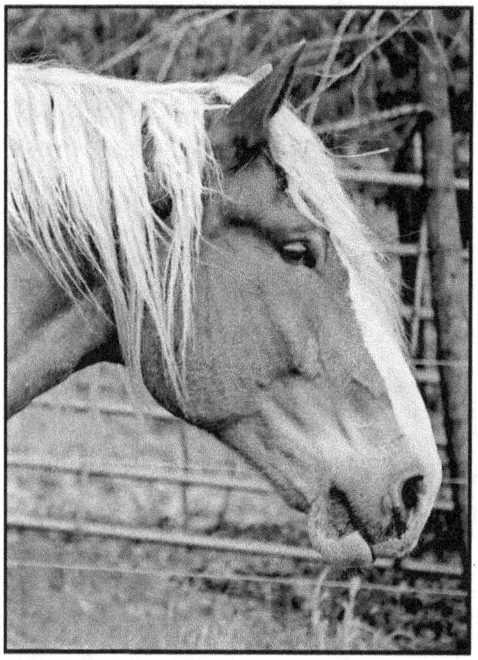

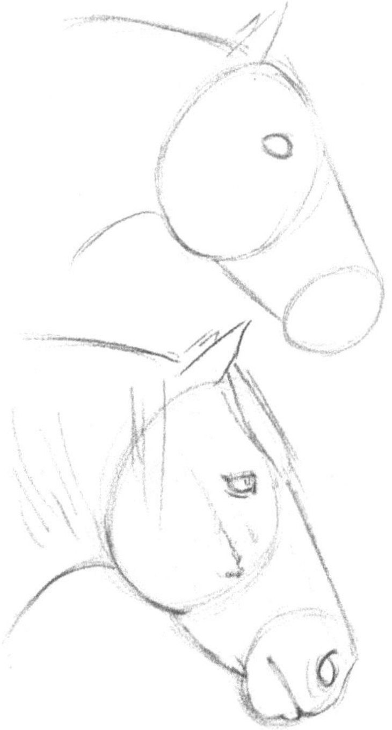

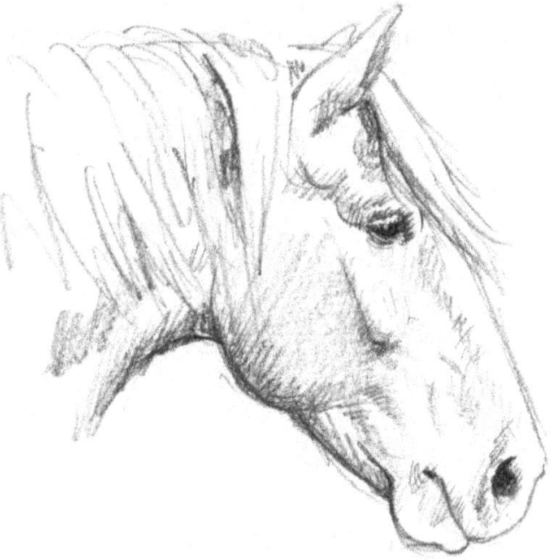

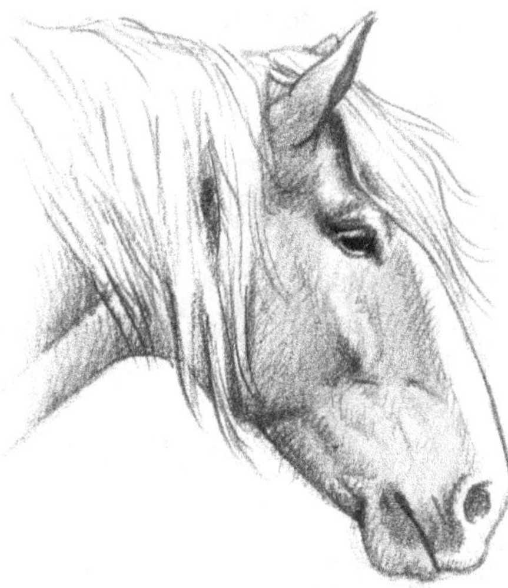

by Ruth Sanderson

A NOTE FROM THE ARTIST

I believe I am an artist today because of my lifelong love of horses. One of the best birthday presents I ever received was Walter Foster's *How to Draw Horses.* I was so excited by it I even held a class on drawing horses on Saturdays for my grade school friends.

Different artists each have their own way of approaching how to draw horses. This book is just one way. My method is based on the observation of real horses, usually ones I have photographed myself, so that the horses I draw and paint look like individuals. Horses come in many shapes, sizes, colors and breeds, and it is fun to be able to draw those differences, and to draw horses in different poses and actions, as I will demonstrate in this book.

If you live near a farm where you can draw horses from life, that is a great way to observe them, see how they move, touch them, and feel their structure. Horses don't usually stand perfectly still, so I suggest drawing them from life loosely with "gesture" sketches. We'll start this book with some gesture sketches, working just with loose lines. After you've been drawing horses awhile, these gesture drawings will feel more natural.

At the end of the 25 lessons in this special edition is a bonus section of 10 large reference photos of mares and foals. Use the methods that you've learned in this book and apply them to drawing the mares and foals.

Paper

Sketchbooks are handy because you can keep all your drawings in one place, but use whatever paper you can get your hands on. Copy paper is pretty smooth, so shading will not be quite as nice as sketch paper or drawing paper, both of which have a slight "tooth" or texture.

Pencils

A #2 "school" pencil is fine. It is basically the same thing as an HB pencil in an art brand. I usually use an HB (any brand) for basic sketching and drawing. F and H pencils are harder and make a lighter line, and sometimes I start with an F. If you find it difficult to erase, I suggest investing in an F or an H pencil. I use a B and 2B for dark areas. B is softer and darker than an HB, and higher B numbers are darker still.

Erasers

The erasers that come on the ends of #2 pencils almost **never** work well. The General brand makes a nice refillable pen-type eraser. I also love kneaded erasers. (Prismacolor is a good brand.) To clean them you simply stretch them out and knead them back into a lump when they get dirty. And if you get bored, you can make little scuptures out of them...

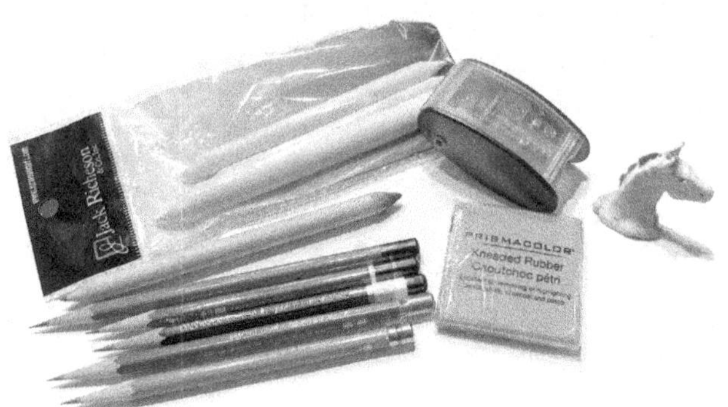

Sharpeners and blending tools

Any sharpener will do, though I prefer a long point for shading, so I use a KUM sharpener (shown) or an old electric brand like Panasonic, which sharpen to longer points than modern brands. I sometimes use a blending stump for smoothing pencil shading. They come in packages of various sizes.

My Graphite Pencil Drawing Hand Positions and Technique

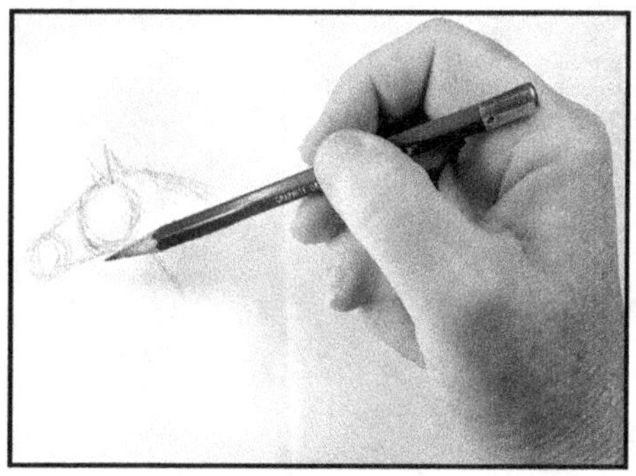

1

The important thing is to draw very lightly at first.

1. For my first sketchy marks I hold the HB or F (harder) pencil at least 2-3 inches from the lead, and move my fingers, wrist, and hand loosely to draw.

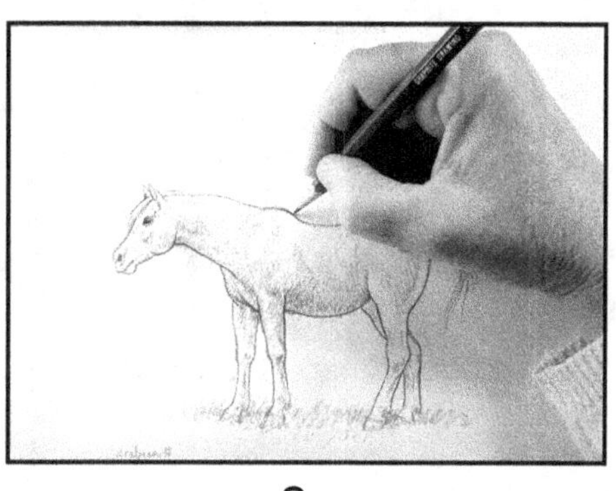

2

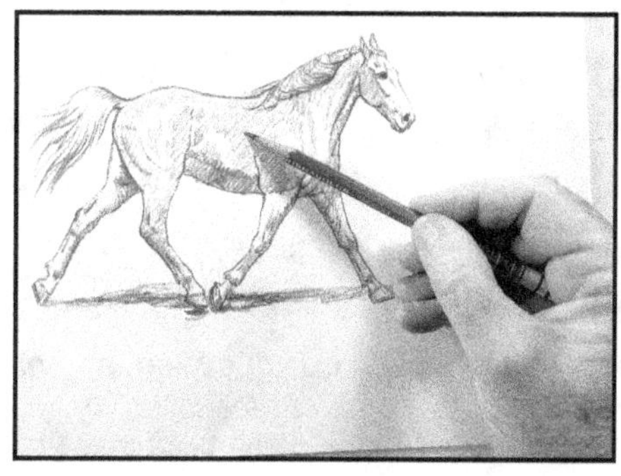

3

2. I sharpen the HB pencil frequently for outlines and hold it in a writing position, also using this for small details like eyes and ears. I sometimes use a sharp B for final details/outlines.

3. For the first stage of looser shading I hold my HB pencil away from the tip, rotating the end of the pencil into my palm, using a back and forth motion with my hand.

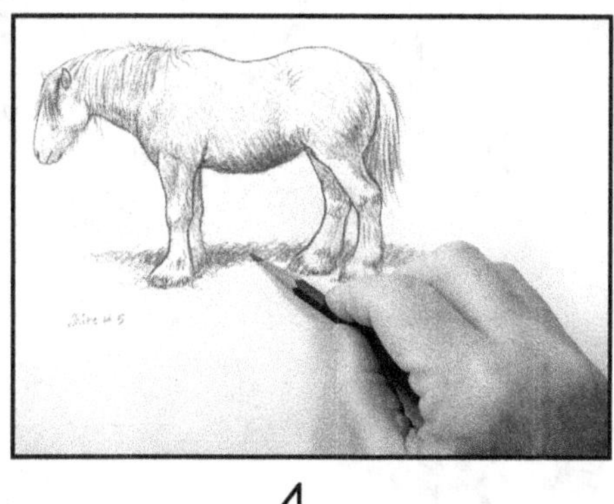

4

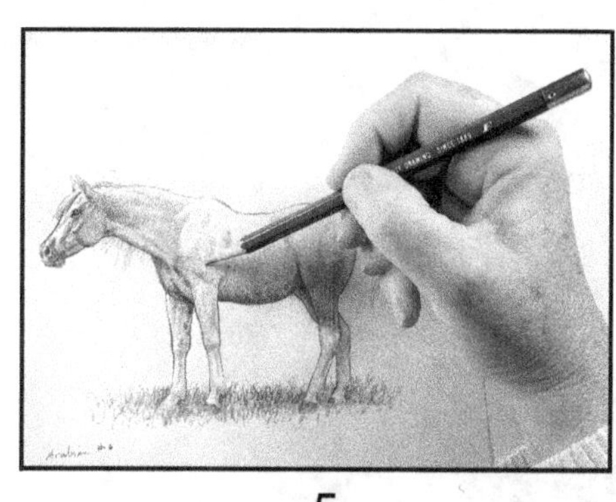

5

4. Sometimes I lay the HB pencil almost flat to create a wide, soft stroke, good for filling in big areas with an even tone, or to create loosely drawn grass and ground.

5. For final shading I hold the HB pencil away from the tip and use a combination of short and long close strokes following the form, some cross-hatching, and then even things out for a smooth look with strokes in a tiny circular motion. I build up the tone slowly with the HB first, then I use a B and/or a 2B for the darkest darks, saving that step for the end.

GESTURE DRAWING

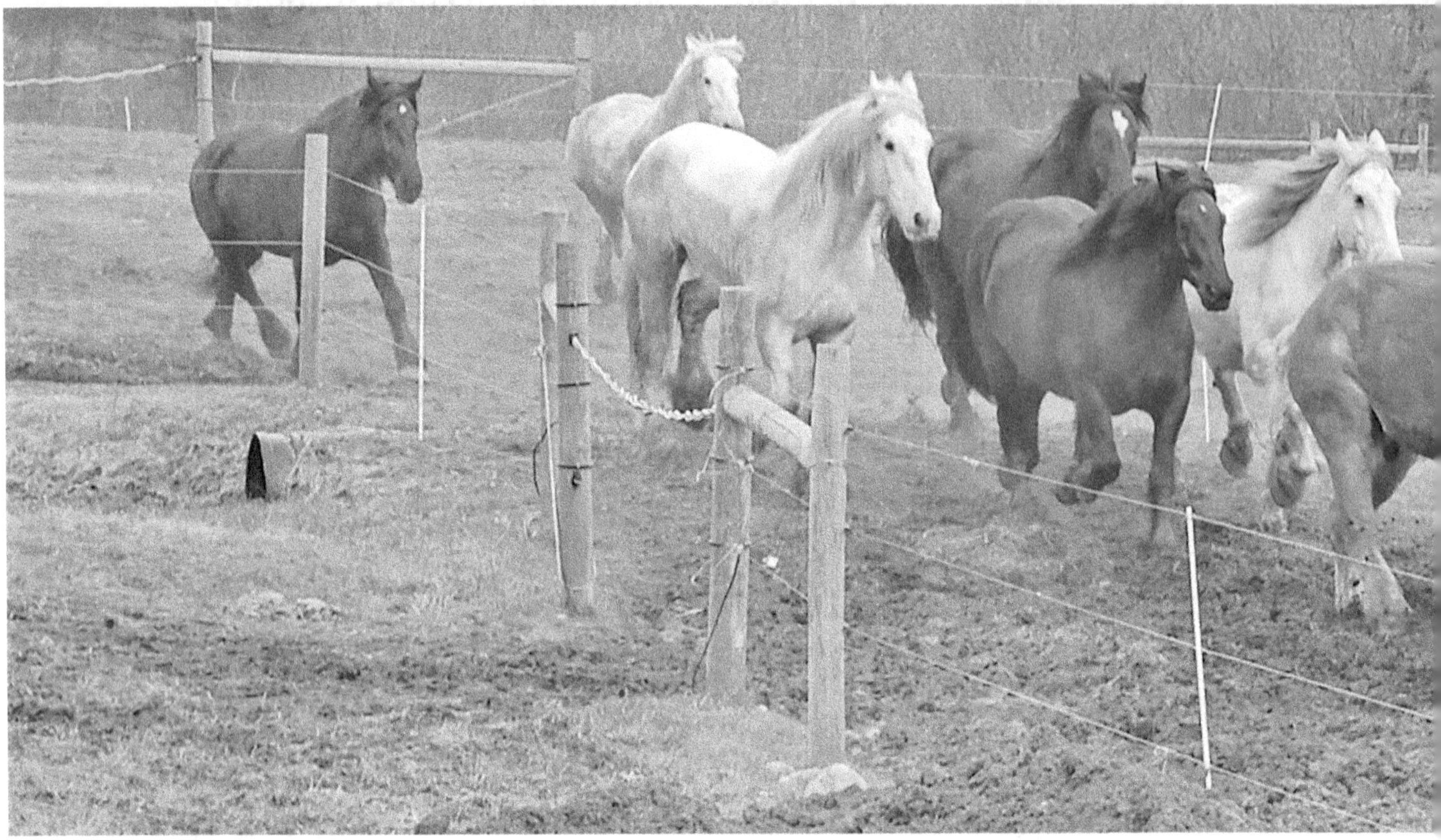

This is a good way to loosen up your hand, and have some fun. Use a pen or marker. Draw with loose, sketchy lines.

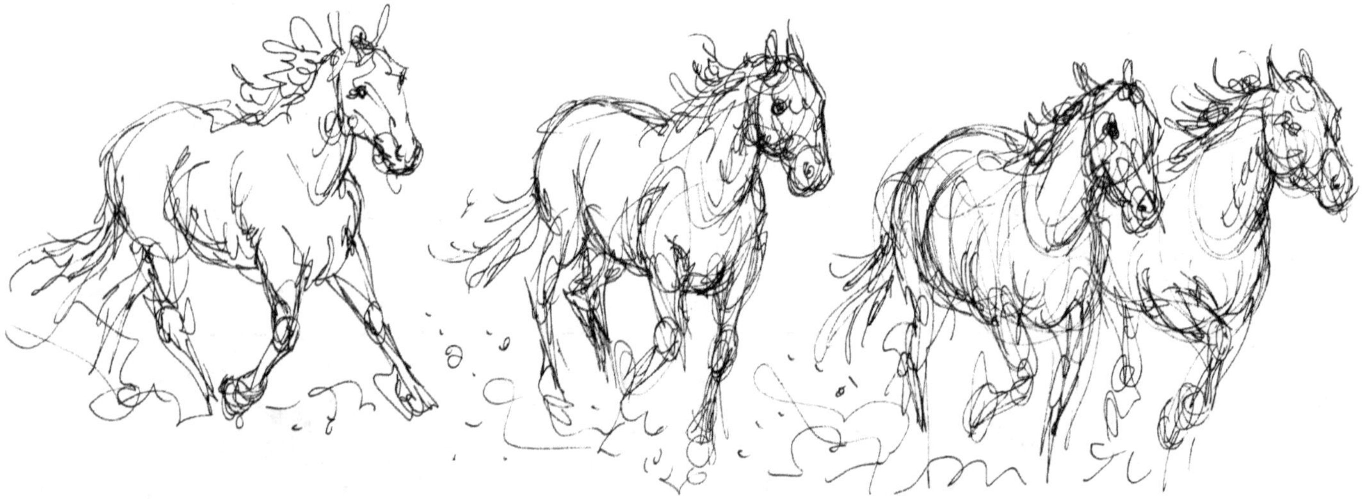

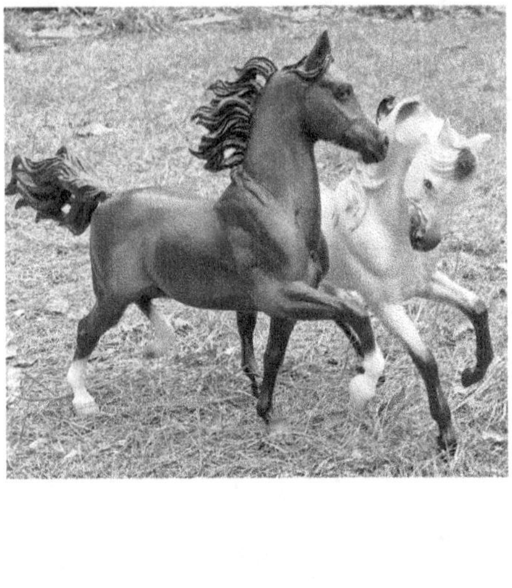

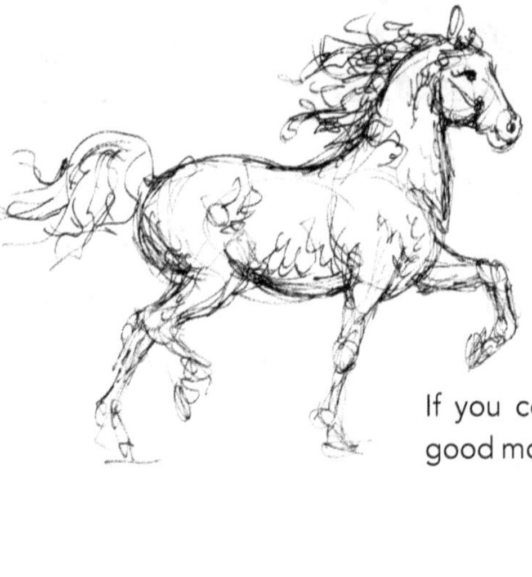

If you collect model horses, they make good models, and they tend to stand still!

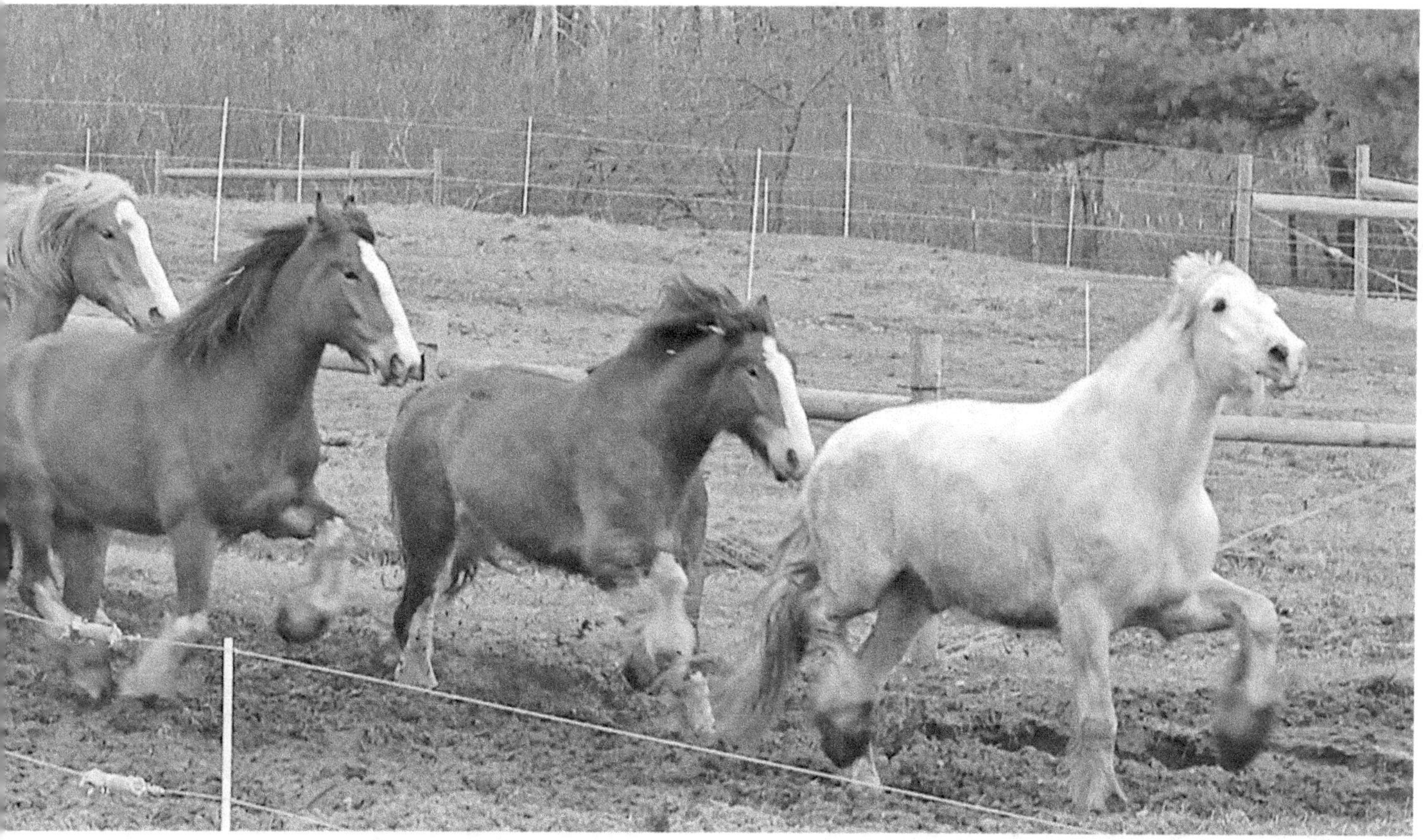

No erasing! Try to capture the spirit and "gesture" of the motion of the horses. Scribbling fast is good!

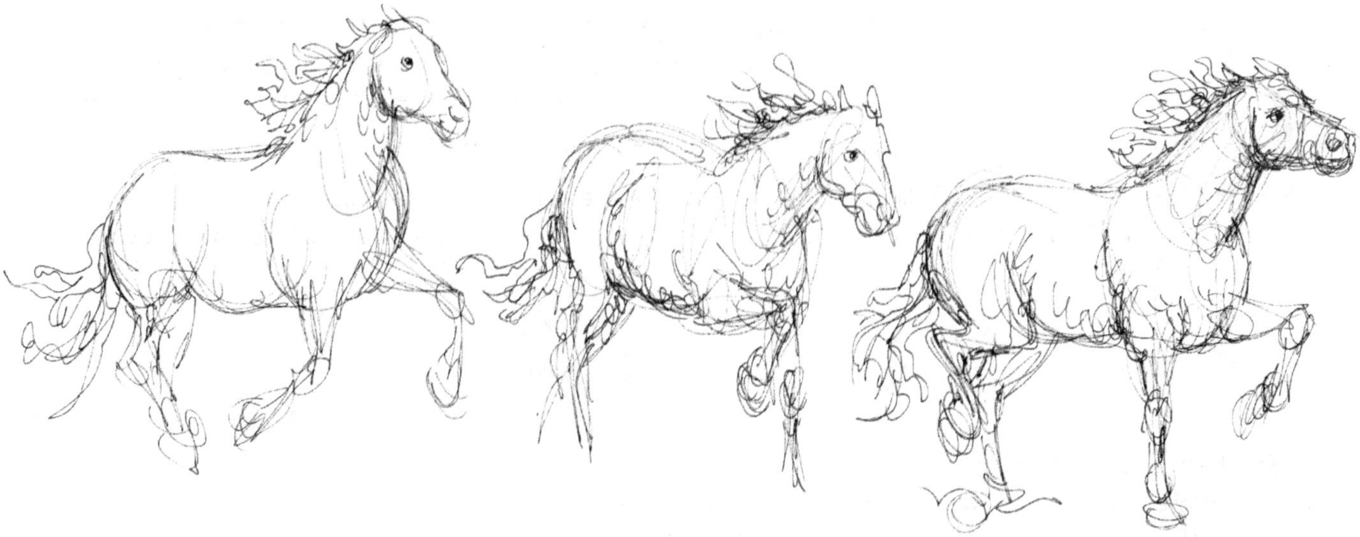

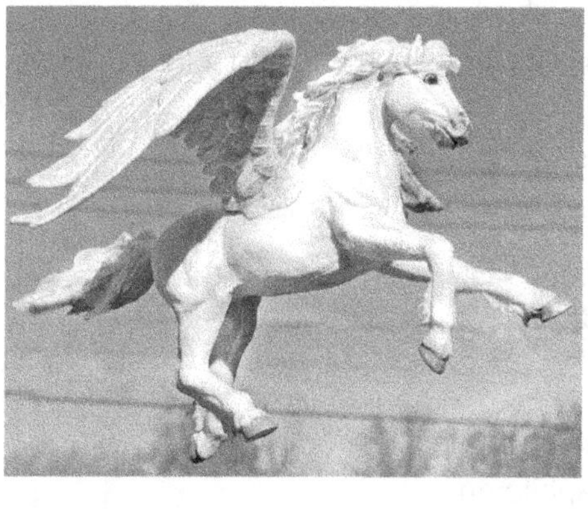

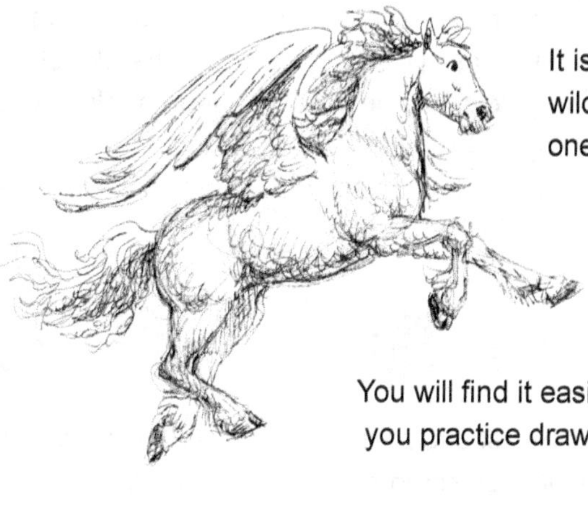

It is rare to spot a pegasus in the wild, but I was in luck when this one flew by our house.

You will find it easier to do gesture drawing after you practice drawing realistic horses for awhile.

REALISTIC DRAWING Basics

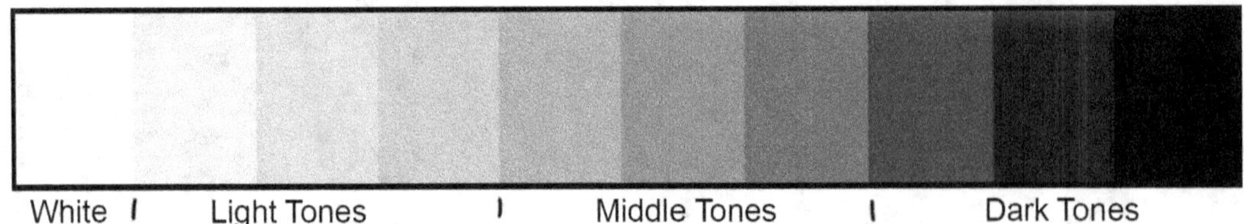

Values: Artists use the term "value" or "tone" to describe how light or dark a section of an object is, and you will find me using these words in my explanations of the steps of drawing realistic horses. Light creates form. When stong light falls on an object, it creates a shadow and a cast shadow. It helps to understand how light falls on basic shapes, such as a sphere, a box, a cylinder, and a cone in order to draw just about anything. I suggest you practice drawing these. Notice that there is often reflected light on the edge of the shadow side of curving objects. You will see this sometimes in horses, too. The reflected light is never as light as the light side of the object, however, so don't overdo it.

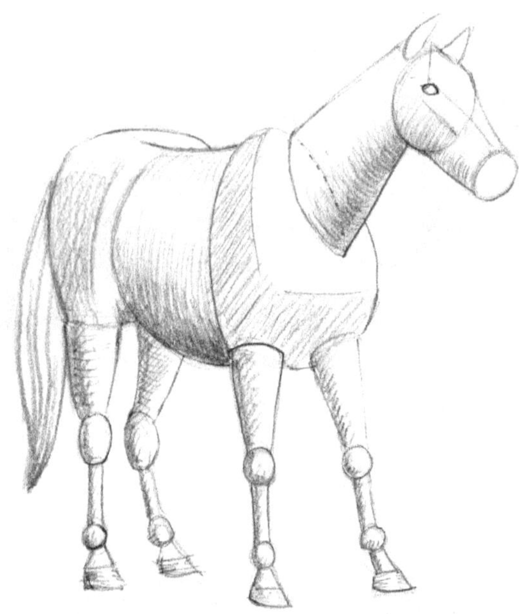

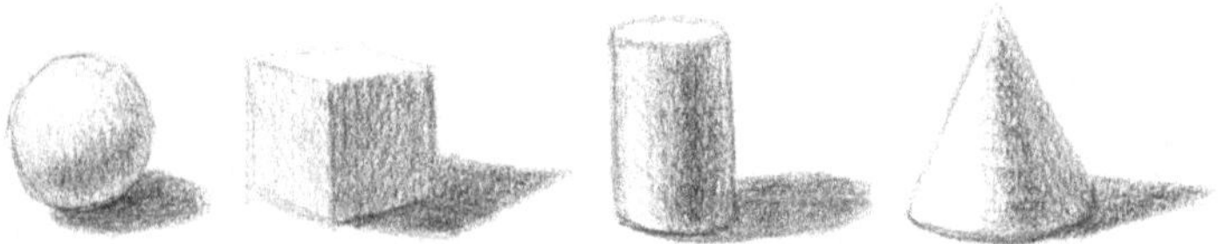

Objects, people, and animals can be simplified into versions of these basic shapes, so that an artist can look for similar shapes and interpret changes in value in a photo to be able to make the subject look more real and three-dimensional.

NOTE: The shadows on a light horse will fall in the range of light and middle values/tones, while the deepest shadows on dark horses will be closer to black. Highlights on dark horses are not actually white, they are usually light or middle tones. But a drawing is not a photo, and I aim for a realistic and pleasing interpretation, not an exact copy of a photo.

This block horse gives you a basic idea of light coming from overhead and in front of the horse. Try to see the simple shapes first in a photo, and if you always think of the horse as having dimension and form, it will help your drawing.

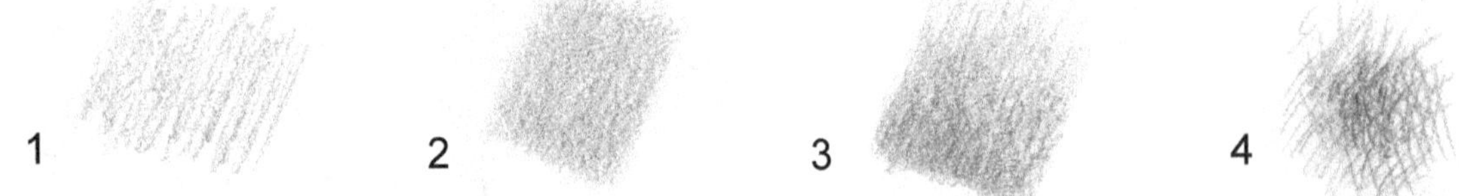

Pencil Strokes and Blending:

1. Start with parallel lines, called "hatching," using light even pressure.
2. Add more light-pressure strokes in the same direction to create an even tone.
3. Overlap and build up more strokes in the same direction to create gradations.
4. Sometimes for complex or darker areas I will add strokes in other directions, called "cross-hatching."
5. When the body part is a curving shape, I sometimes use short strokes to look like fur, with a curve to follow the form.
6. For soft changes in tone I use tiny oval strokes very close together.
7. Sometimes I use a blending stump and rub to smooth out pencil lines. (this is half blended.)

8. The residue on the stump can be used to softly shade other small areas that are white.
Clean the blending stump by rubbing on scrap paper if it gets too filled with graphite dust.

How to "Read" a Reference Photo

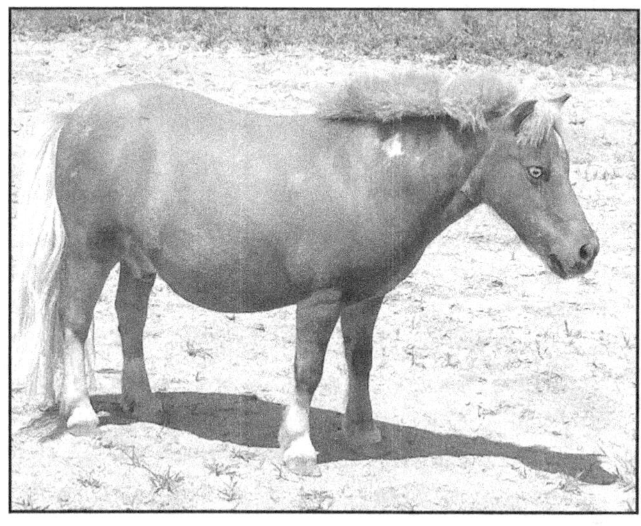

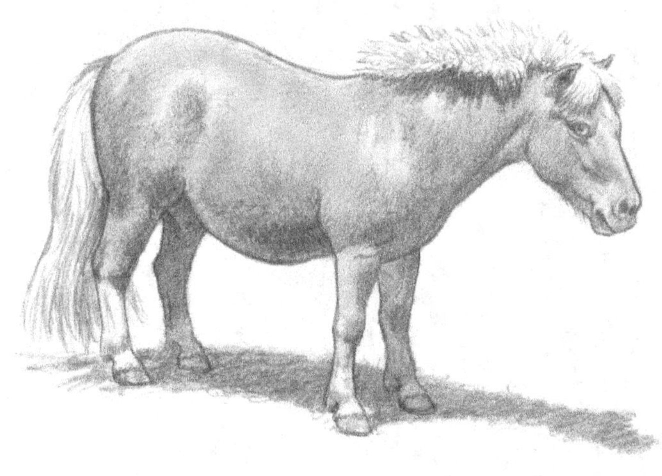

When you look at a reference photo, try to determine where the light is coming from. On bright sunny days there will be a strong cast shadow. Notice in this photo of a pony that the cast shadow is below him and to the right. This means the light is coming from above the viewer's left shoulder, since the side of the horse facing us is in the light. This is mid-day lighting, where the sun is almost directly overhead. It makes for nice lighting and strong shadows.

Imagine his belly as a ball and see how it looks similar to the shading on the ball shape on the left page. A shadow is created as his belly curves under, away from the light. On cloudy days, the shadows won't be sharp, and a horse's coat will look duller. Horses in strong sunlight are easier to draw to get a dimensional look.

I will often exaggerate the lighting effects in a drawing, making the horse appear a bit shinier than in the photo reference. The area around the point of the hip and the shoulder often have shiny highlights, and note how I have "pushed" them to be even shinier. As I said before, an artist's job is to interpret and not just reproduce a photo. I actually aim to make the drawing more interesting than the photo, and I try to capture the spirit of the horse.

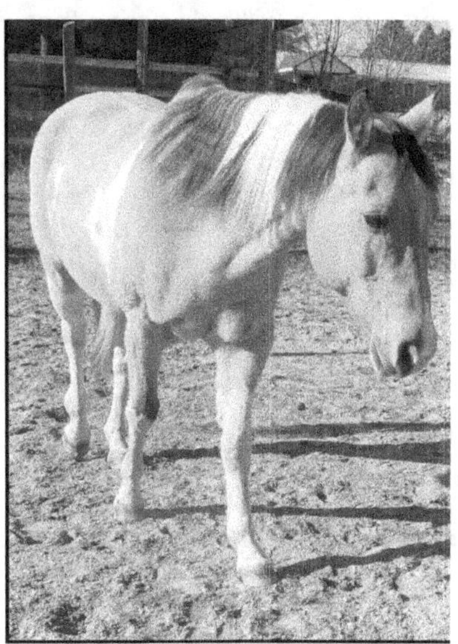

The photo on the left shows a typical camera distortion when taking a photo from the front of a horse. The head is always too big, the legs too short, the hind end looks much too small. Using a telephoto lens and standing further back helps. Professional artists using photos will often fix the distortions in Photoshop so the proportions look correct. The photo on the right is made up of at least three photos that I pieced together and adjusted until the pose felt right. Hind end is still a bit small.

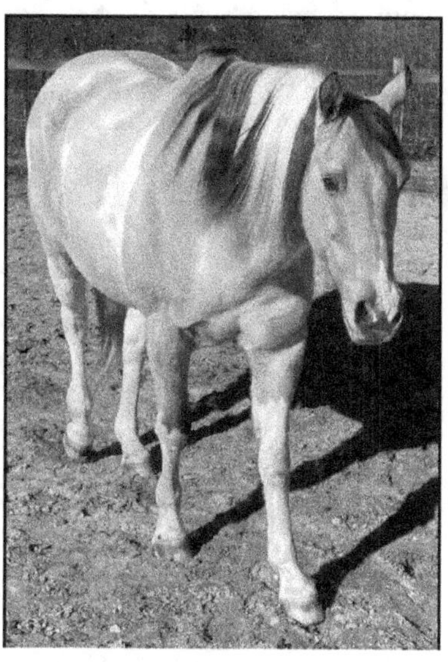

The long shadows mean the light is coming from the side, so there is no strong shadow under his belly. But there is a shadow on the right side of his legs, his chest, and his face. There are good highlights on his mane and coat.

HORSE HEAD Basics

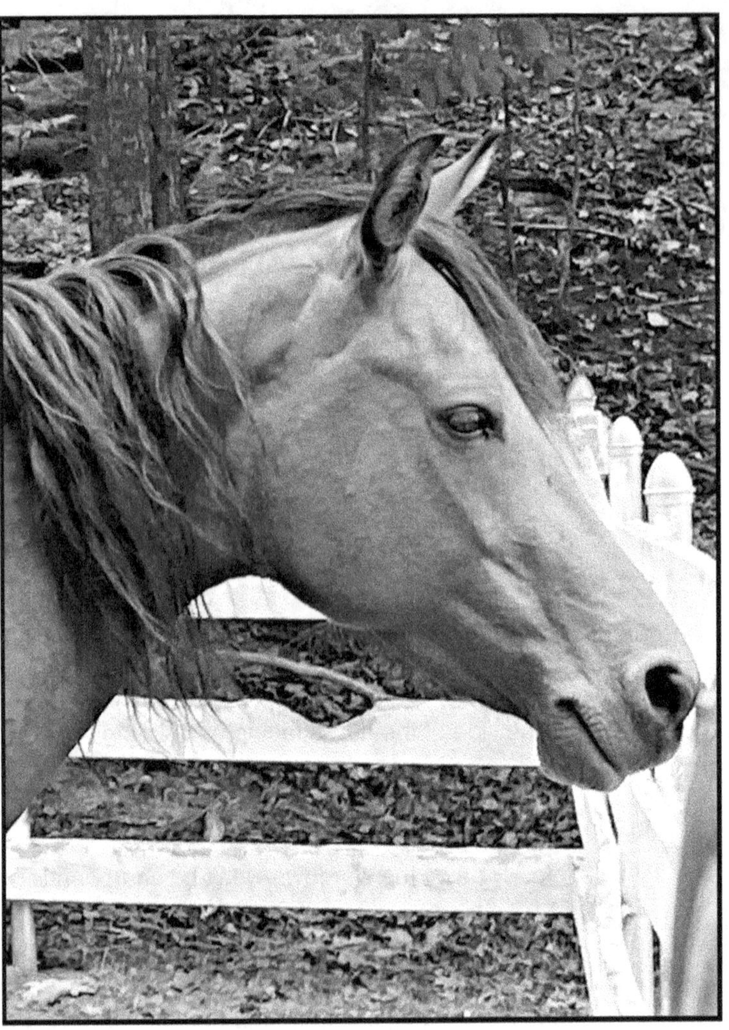

OBSERVATION is the key to realistic drawing.

EARS
Horse ears swivel forward and back and show their mood. Ears forward means they are alert, and interested in what is in front of them. They cock an ear back when paying attention to something behind them. Both ears flopped means they are relaxed. Ears flat back means they are mad! Look at the muscles below to understand how they do this.

EYES
Sometimes the eyelashes are prominent and hide part of the eye, sometimes they are light, and sometimes they don't show. Eyelids and creases differ. Study the details of each horse. Horses have a bony indentation above the eye that deepens with age. This is a young horse, so it is not too prominent.

MUZZLE
The muzzle is the term for the area that includes the nostrils, the mouth, and the chin. The nostrils make the shape of a 6. The mouth curves up slightly, but down right at the end. The chin is usually teacup shaped.

Study the shape of the features of each horse carefully. Like people, no two horses are identical.

PLANES of the face

Good lighting will help define the planes of the face. I always look for the straight bone at the top of the cheek, which is often defined sharply by a shadow below and light above. There are often prominent veins at the corner of the cheekbone. There are many muscles between the edge of the jaw and the muzzle. Careful obsevation and shading will help define these.

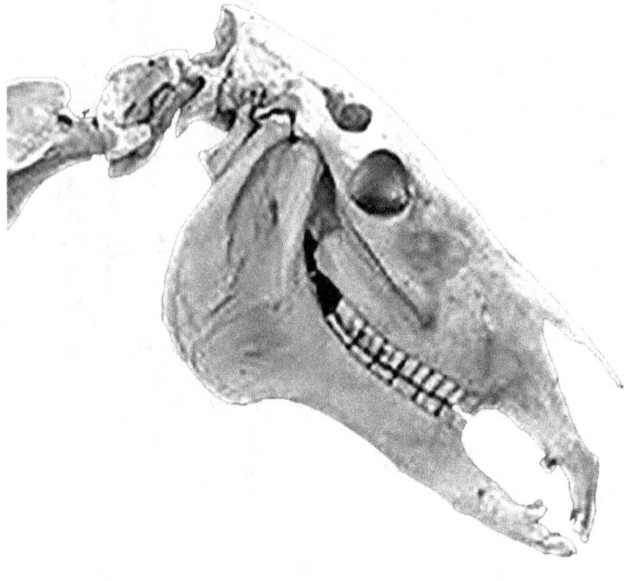

HORSE HEAD SKULL

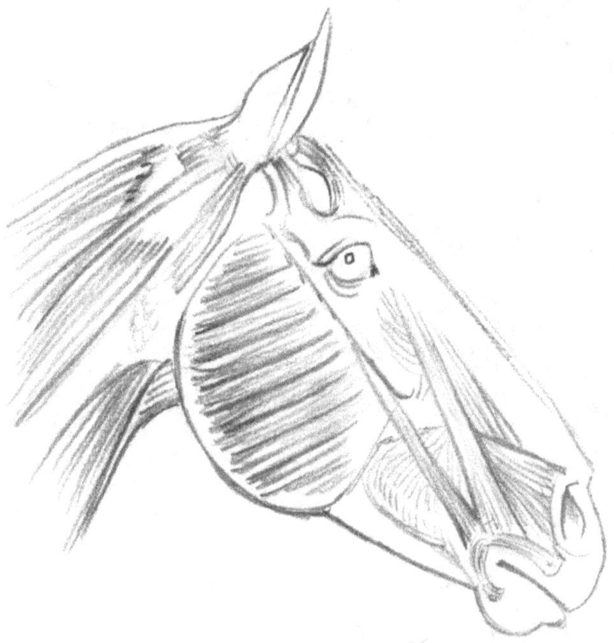

SURFACE MUSCLES of the HEAD

HORSE HEAD Details

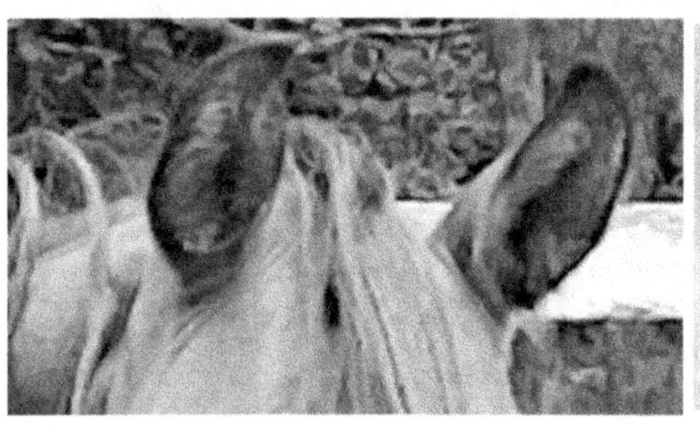 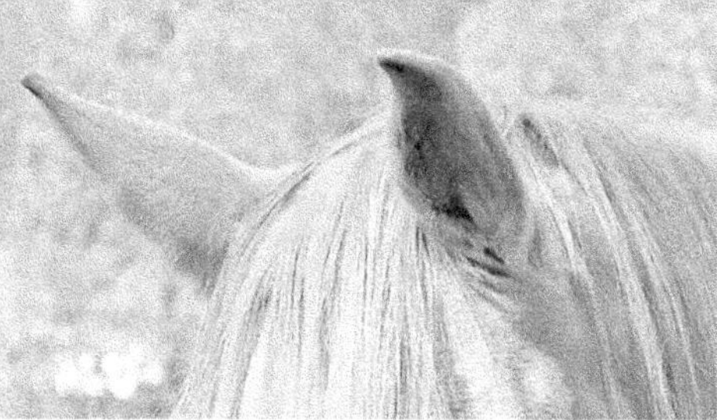 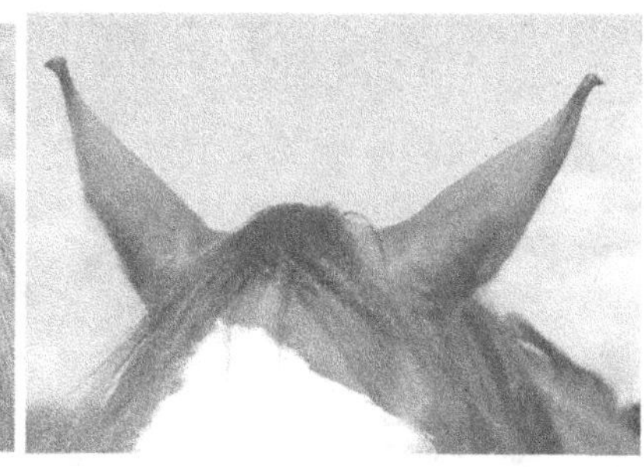

Some ears have a dark edge and usually lighter horses have a light one. Look for not only the shape of the inside of the ear, but the base of the ear that makes it swivel. Sometimes the mane or forelock covers it, but see if you can find it.

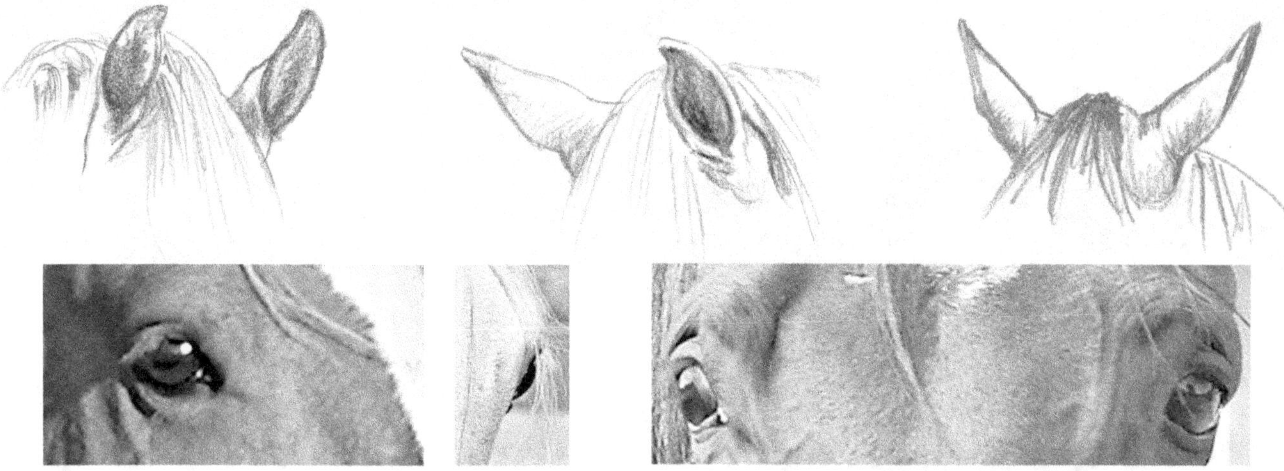

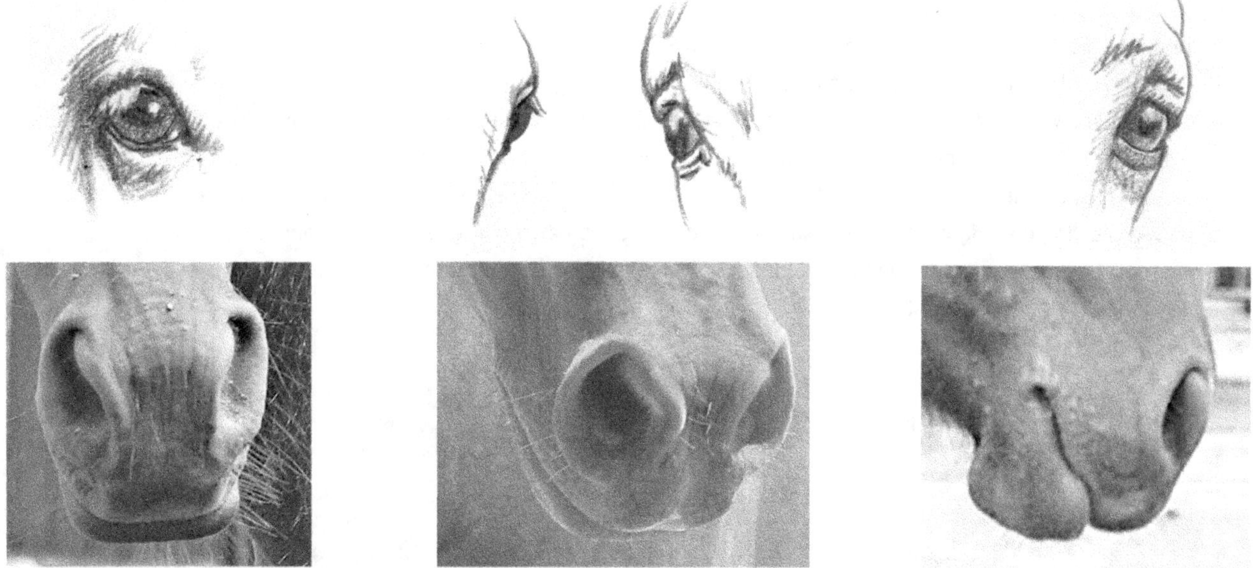

Eyes that show a white highlight really bring a spark of life to a drawing. When a photo of the eye is complex and very reflective (as the ones on the right are) sometimes I will simplify it, accenting with a light highlight.

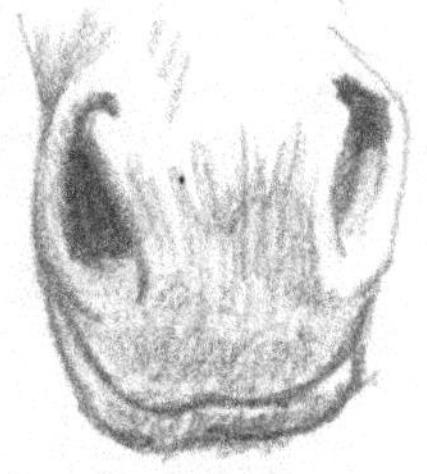 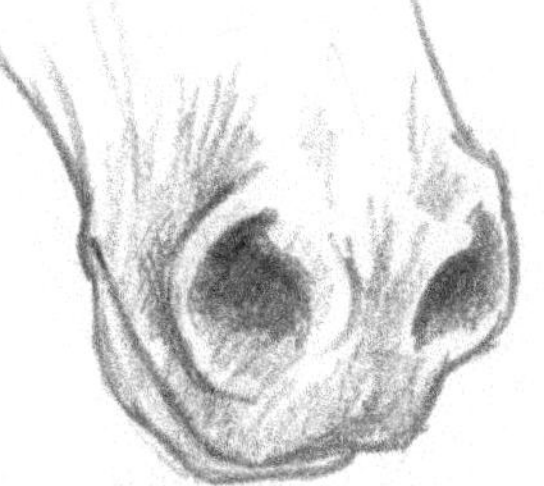 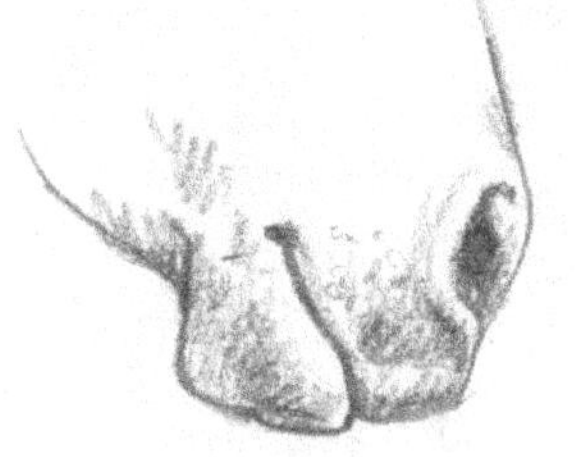

Nostrils are narrower at rest or when a horse is walking. On exertion the nostrils flare and widen to let in more air. Look for the subtle curves of the mouth that are different on each horse.

MORGAN

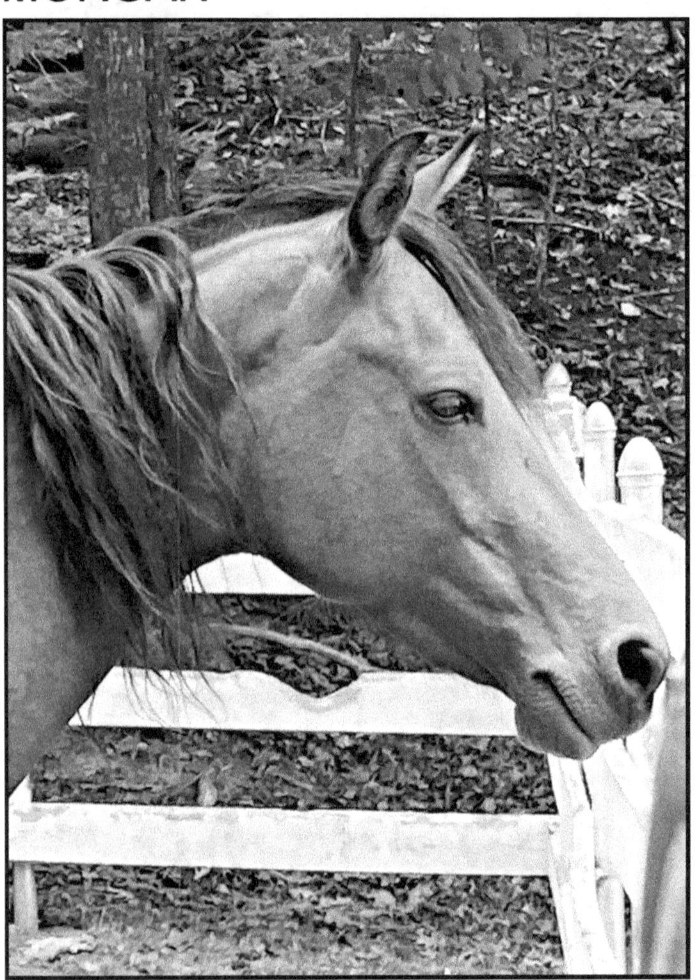

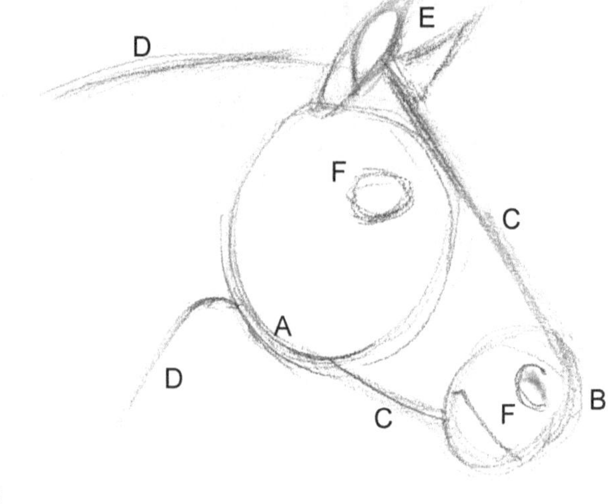

1. A. Start with a big oval, using the curve of the jaw for the shape.

    B. Draw a small oval for the muzzle area.

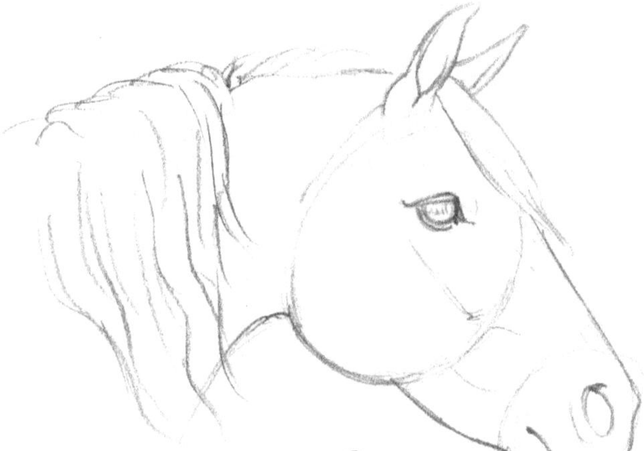

    C. Draw a line for the top of the face, and one between the cheek and the chin.

    D. Draw the top and bottom arching lines of the neck.

    E. Ears can be simple inverted Vs at first. For inside of near ear, draw an inverted teardrop, then add a tip pointing in, and the base.

    F. Draw an oval where the eye will go, a 6 for the nostril, and a slightly curved line for the mouth.

2. Study the photo and start refining each part of the face to match the lines and shapes you see, erasing initial guidelines. Indicate mane.

3. Draw the shapes creating the edges of shadow and fill in the shadow areas loosely. Darken eye and nose.

4. For a finished realistic look, carefully build up the shadows and details with an HB, then a B and/or 2B for darkest darks.

Follow these steps for all the head portraits.

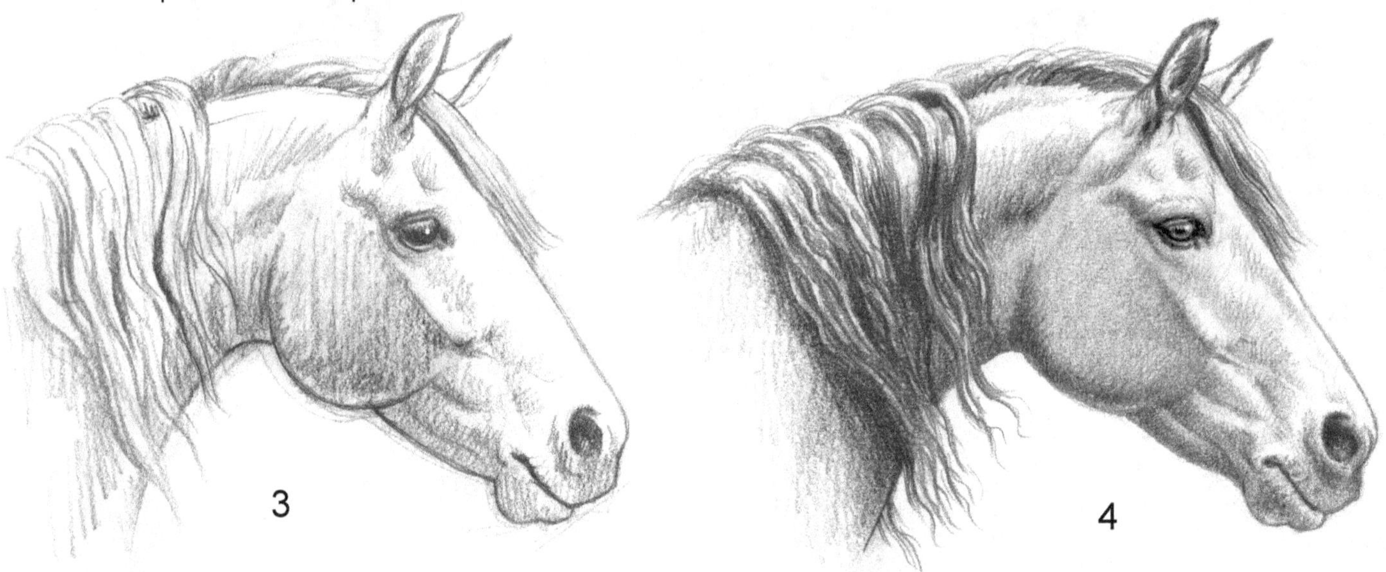

Use your eraser to pull out highlights and "clean up" any "dirty" areas. Use a blending stump if you want a smoother look.

BELGIAN

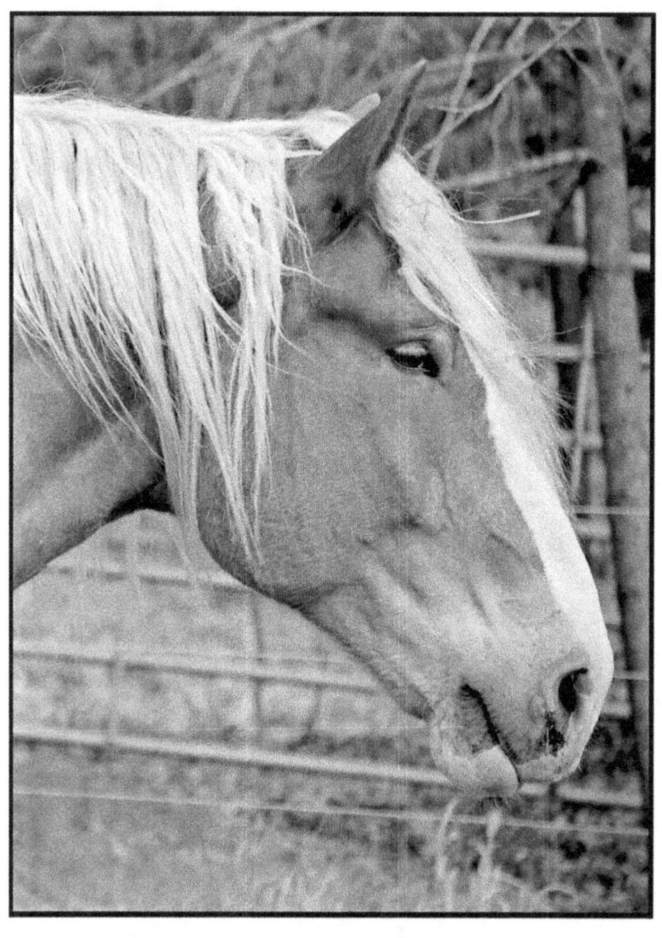

Notice the wider head of this big draft horse. That is a normal-sized eye on a very large head!

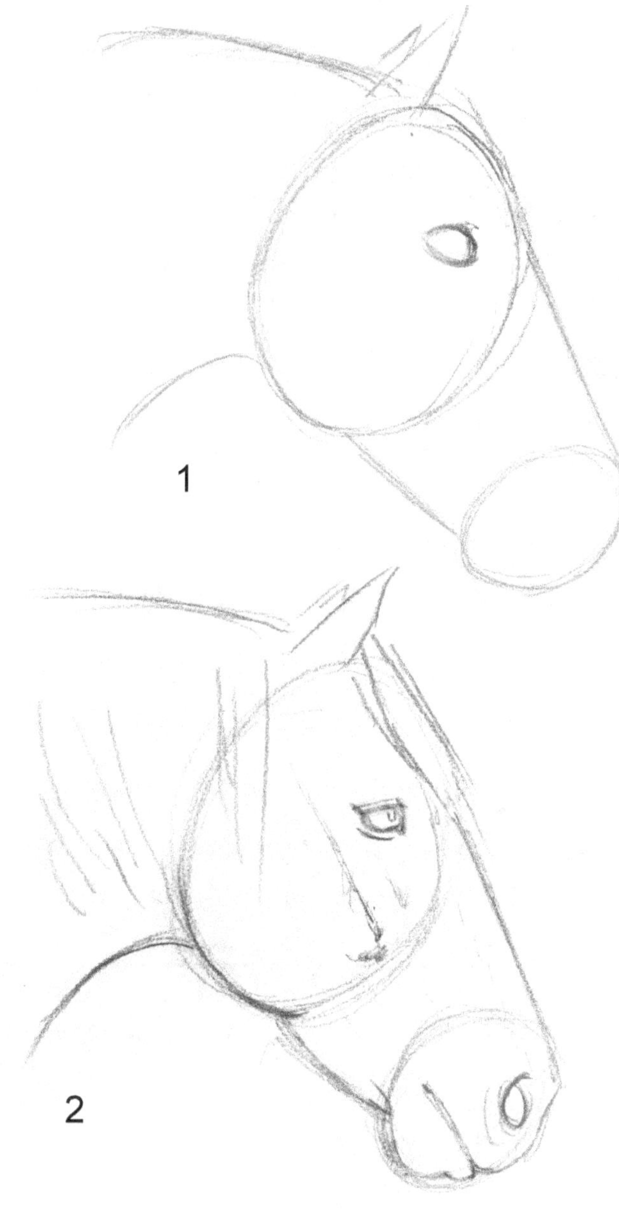

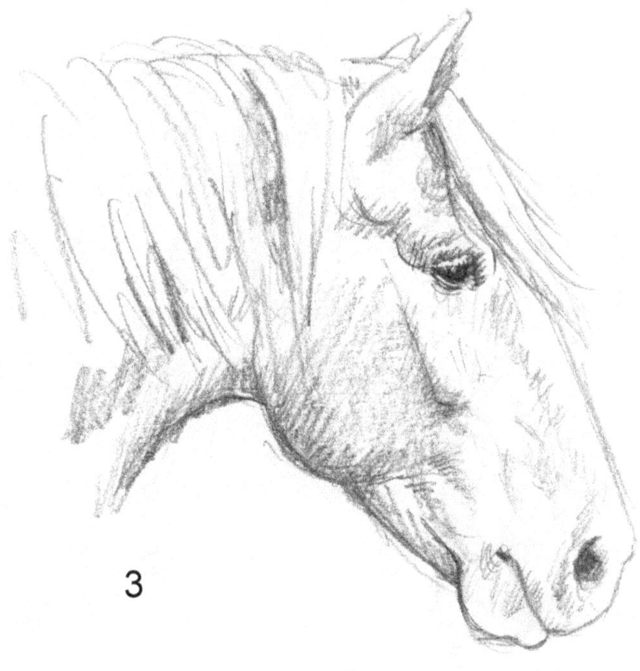

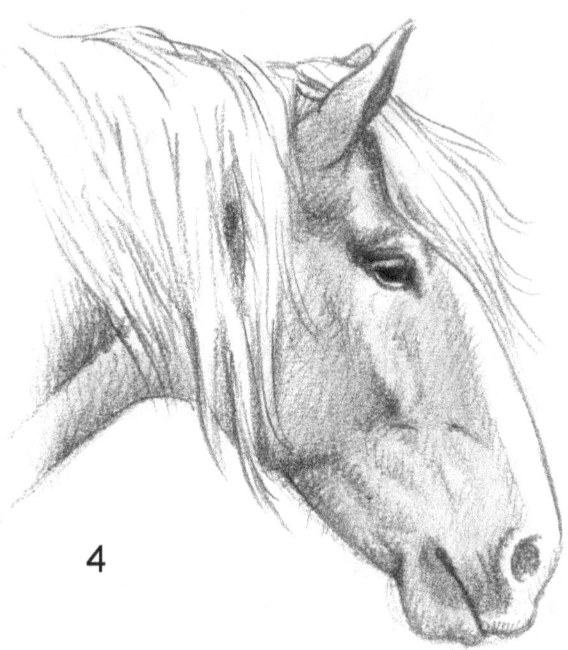

AMERICAN PAINT HORSE

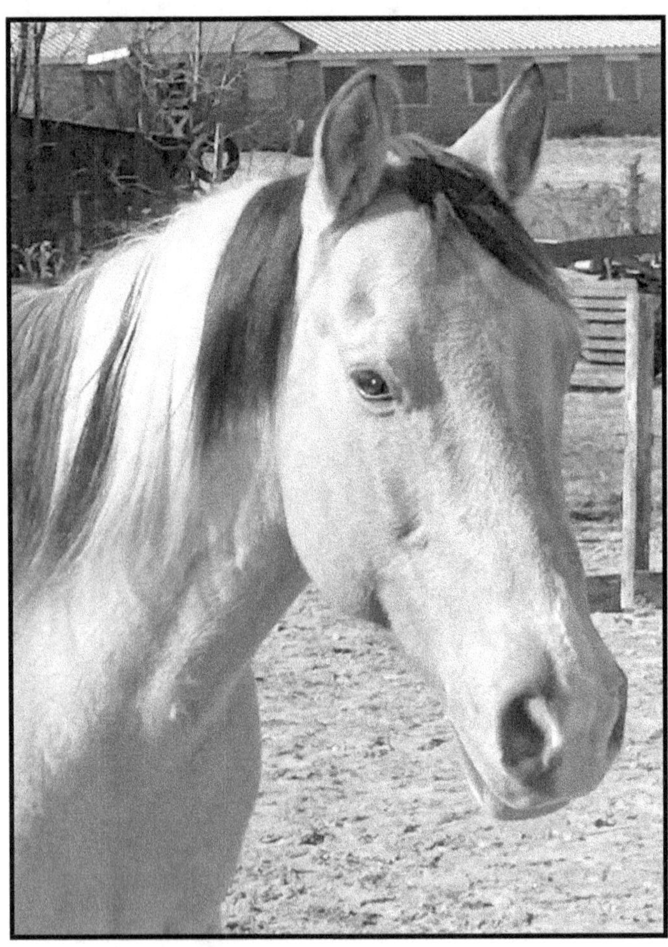

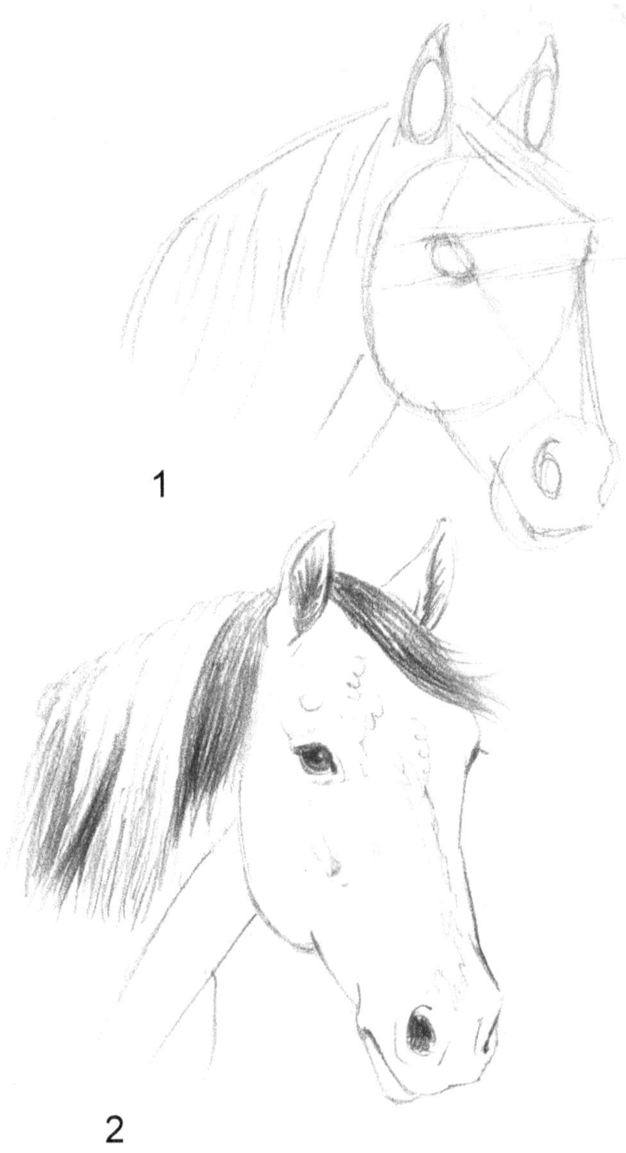

Reminder: Draw lightly at first. Start with simple shapes. Keep referring to the photo as you draw. For views showing both eyes I draw a diamond shape and two parallel lines to line up the eyes.

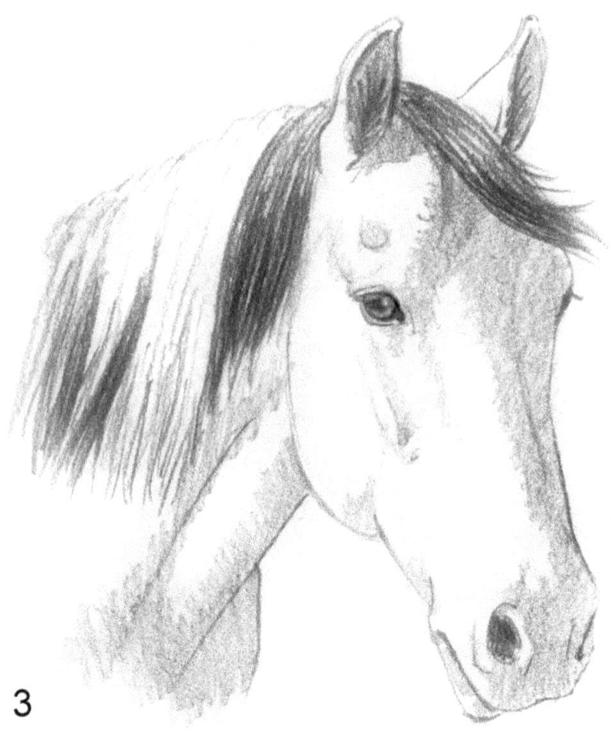

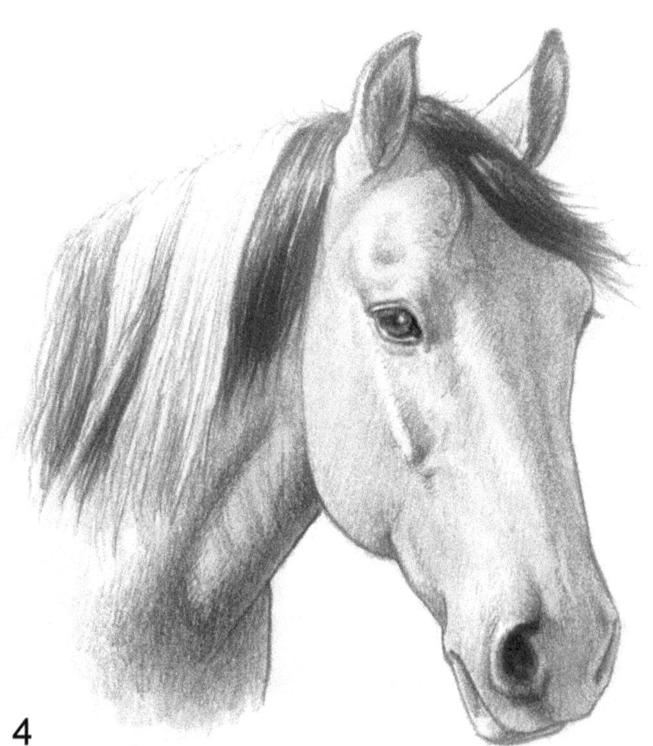

THOROUGHBRED FOAL

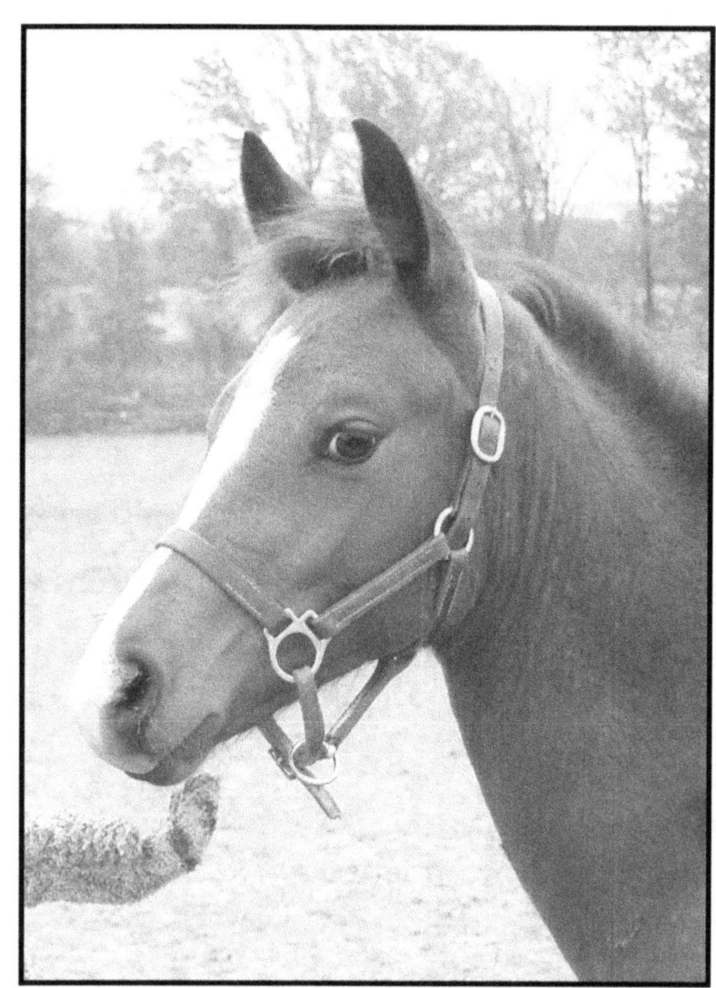

Sketch his halter with simple shapes first. Foals are born with adult-sized ears. They have a slight "dish" to their face, and very small muzzles.

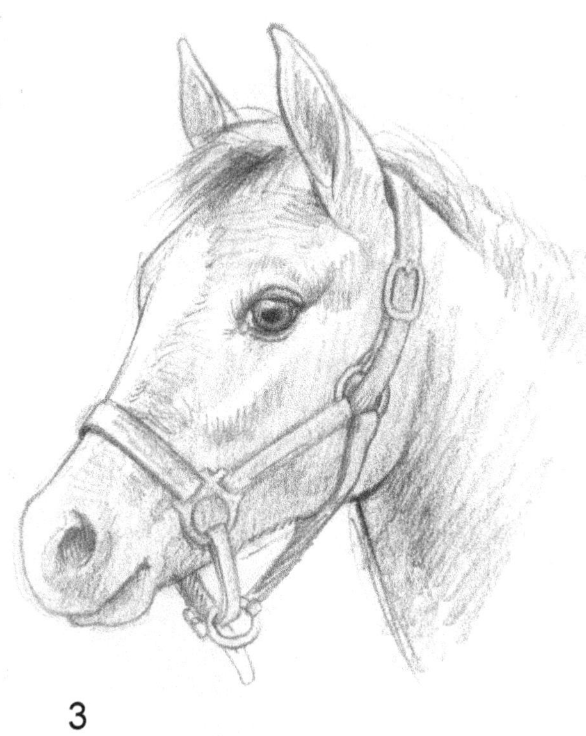

1

2

3

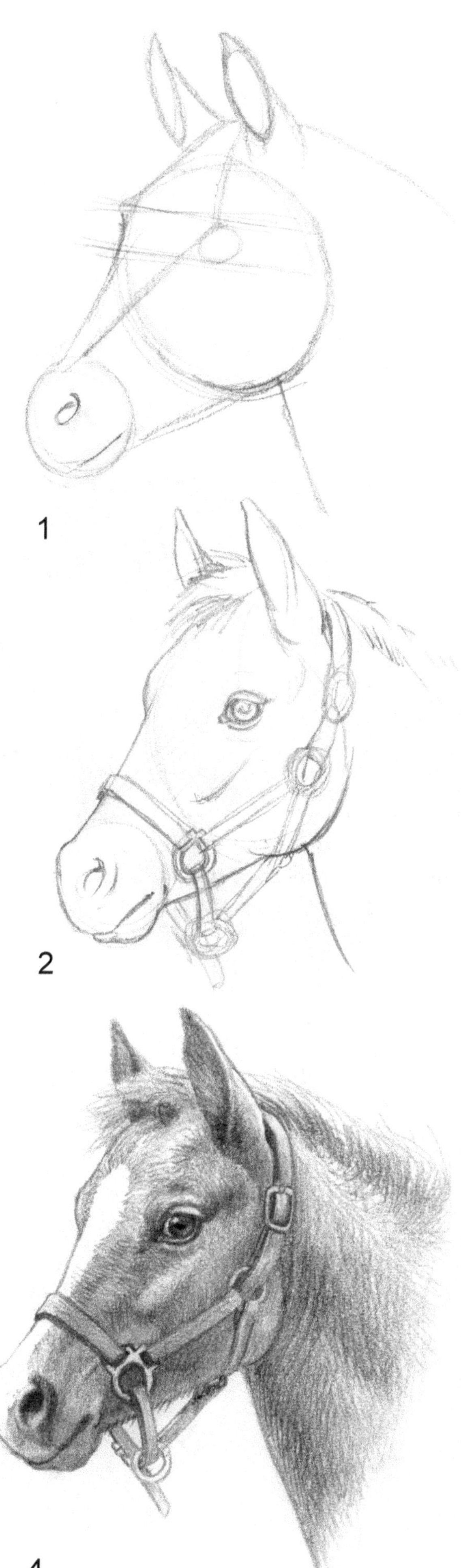

4

APPALOOSA

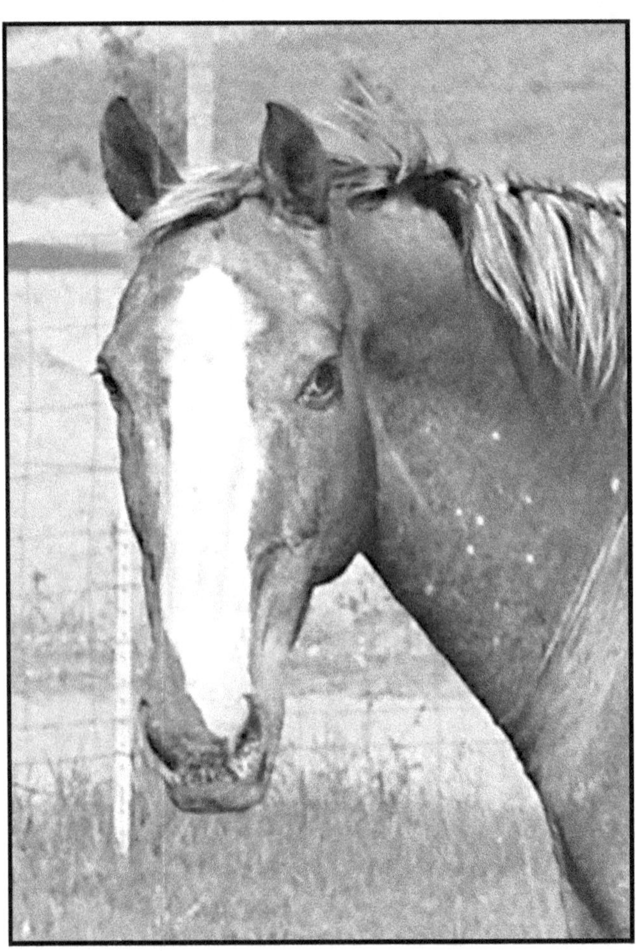

1

This Appy has just a few white spots on his neck. Scrunch up your kneaded eraser to a point and erase to create the spots. You can also draw around them, but that's a bit harder.

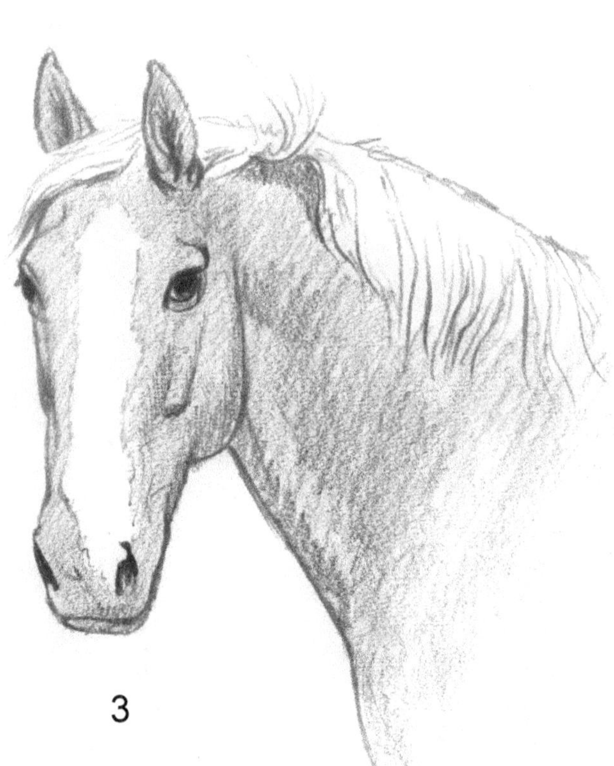

2

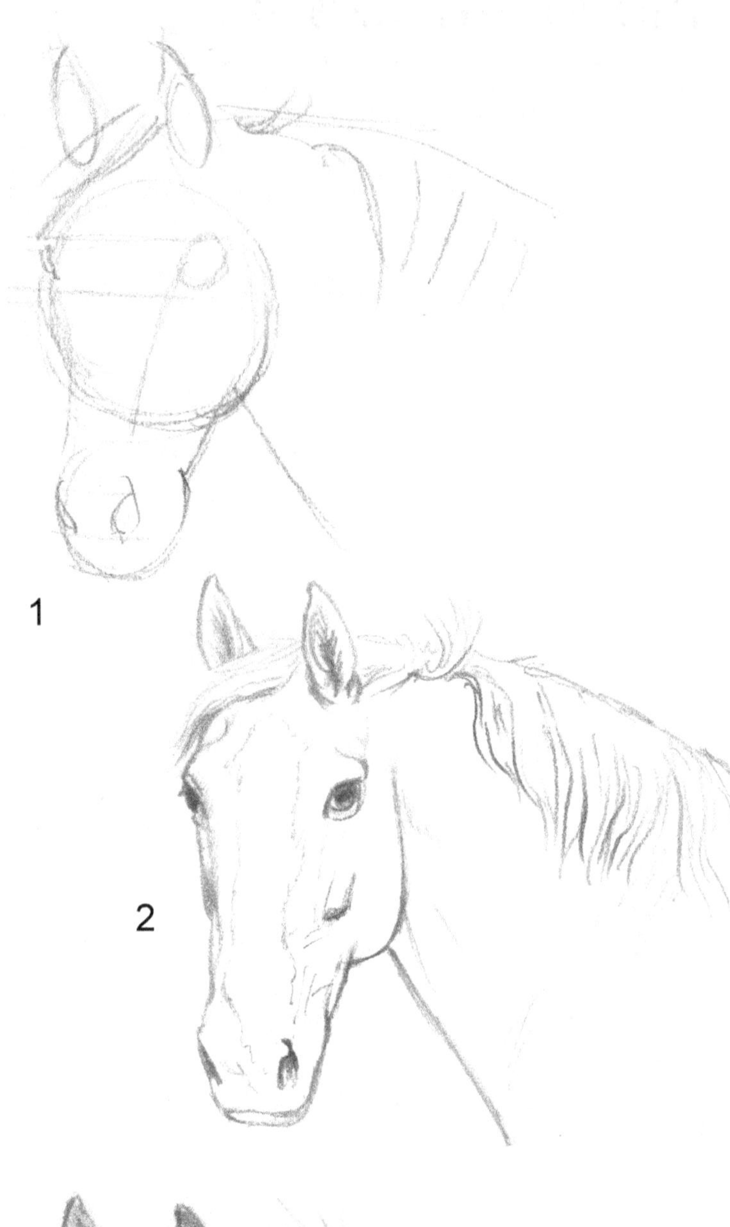

3

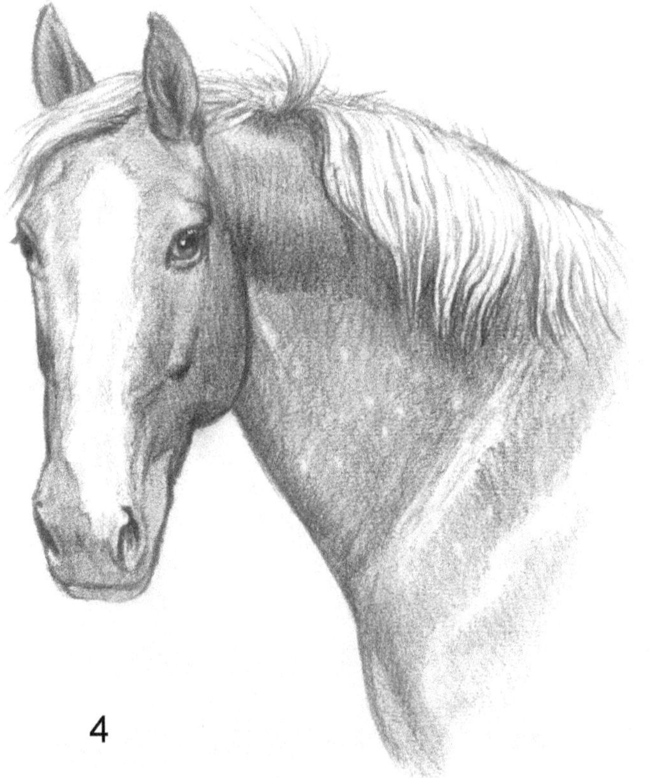

4

HAFLINGER

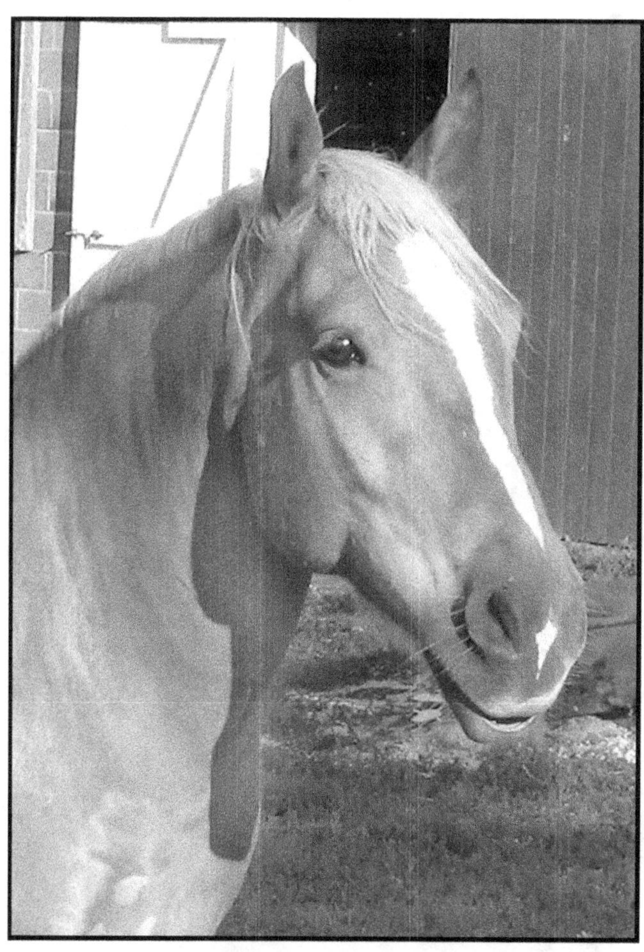

This handsome Haflinger has great direct lighting on his face, making it easy to see the bones and muscles. For step 4 I added a light even tone over his whole face, and built up shadows. Then I used a blending stump to make his coat look really smooth, and erased highlights.

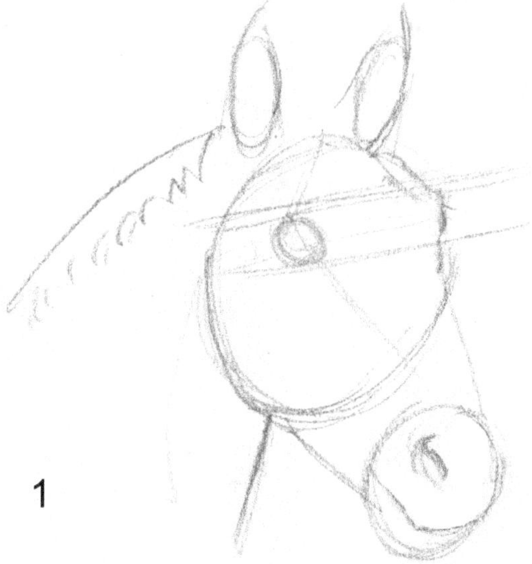

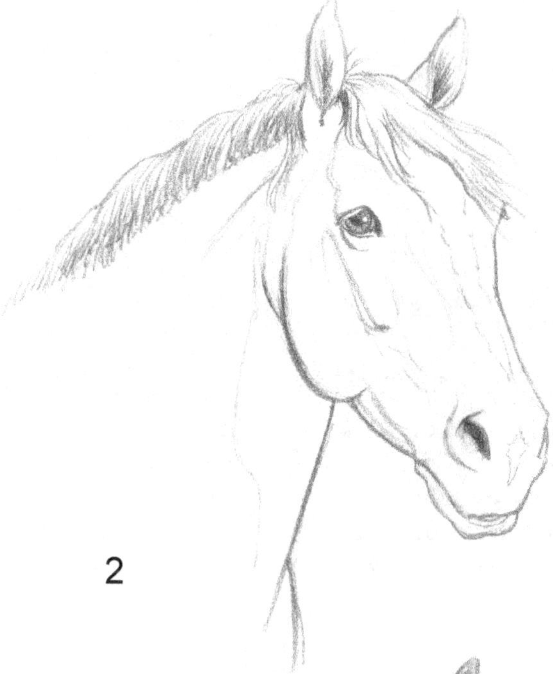

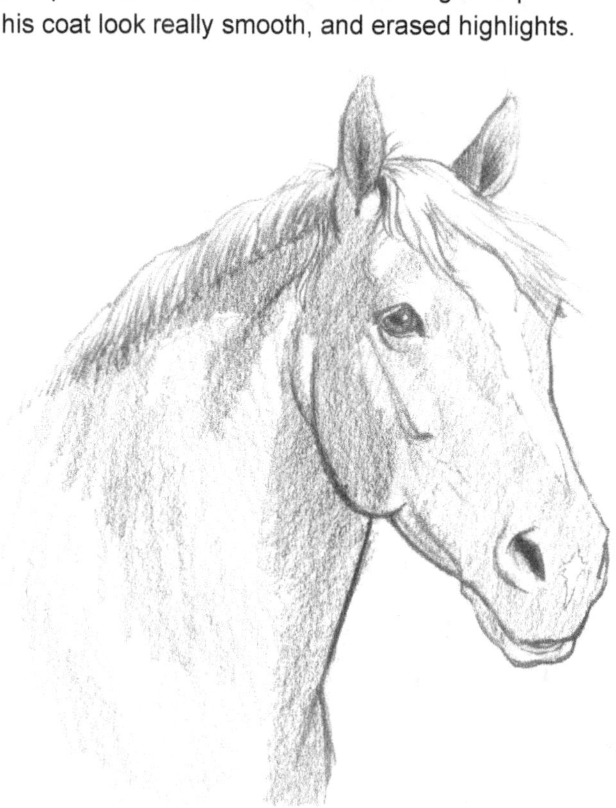

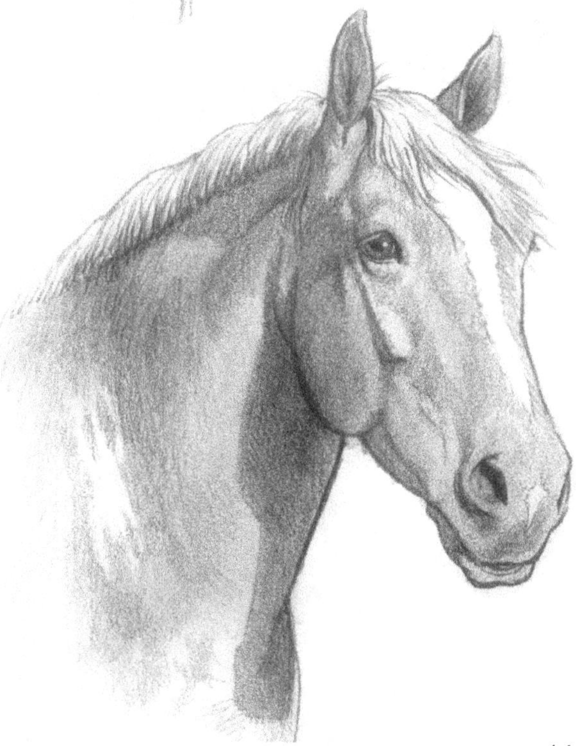

ARABIAN

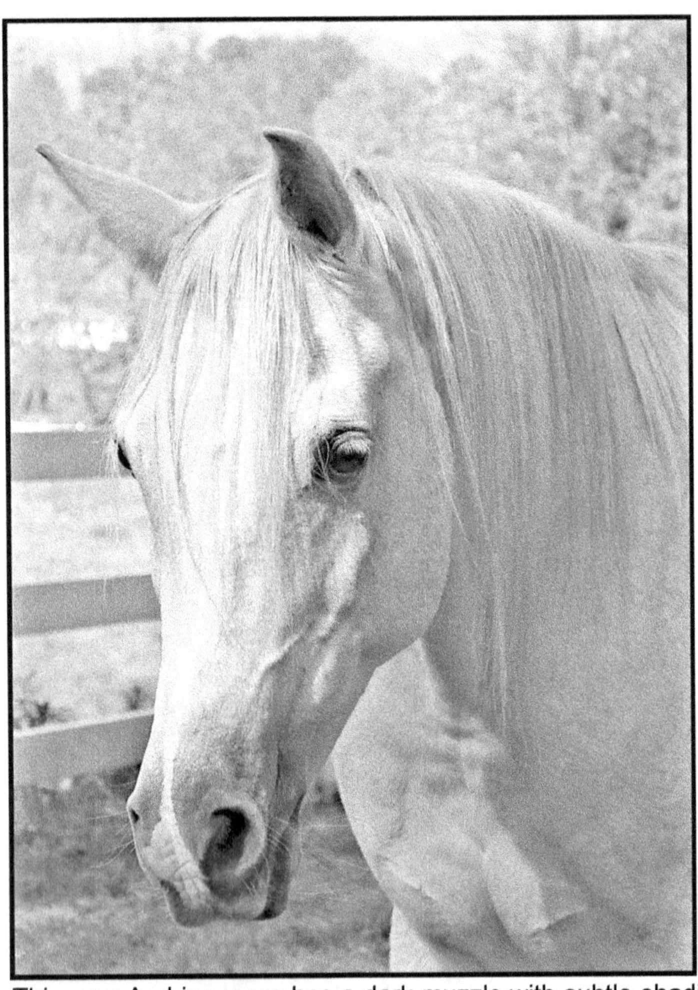

This gray Arabian mare has a dark muzzle with subtle shading going up the light side of her face. I left the front of her forelock white to simplify it, but you can add more strands and shadows. Art is all about interpretation. Finish it your own way.

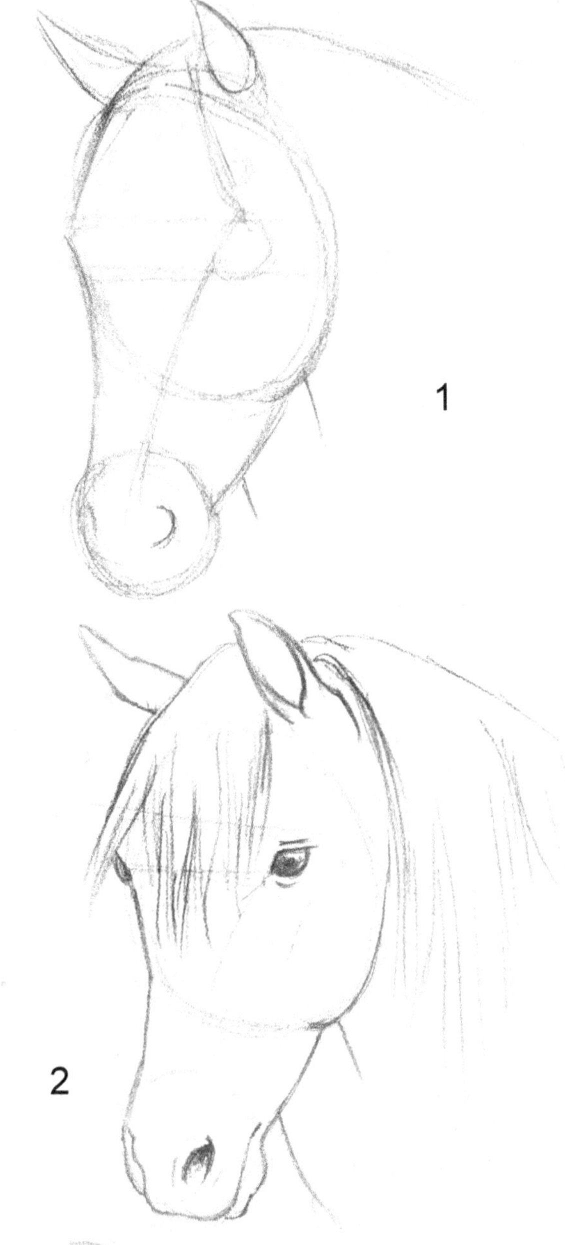

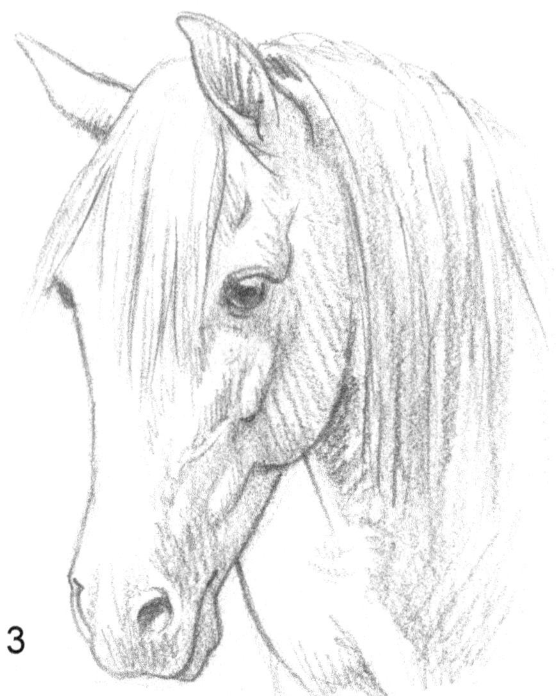

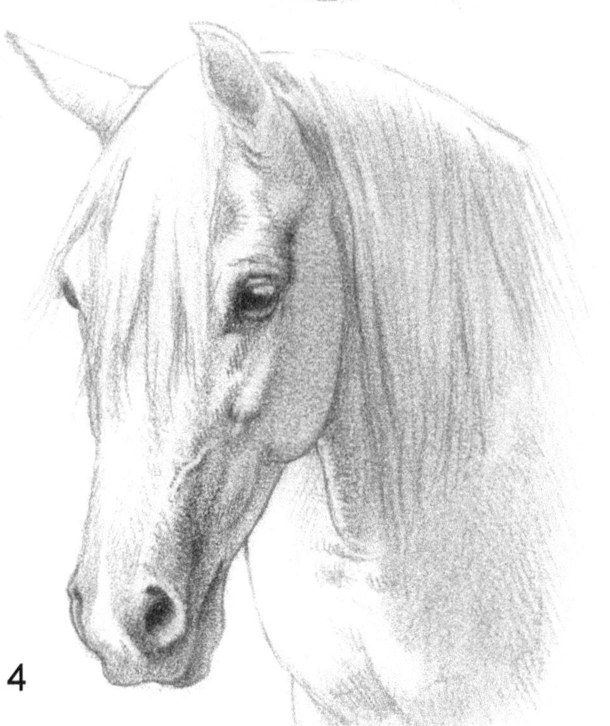

QUARTER HORSE

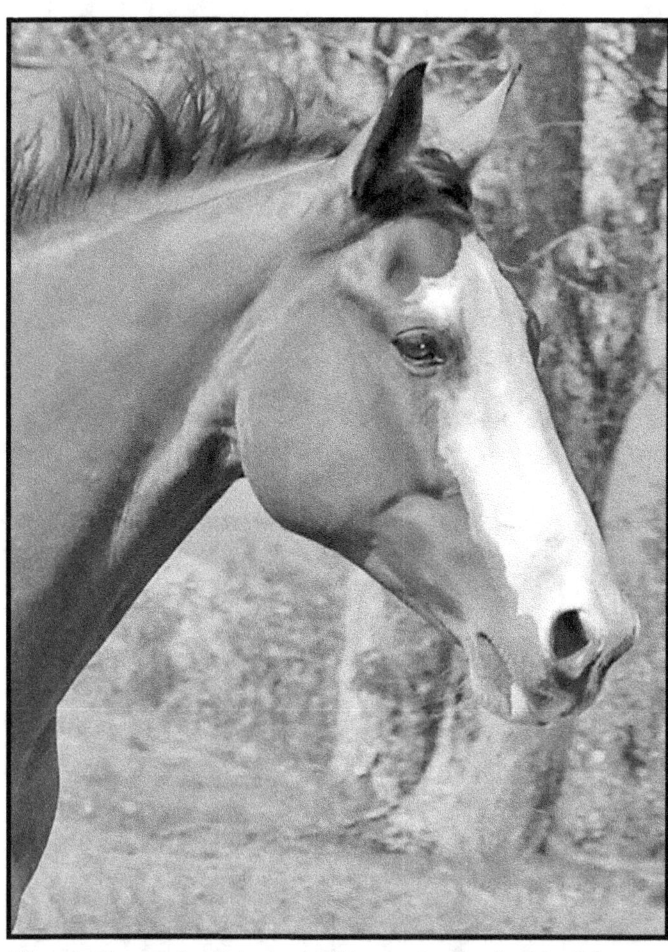

The challenge for this portrait is capturing that half-tone strip next to his white blaze. Draw it carefully. The light is coming from the left side, so the shadows on his face are quite different than in most of the other photos..

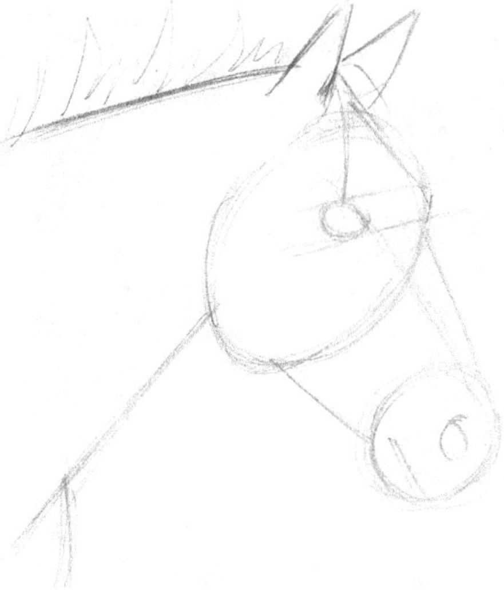

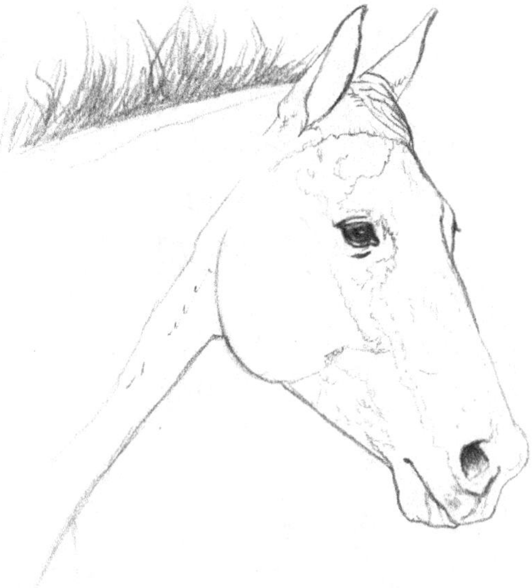

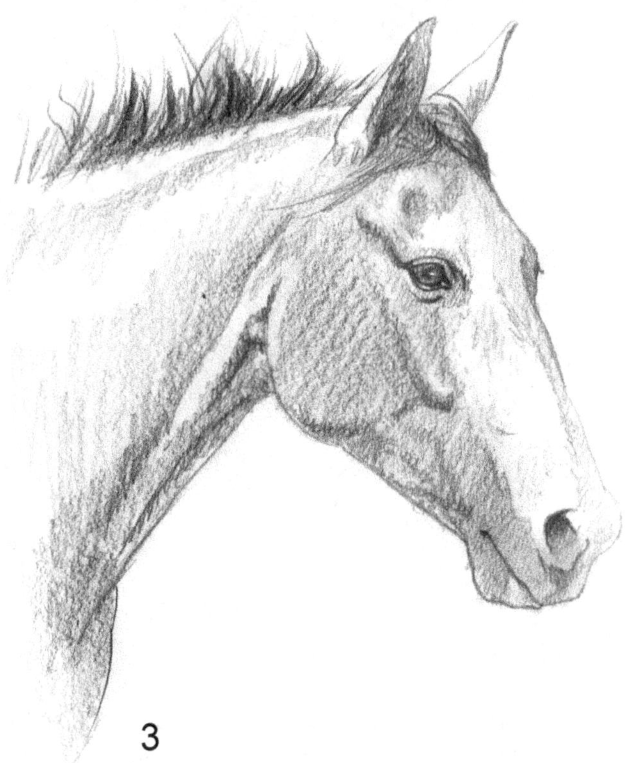

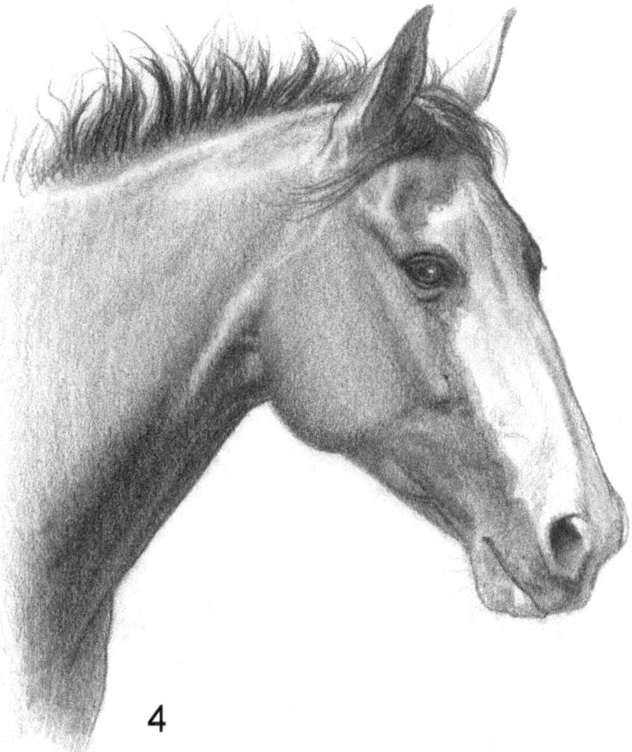

Advanced Lesson: Colored Pencil on Toned Paper

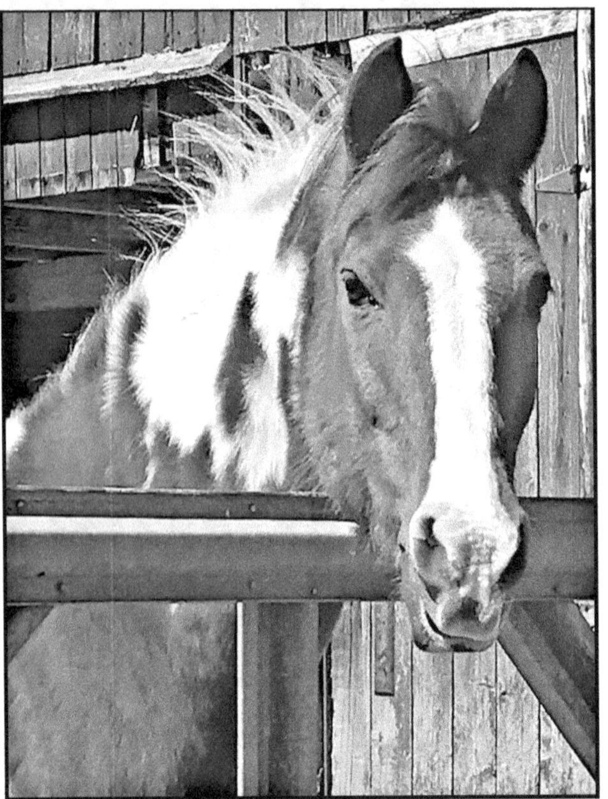 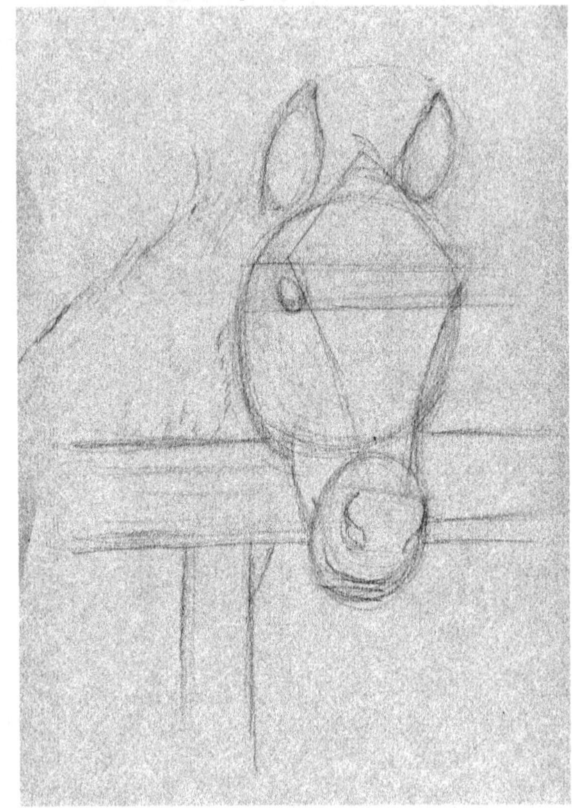

1

Horses with a lot of white come out quite well on toned paper. I used a Col-erase Prismacolor black pencil, and a Prismacolor white pencil, on 9x12 gray charcoal paper. You can use black and white charcoal pencils if you prefer.

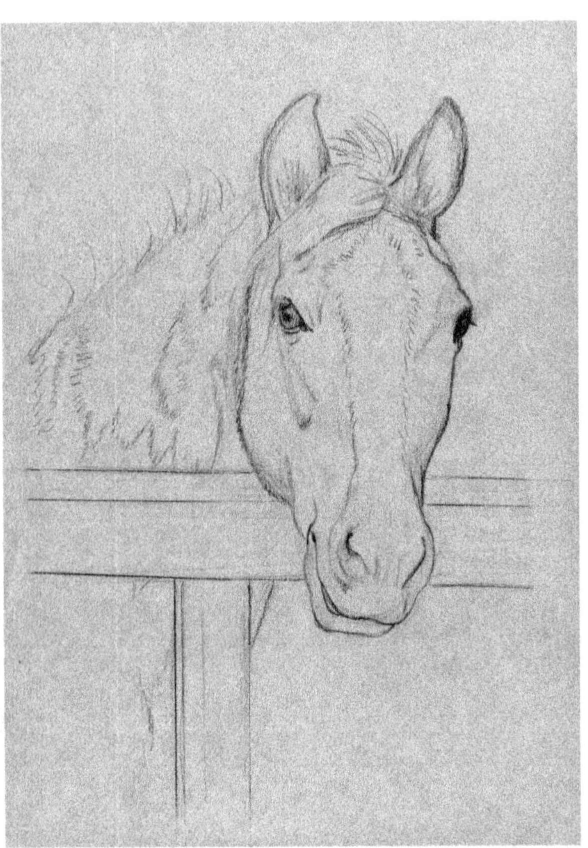

2

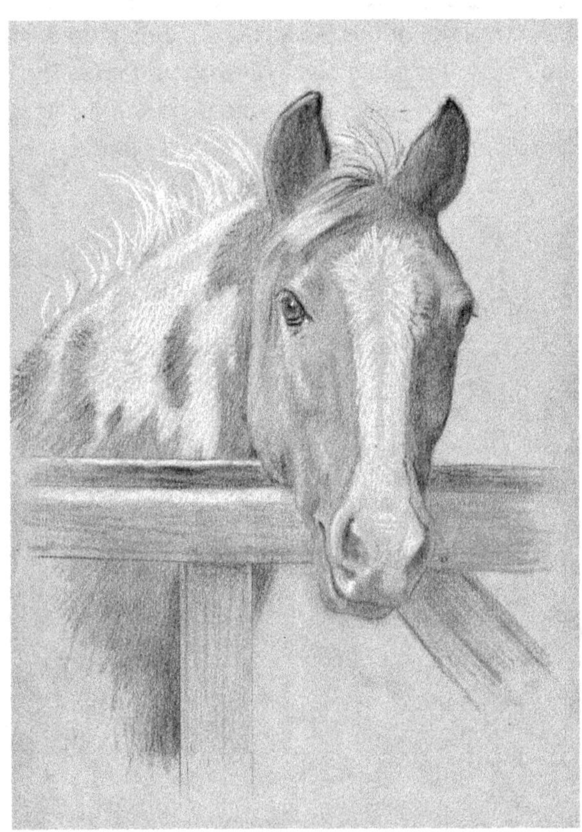

3

1. Using an erasable black colored pencil, or a charcoal pencil, follow the first basic steps for heads, detailed on p. 9. Draw a diamond shape for the front of the face, and two parallel lines to line up the eyes. Indicate the fence.

(Continued on opposite page.)

ARABIAN

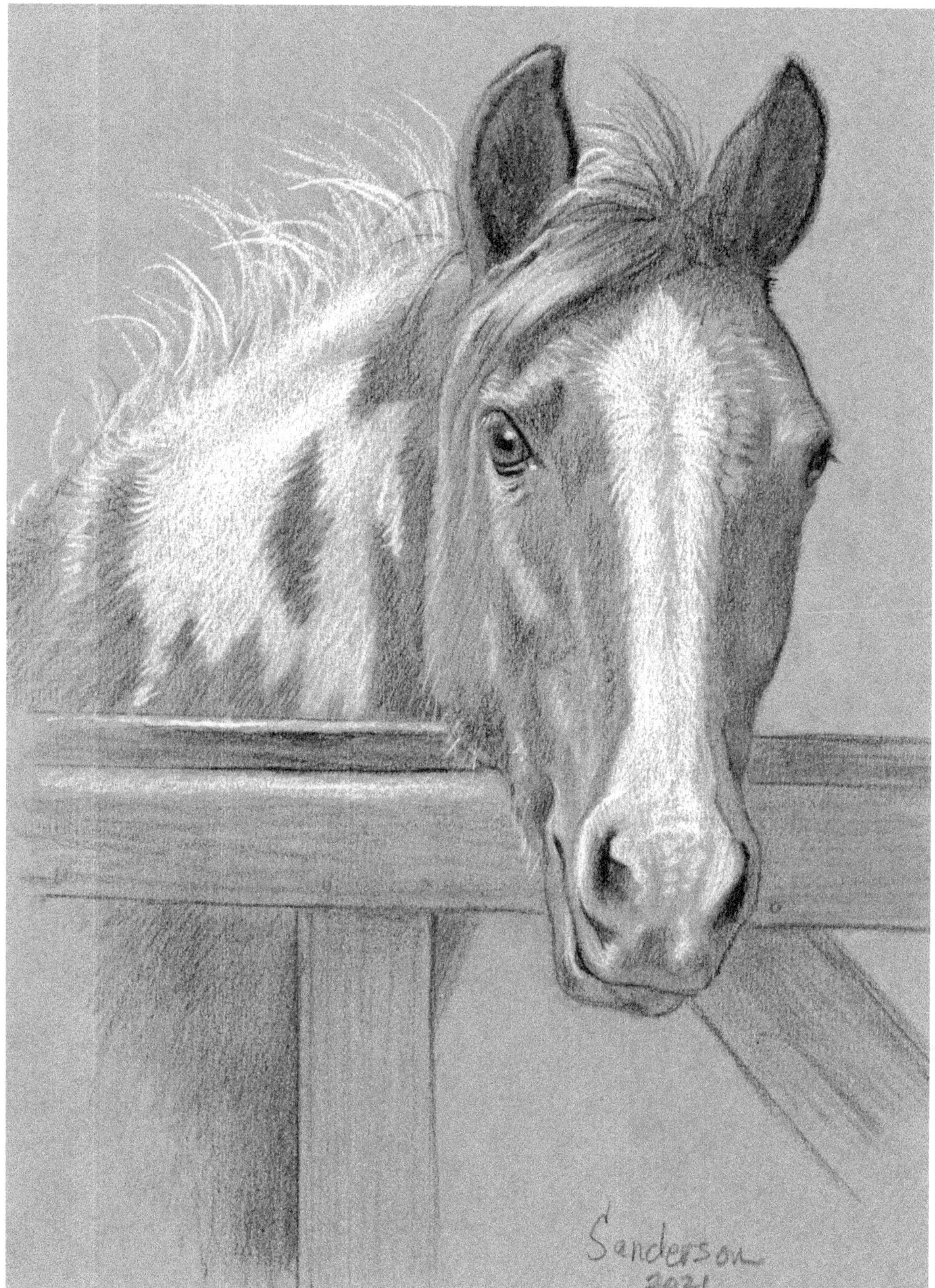

2. Study the photo and refine the outline to match what you see. Erase your first block-in lines as you go. Indicate the white blaze and the white spots on his coat with little lines that show the direction the fur is growing.

3. I erased most of the black lines for his mane, and drew them in white, leaving just a few at the base. In general, try to avoid mixing white and black lines. With the white pencil, start to build up the light areas where his coat is white, following the direction the fur is growing. The gray paper becomes the half-tones/shadows of the white coat. Add fence highlights. Add highlight on his eye. Start shading with black pencil on the colored areas of his coat, and add tone on the fence.

4. Build up the white coat carefully with tiny strokes of a sharp white pencil. Don't bear down too hard or the pencil will break. The more you go over and over an area, the whiter it will get. Be patient! I like the look of some of the gray still showing through, so it looks like soft fur. I added just a few white highlights on the color side of his face.

HORSE BODY Basics

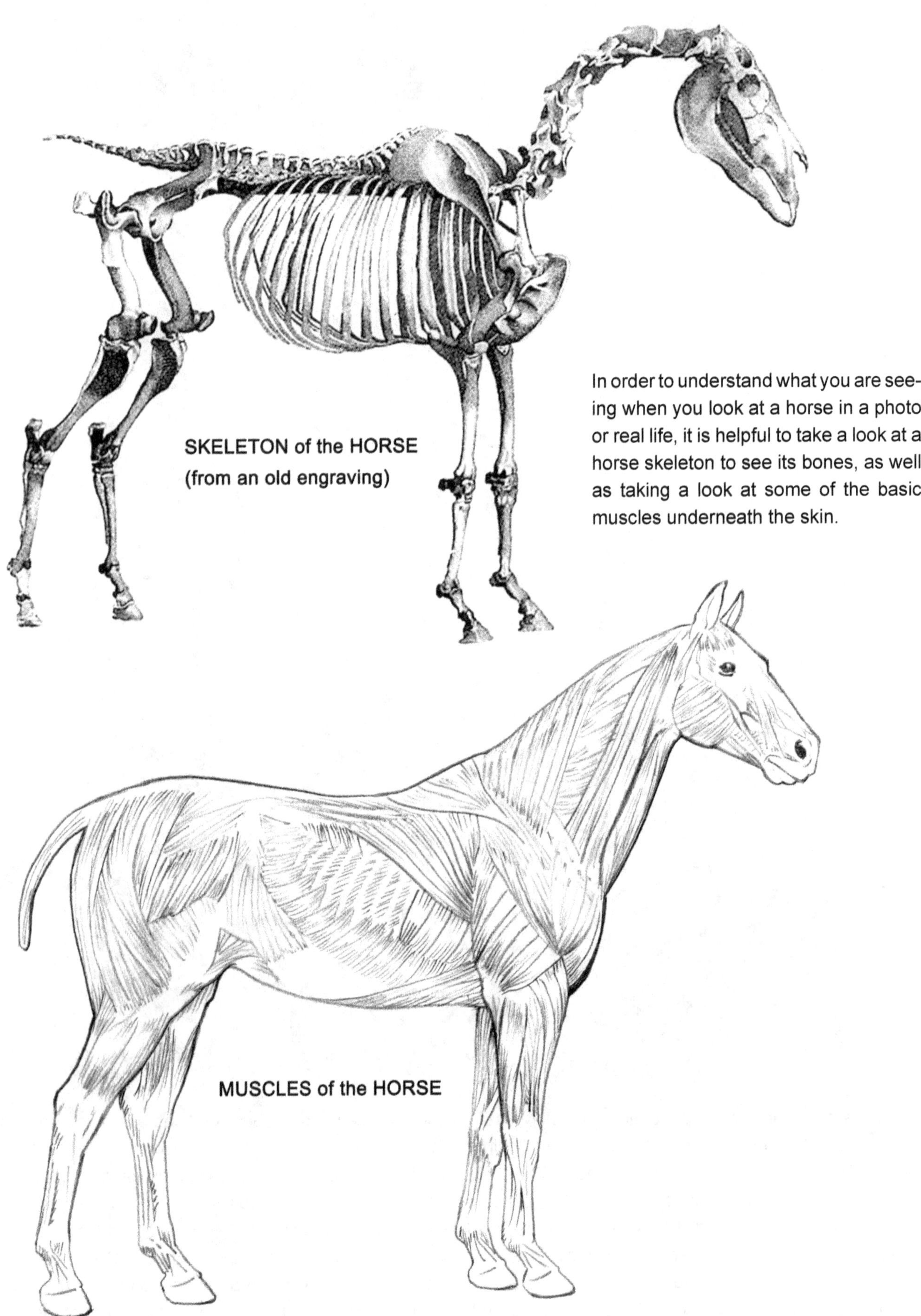

In order to understand what you are seeing when you look at a horse in a photo or real life, it is helpful to take a look at a horse skeleton to see its bones, as well as taking a look at some of the basic muscles underneath the skin.

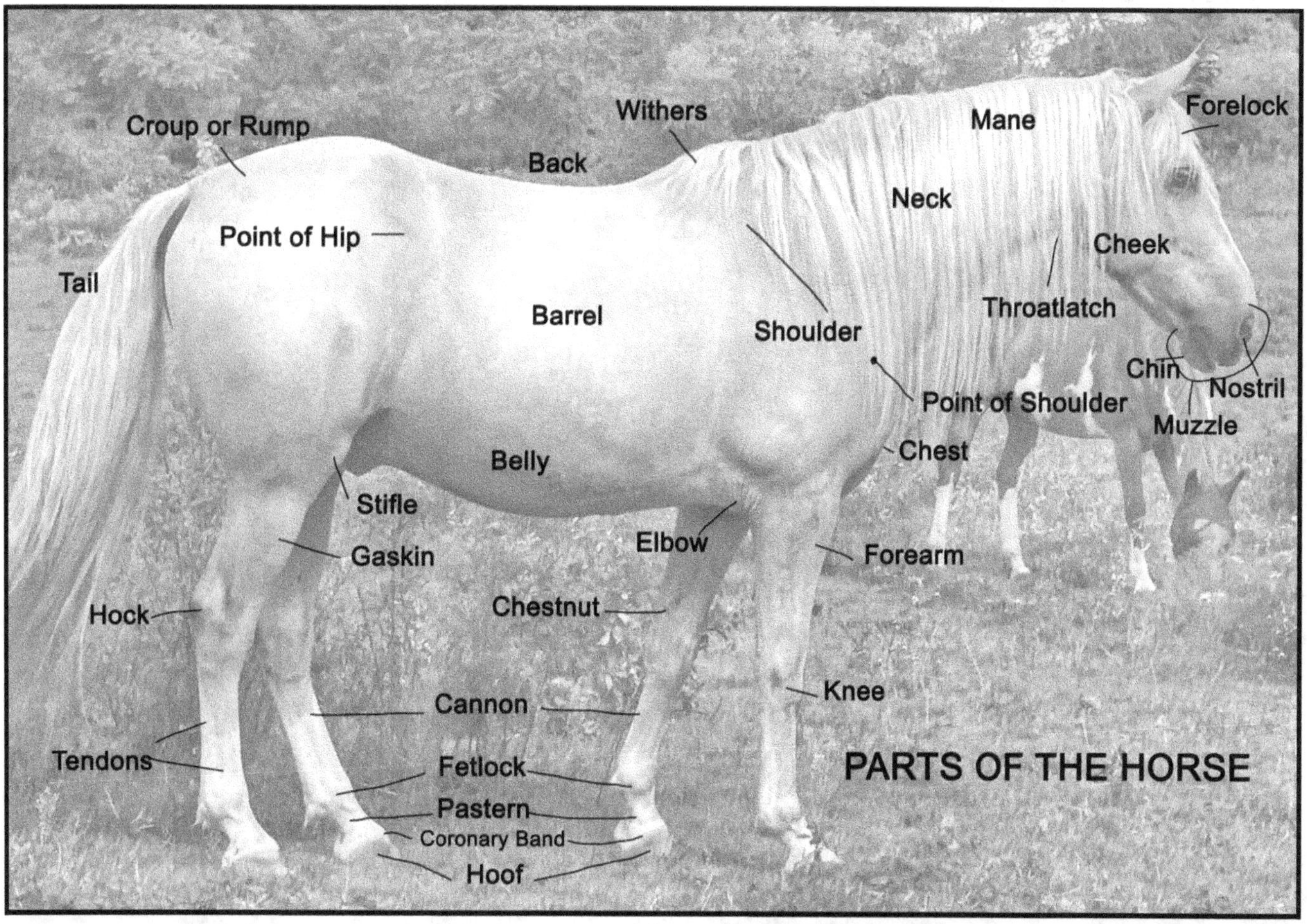

Croup or Rump
Withers
Back
Mane
Forelock
Point of Hip
Neck
Cheek
Tail
Throatlatch
Barrel
Shoulder
Chin
Nostril
Point of Shoulder
Muzzle
Chest
Belly
Stifle
Elbow
Gaskin
Forearm
Hock
Chestnut
Knee
Cannon
PARTS OF THE HORSE
Tendons
Fetlock
Pastern
Coronary Band
Hoof

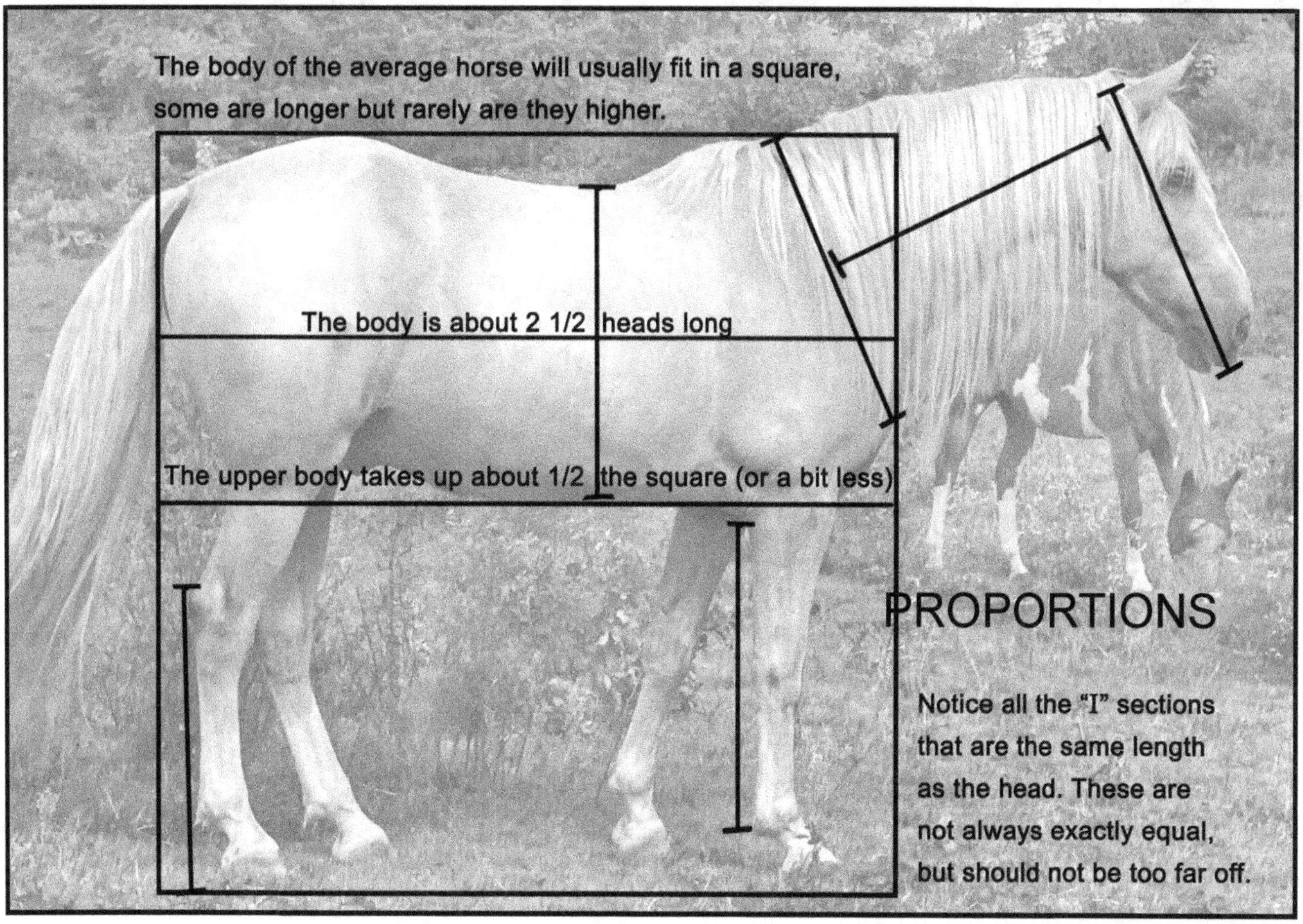

The body of the average horse will usually fit in a square,
some are longer but rarely are they higher.
The body is about 2 1/2 heads long
The upper body takes up about 1/2 the square (or a bit less)
PROPORTIONS
Notice all the "I" sections
that are the same length
as the head. These are
not always exactly equal,
but should not be too far off.

HORSE LEG Details and Tips for Drawing

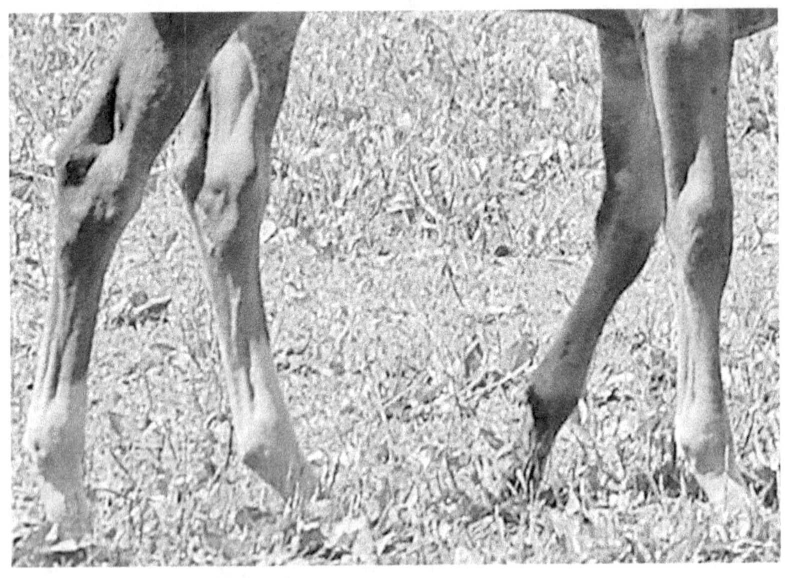 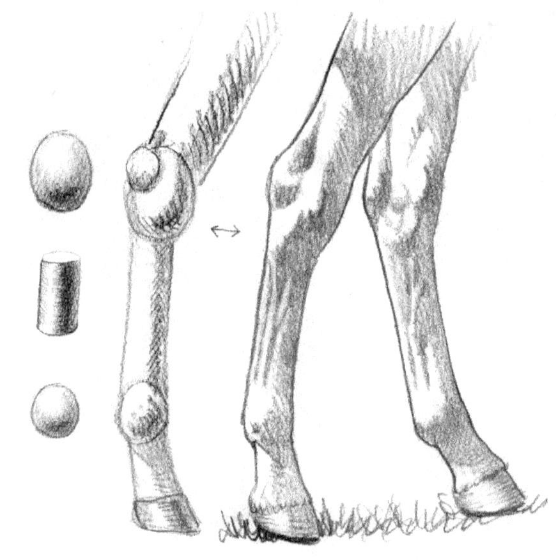

Look to simplify shapes first. It will help you shade complex areas around bones and muscles. It is not necessary to draw every tiny detail in the legs in a small drawing, but a few indications of bones and tendons will go a long way in drawing decent convincing legs. It does take practice, so keep at it and you will improve. Always look for form first, not outline.

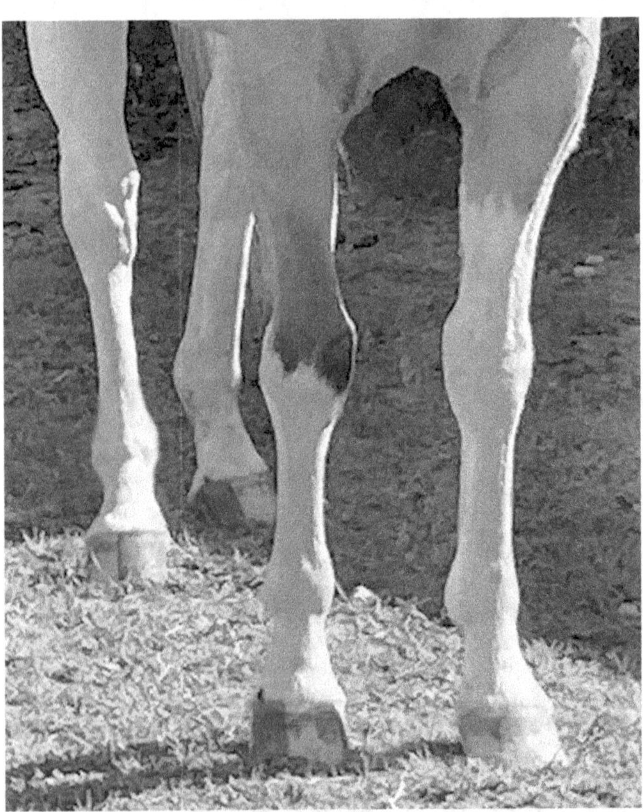 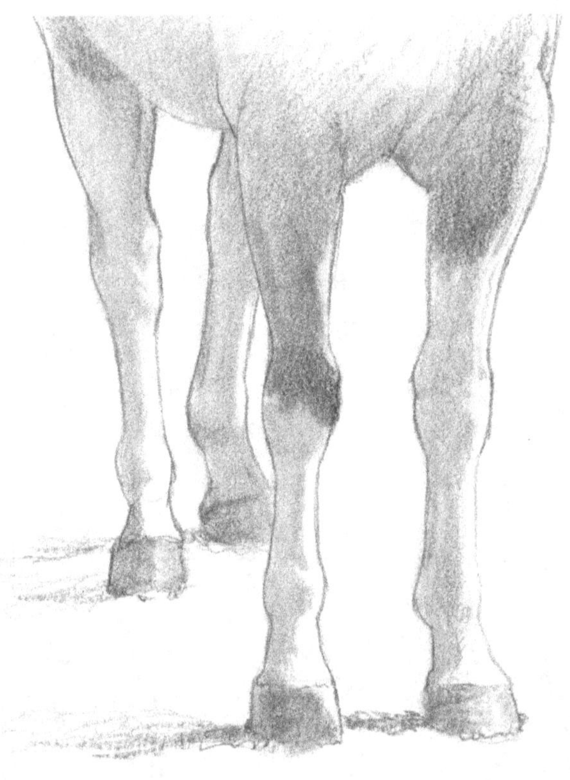

The lower leg on a horse is mostly tendon and bone, and usually you can spot the knobby parts in a decent photo, and the tendons from the knee to the pastern. When light hits them, they create shadows that will help define the form as you draw them. Note how the front view and side view leg shapes look quite different. The legs of a foal (top) are thinner.

 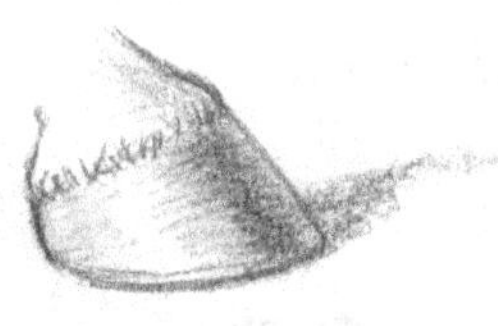 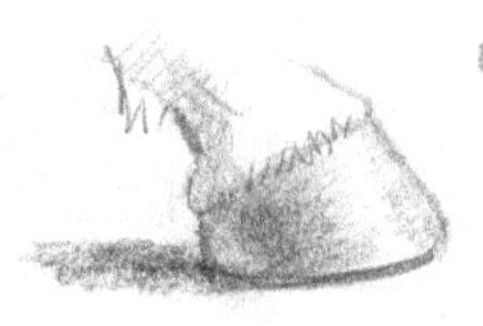

Hooves are sort of a cross between a cone shape and a cylinder. They are tricky to shade because some hooves are light, some are dark, and some have light and dark areas. I think of the lighting first, and simplify them.

Remember, **OBSERVATION** is the key to realistic drawing.

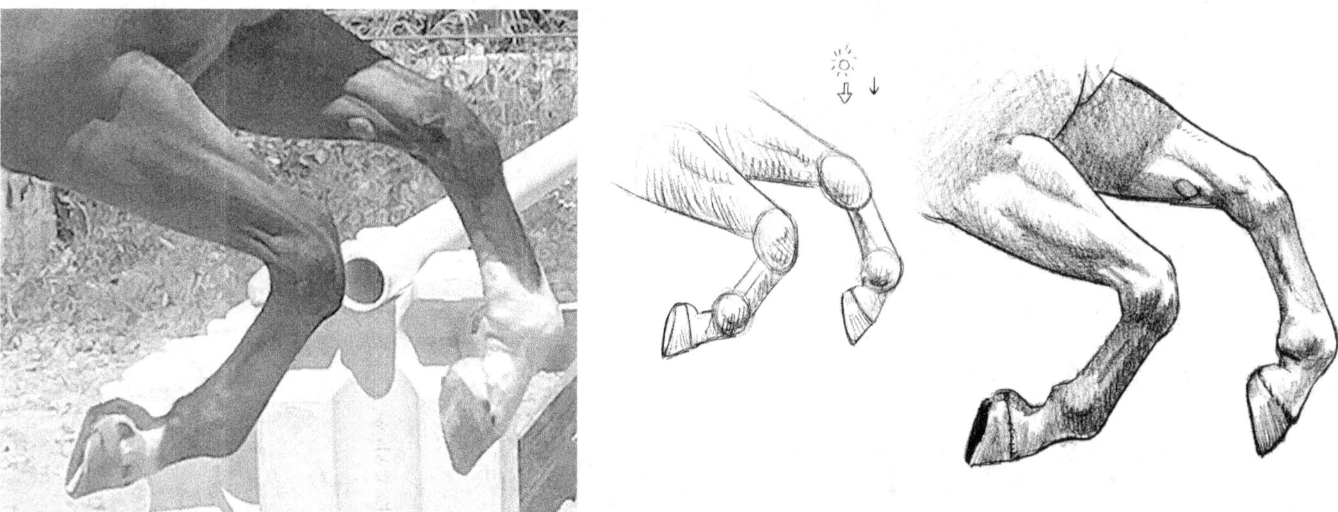

Look at all the muscles of the upper legs on p.19. You can see them here nicely defined by the light. Notice how the front of the knees in a side view are almost flat. When part of the horse is in shadow you don't need to draw too much detail in that dark area. Concentrate on the sharply defined areas in the light. Start with simple shapes.

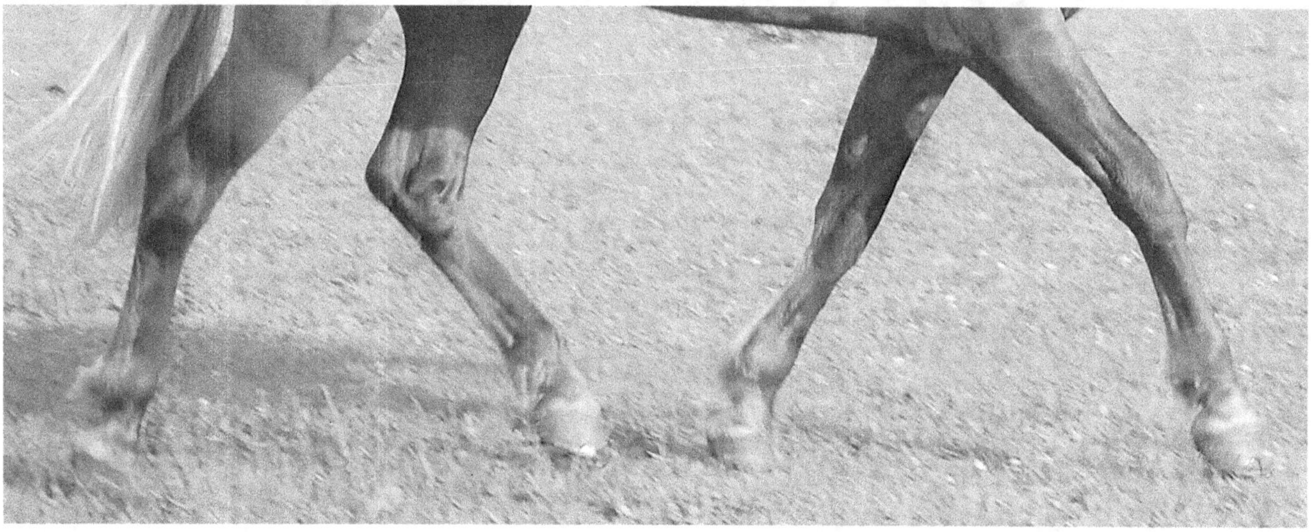

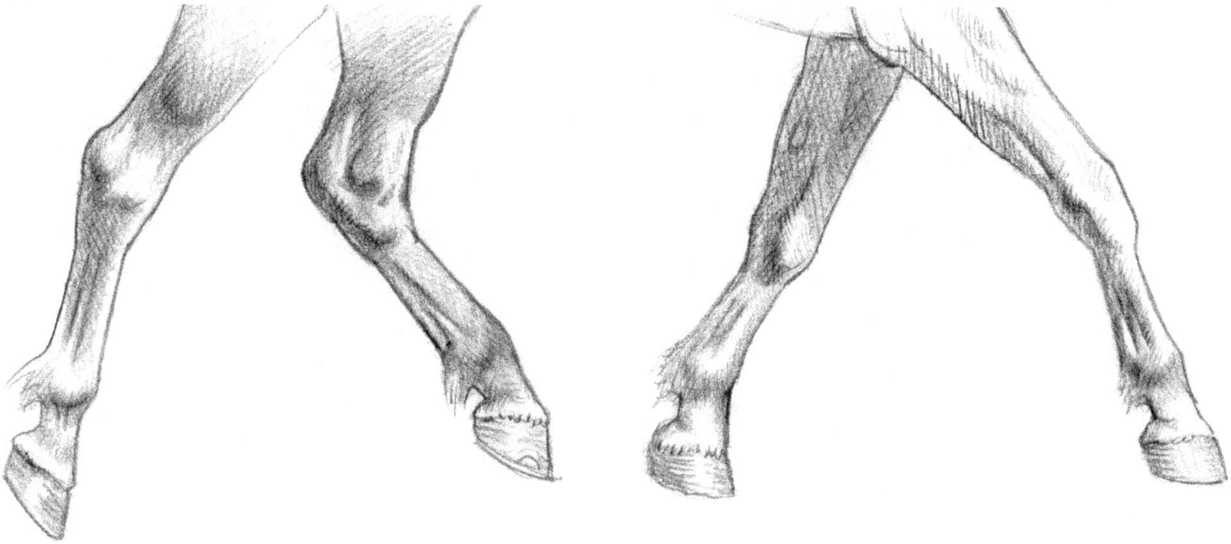

Can you spot the places where I have picked out cylinder shapes and sphere (ball) shapes to emphasize them when I shaded these trotting legs? Remember, always look for form first, not outline.

TENNESSEE WALKER

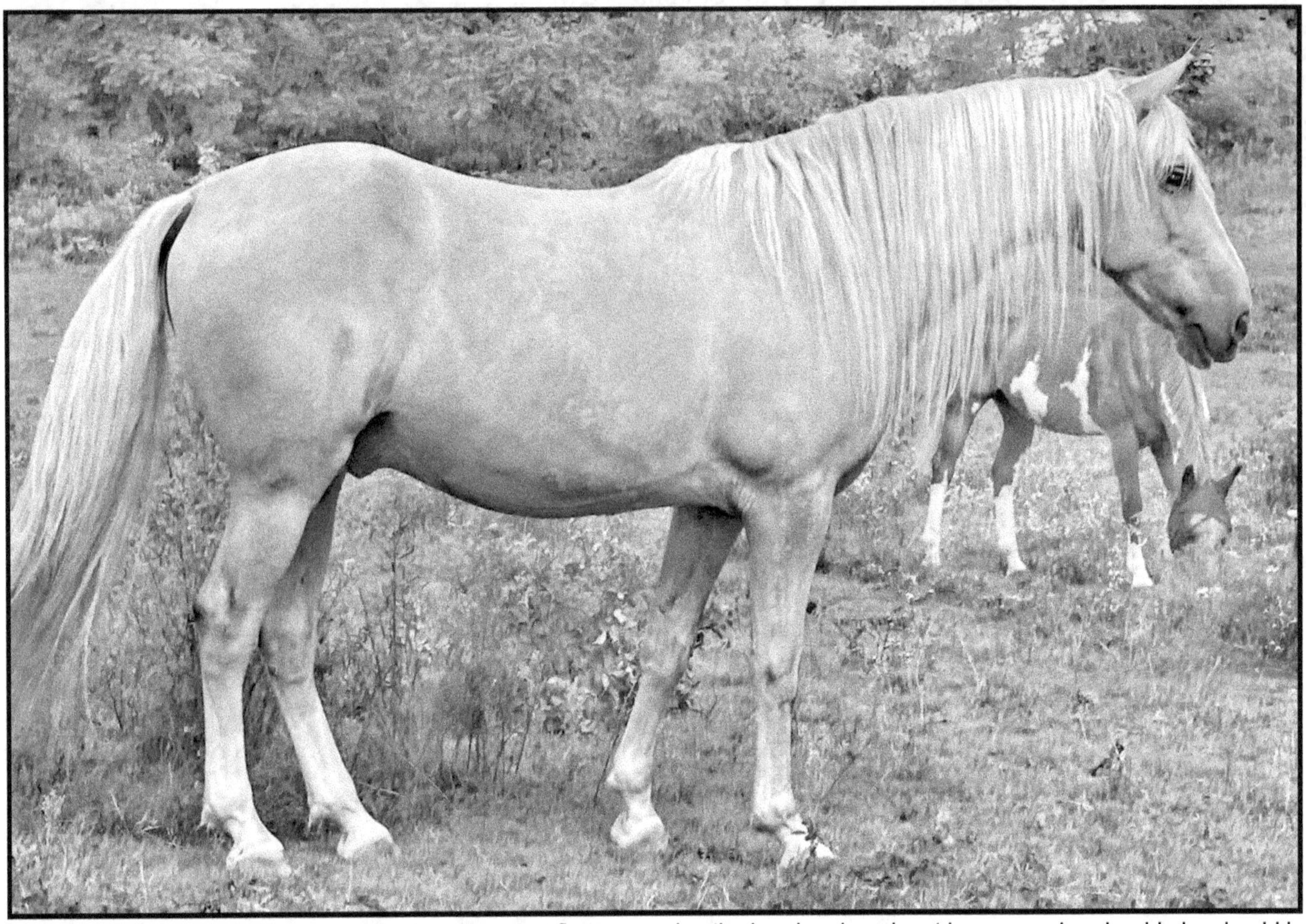

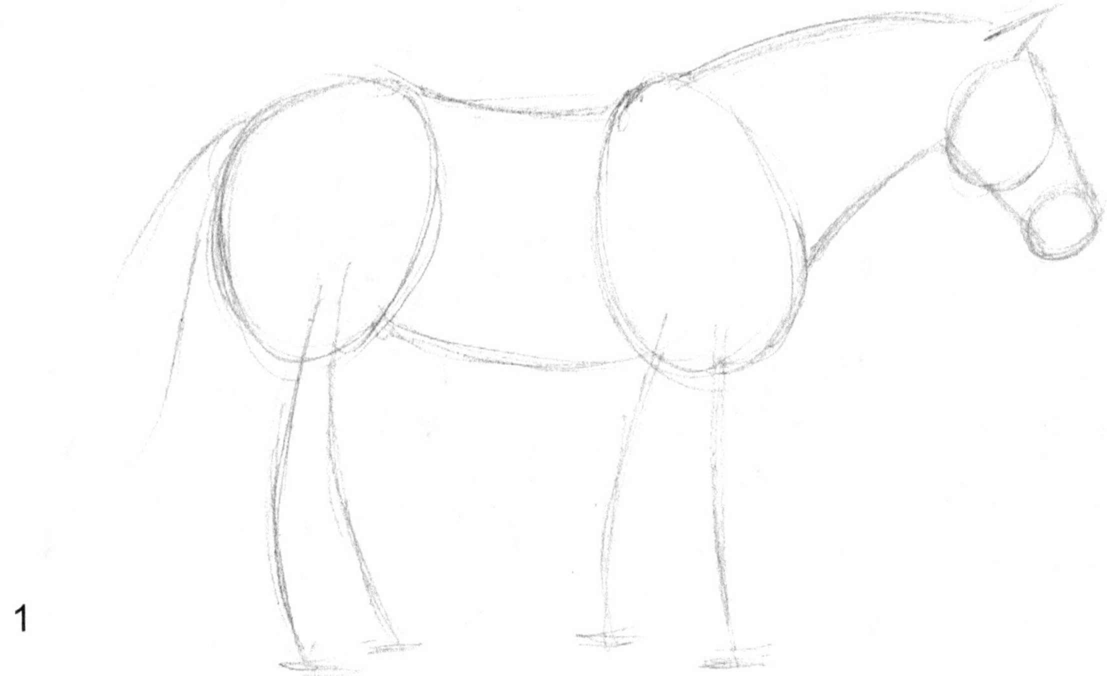

1. Block in the head with simple shapes first. I suggest first measuring the head and mark out how many heads wide he should be and put light marks on your paper so you won't run out of room. (You can use the end of the pencil and your thumb, you don't need a ruler.) See Proportions on p.20 to help you figure out proportions. Drawing lightly at first helps--you can just erase and start again.

Draw an egg shape for the horse's front end, with the small part of the egg making up the withers. Draw an upside down egg shape for the rear end. The withers and the top of the hindquarters are usually at the same height. Connect the two shapes with lines for the back and belly, curving them in a similar way to the photo. For placement of the legs, at first I draw very simple "gesture" lines for placement. Note that the feet closest to us are lower, due to perspective. I mark where the bottom of the hoof would be.

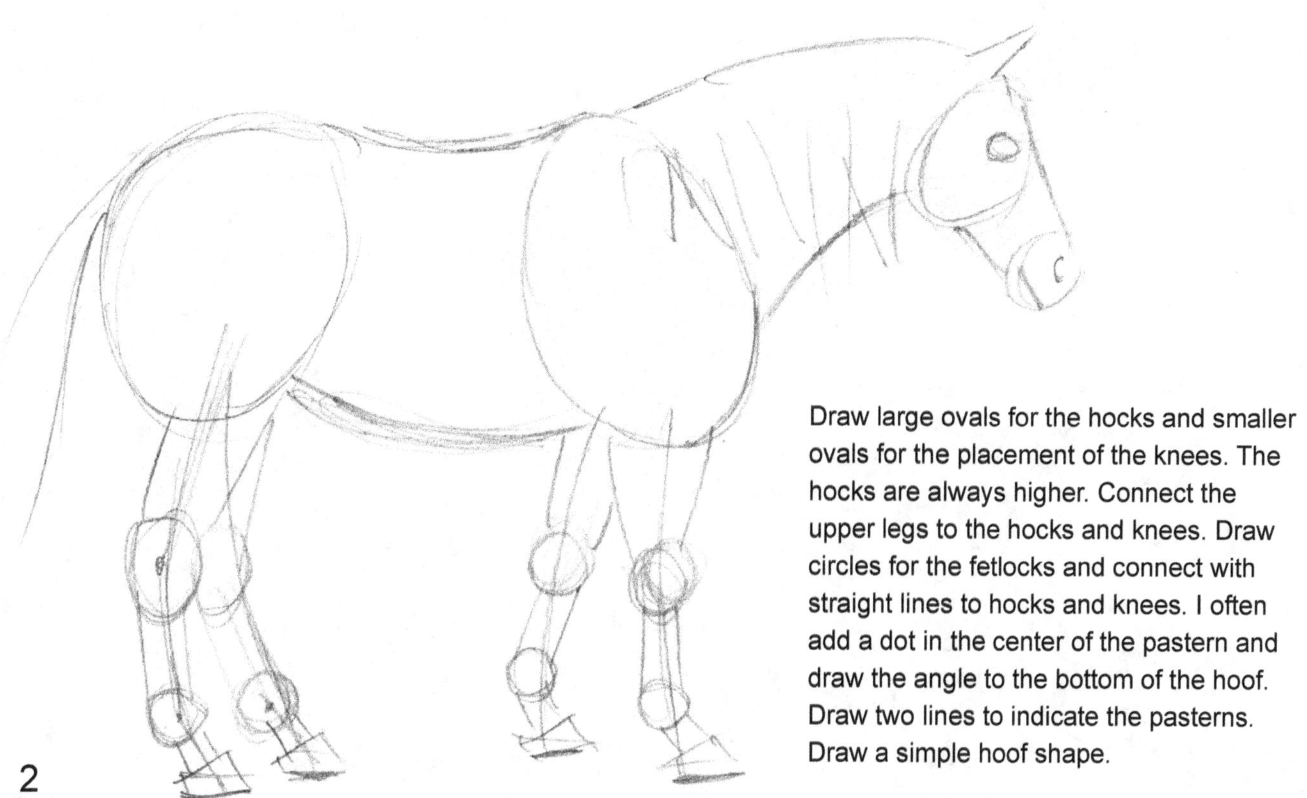

Draw large ovals for the hocks and smaller ovals for the placement of the knees. The hocks are always higher. Connect the upper legs to the hocks and knees. Draw circles for the fetlocks and connect with straight lines to hocks and knees. I often add a dot in the center of the pastern and draw the angle to the bottom of the hoof. Draw two lines to indicate the pasterns. Draw a simple hoof shape.

2

2. Now is the time to **check your proportions** and make any changes. Look at the photo and at your drawing. If you are unsure, use the head as a unit of measurement, like the chart of body proportions. Is the head too big or too small? Do the legs look too long or too short? Body too long? Is he too fat or too thin? Adjust.

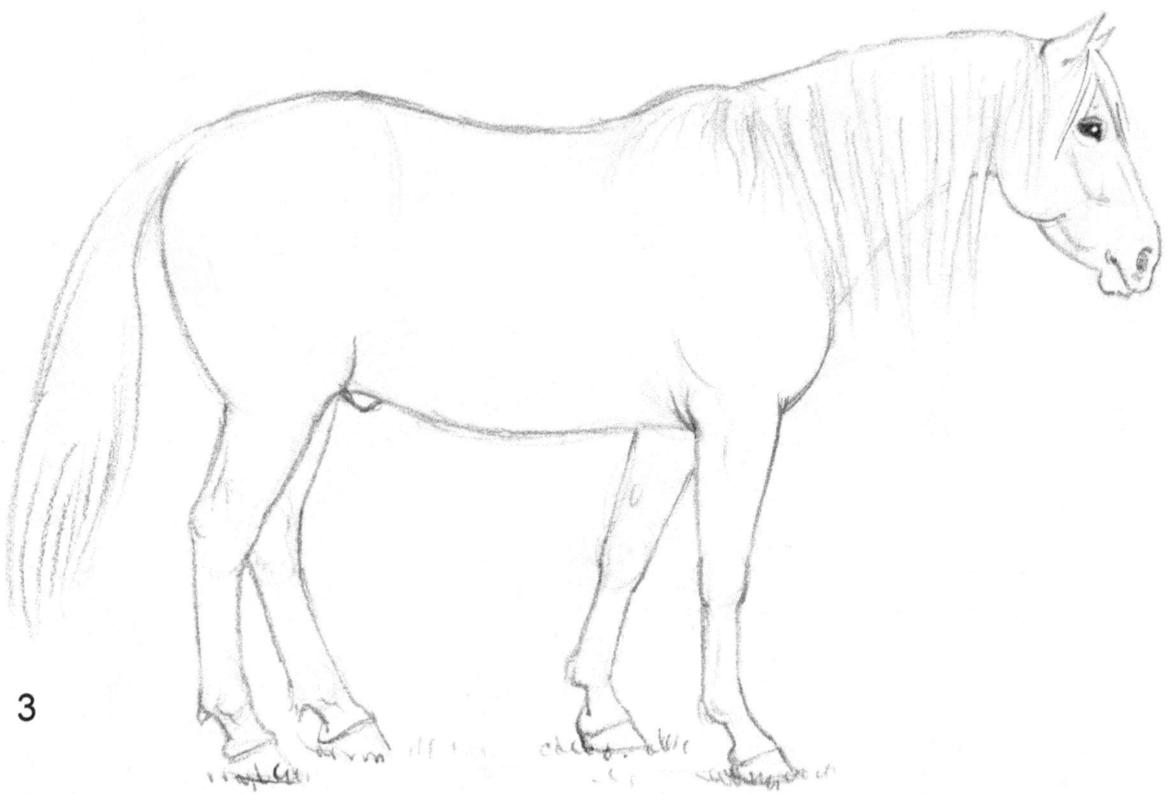

3

3. Looking carefully at the photo, start to refine the block-in shapes into the lines of the exact outlines of shapes and angles that you see. Add a few lines to indicate the muscles and bones that are prominent. I erase most of my initial block-in shape lines as I go. Notice how much thinner his legs are now.

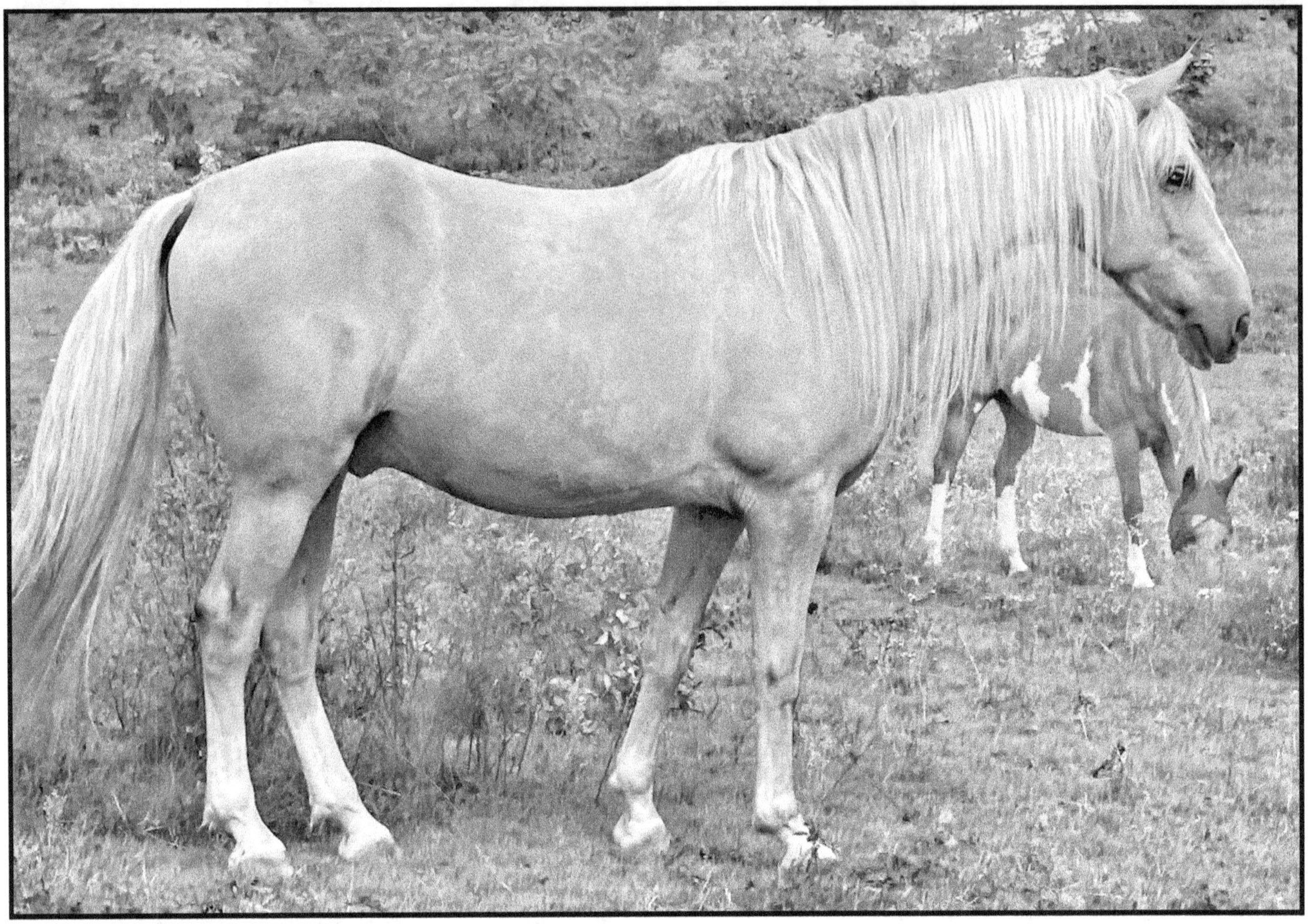

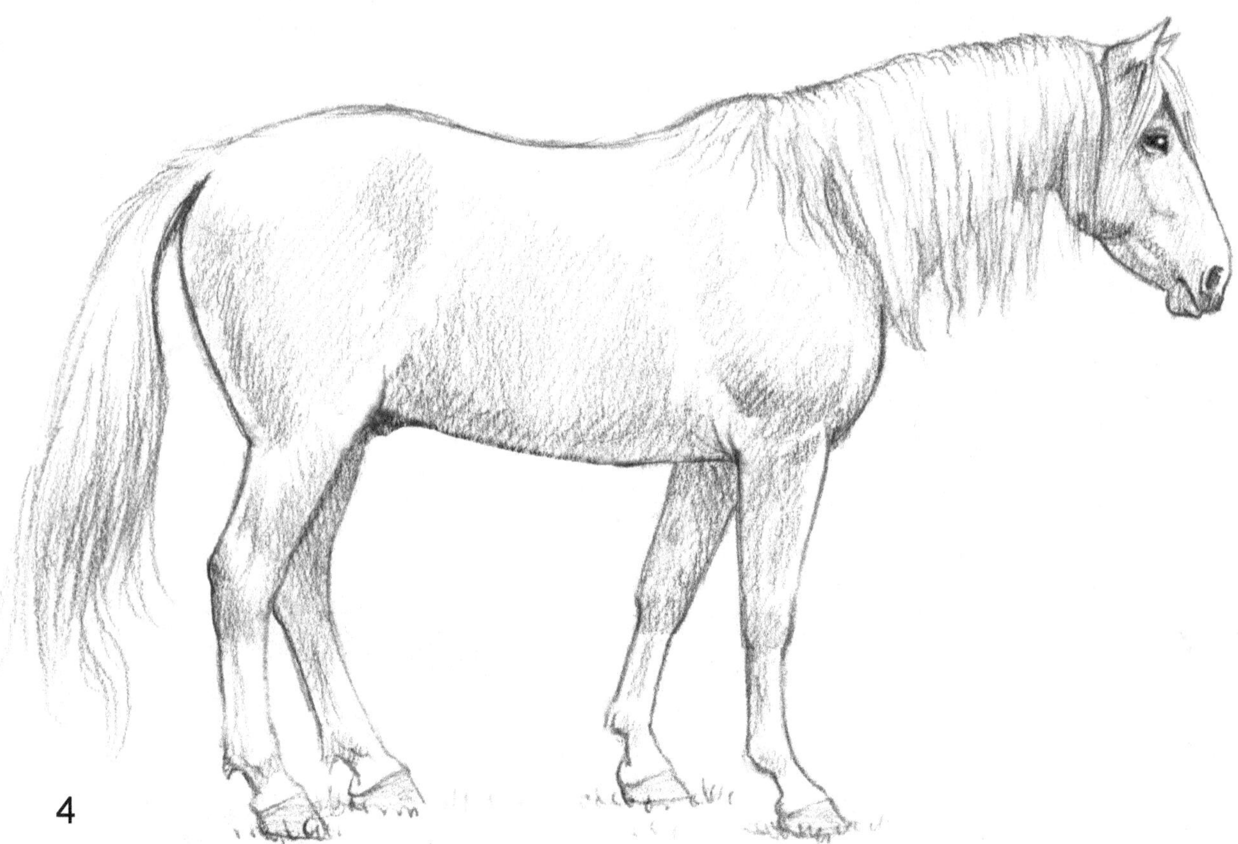

4

4. Start to indicate the areas of tone and shadow with loose strokes, holding the HB sideways, away from tip.
Some artists outline areas where tones change, but I usually do it by eye as I go, especially for small drawings.

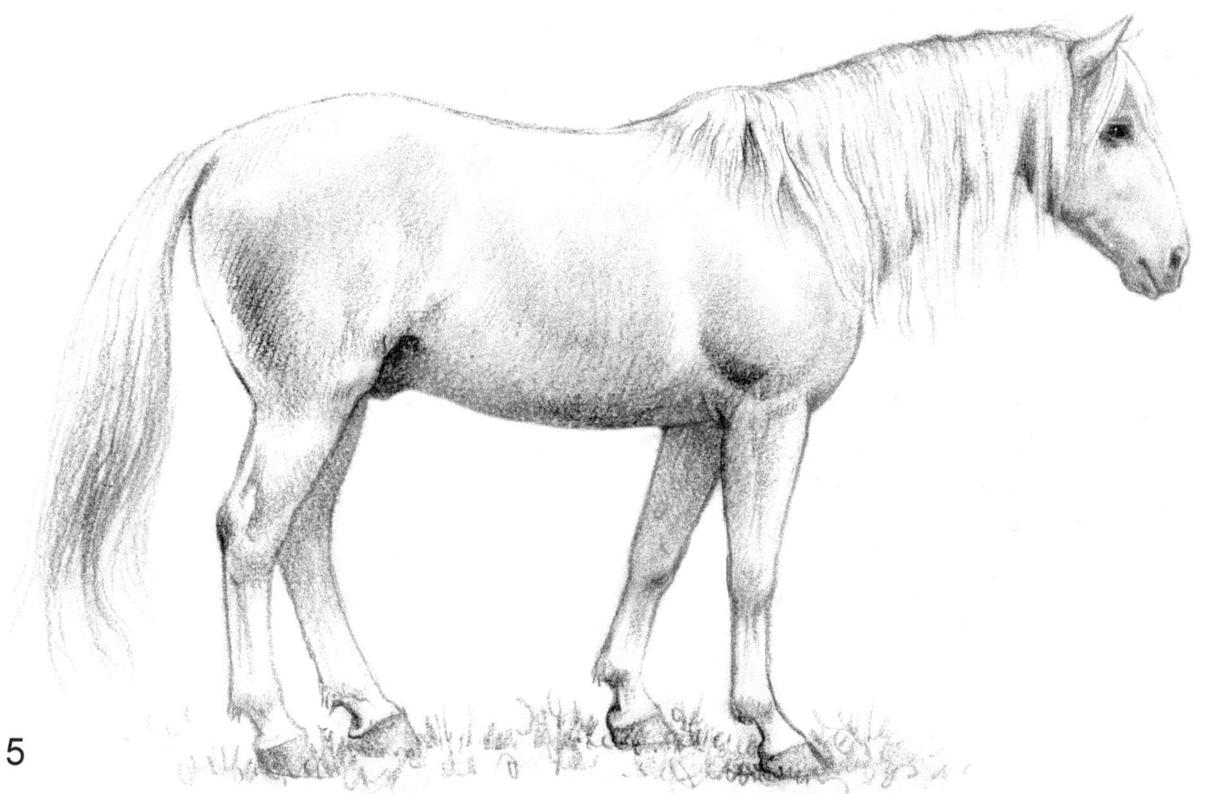

5

5. Add more shading with the HB. Try to simplify the shading into three basic values at first--a medium tone, a shadow tone, and then highlights that are left white or erased. Note: I erased areas of his mane to create more interesting uneven shapes. It helps to squint often at a reference picture to eliminate detail and see basic values.

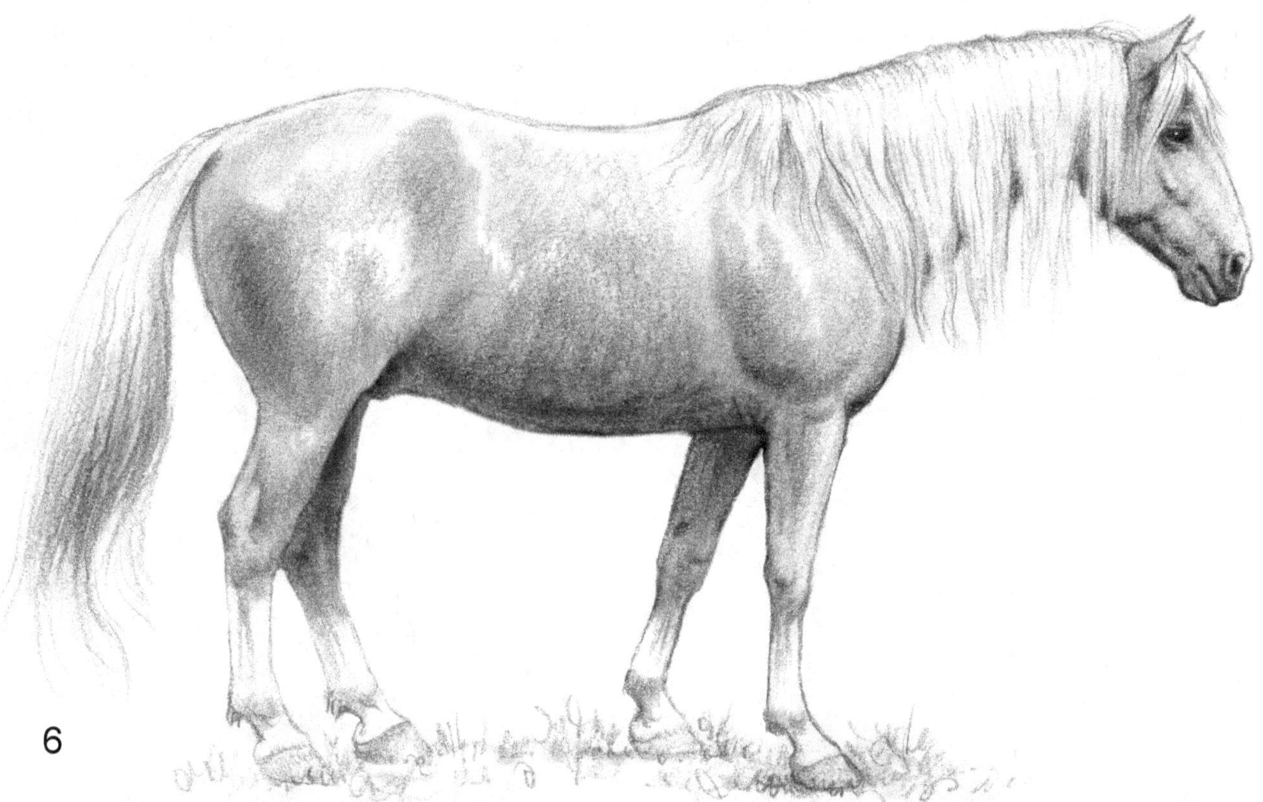

6

6. Use the HB to develop more tones on his body and legs. Add B and 2B to deepen the shadow areas, and (optional) carefully use the blending stump to soften the pencil strokes over his whole body. Note: Horses have subtle highlights and shading that I simplify for small drawings. I use the kneaded erasor to enhance areas of highlights to make them "pop." I don't just copy a photo, I interpret it artistically, and so can you!

MORGAN

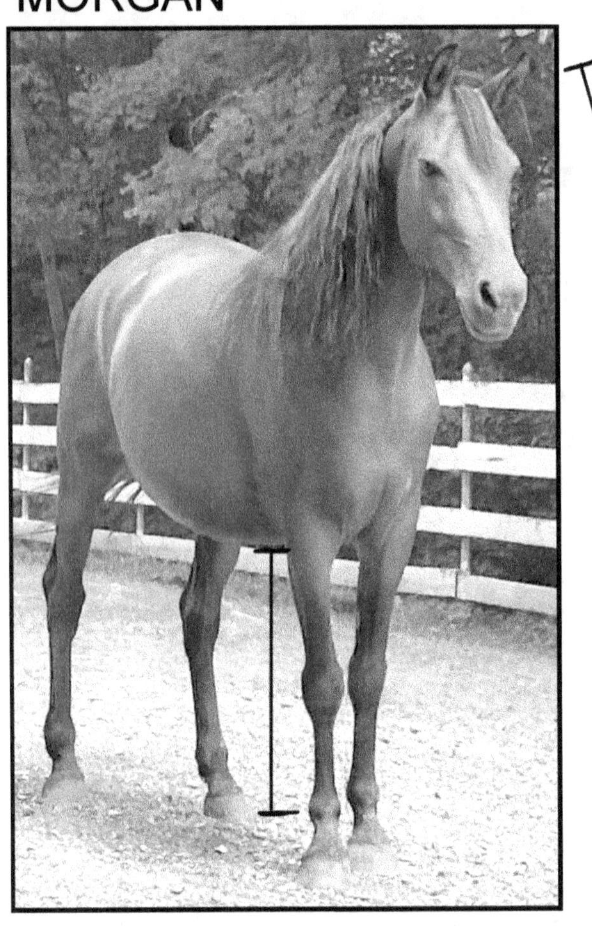

Head

Use the head any time to measure the relative proportions of different parts of the body, if you sense that your proportions are off. A very common mistake is to make the legs too long, for instance. Proportions are very important!

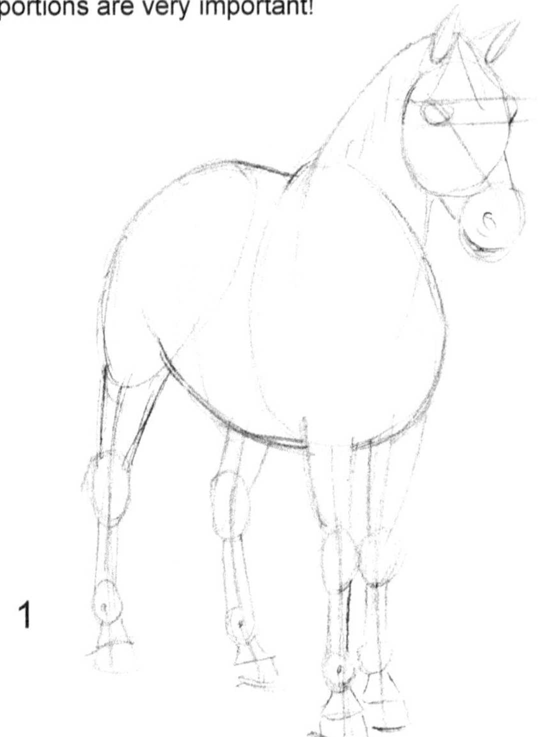

1

1. For 3/4 front views, draw the chest egg-shape first, then an egg shape for the closest hindquarter. Place the head ovals, noting where the bottom of the muzzle lines up on the body. Draw two parallel lines where the eyes will go, and a diamond shape to indicate the front plane of the face. Draw neck lines, a curving belly line, and a small back line. Indicate legs with simple gesture lines, and mark bottom of hooves. (continued on next page...)

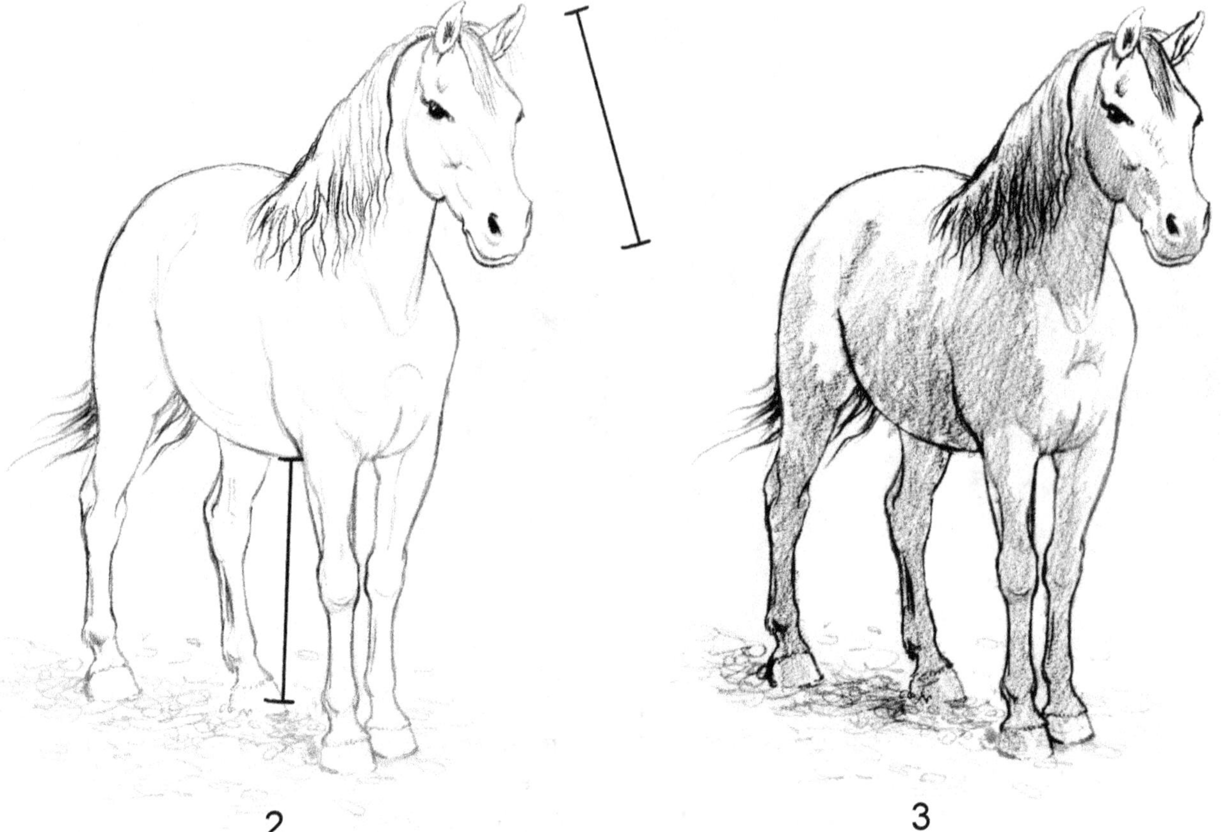

2

3

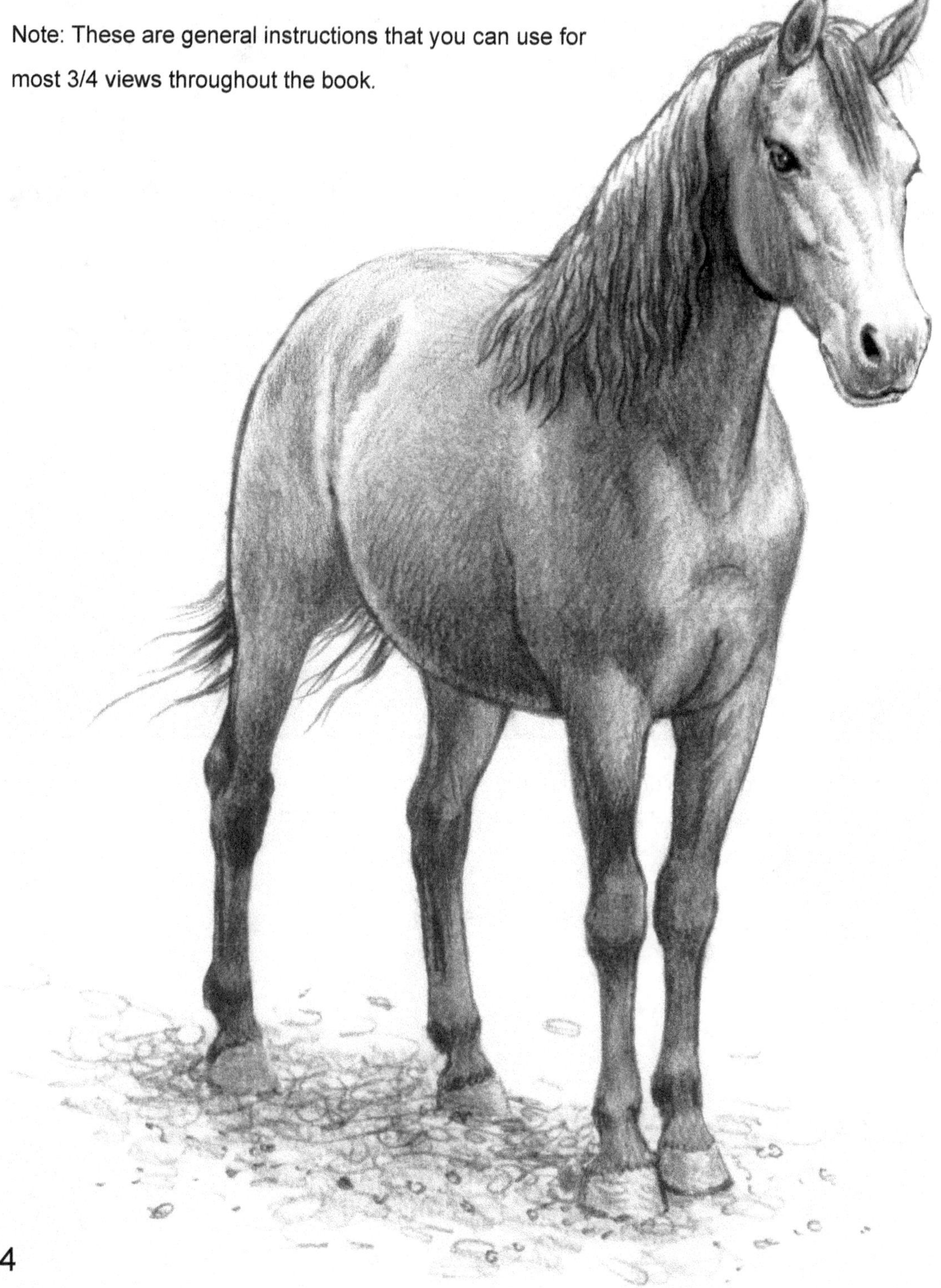

4

1. (Opposite) Draw large ovals for the hocks and smaller ovals for the placement of the knees. Connect the upper legs to the hocks and knees. Draw circles for the fetlocks and connect with straight lines to hocks and knees. Draw two lines making a cut-off cone shape to indicate the pasterns. Draw a simple hoof shape.
2. (Opposite) Looking carefully at the photo, start to refine the block-in shapes into the lines of the exact outlines of shapes and angles that you see. Add a few lines to indicate the muscles and bones that are prominent. I erase most of my initial block-in shape lines as I go. Pay attention to the subtle curve between the pastern and hoof.
3. (Opposite) Start to indicate the areas of tone and shadow with the HB using loose parallel strokes.
4. Build up the tones slowly with the HB pencil, with strokes following the curves of the body, and add B and 2B for darkest darks. Use a blending stump to soften the shading if you want. Erase some selected highlights.

SHIRE DRAFT HORSE

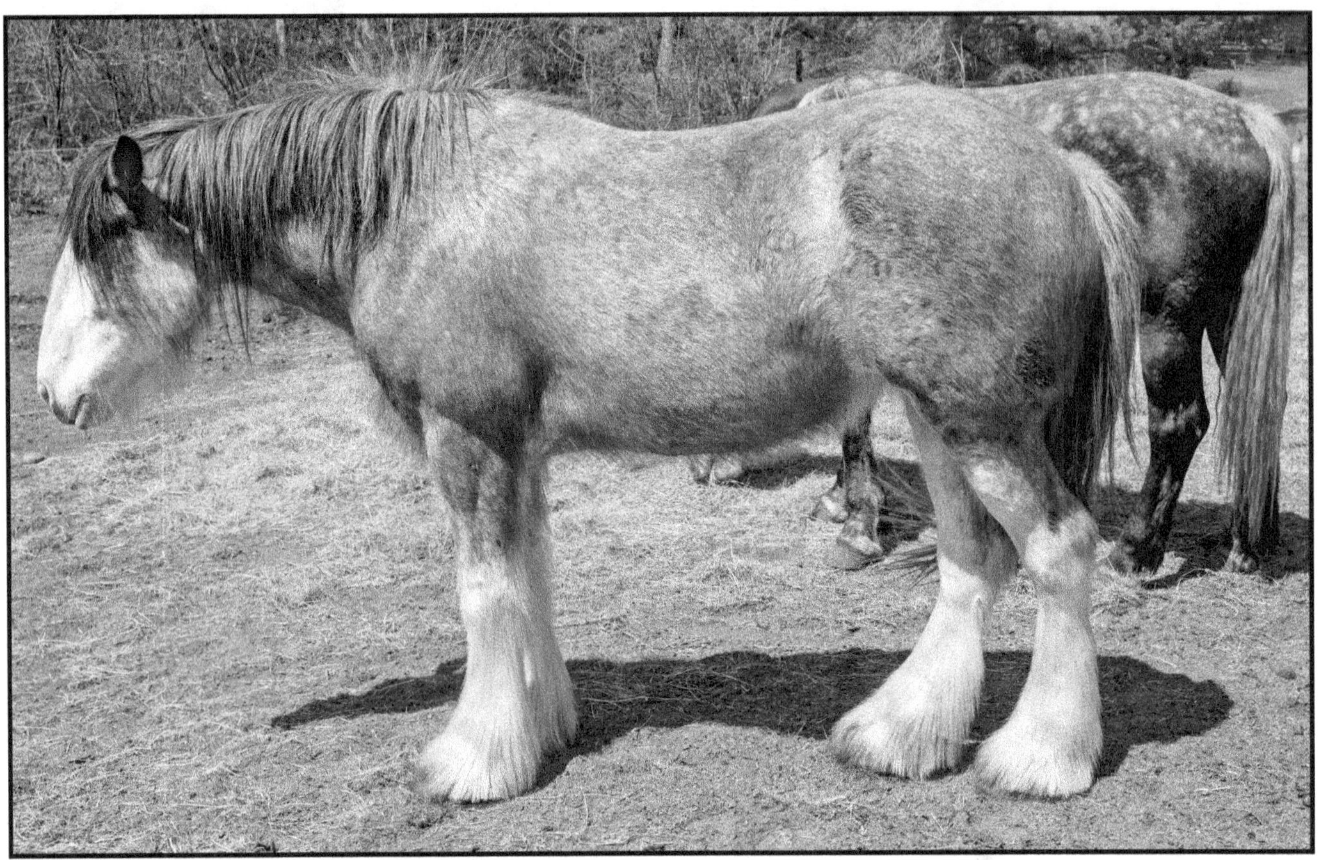

Notice how hairy the lower legs are on this draft horse mare. They are called "feathers," and though they cover the bones, you can still make out the form underneath, because of the sunlight falling from above.

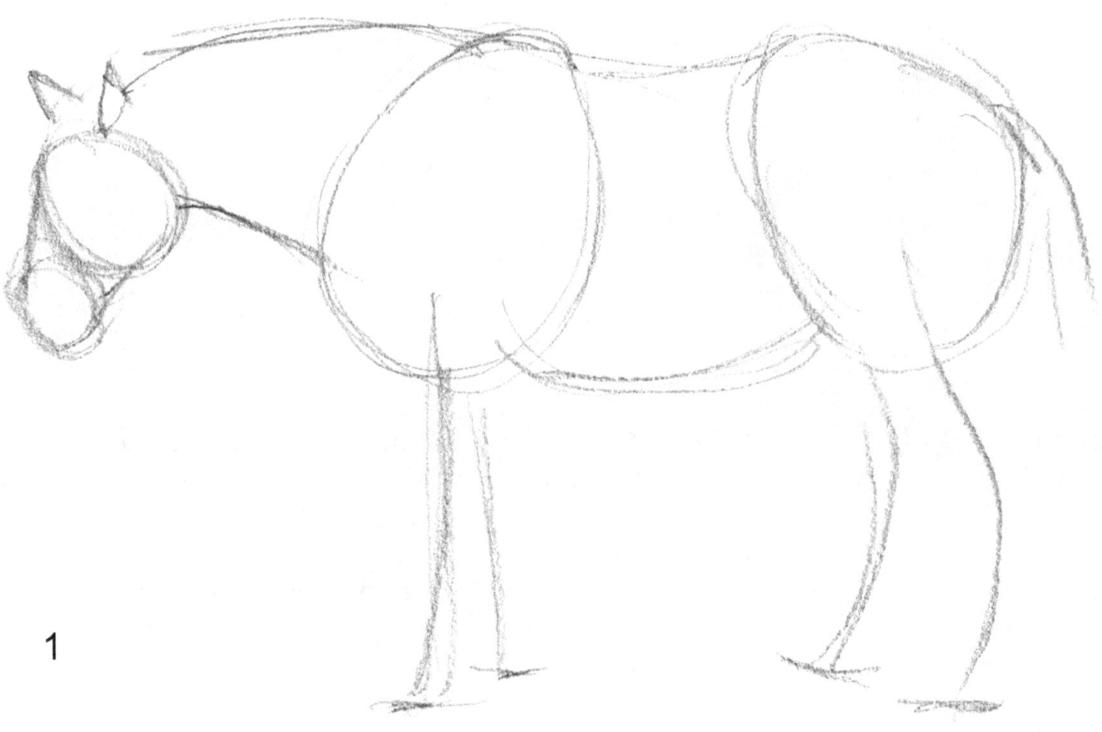

1

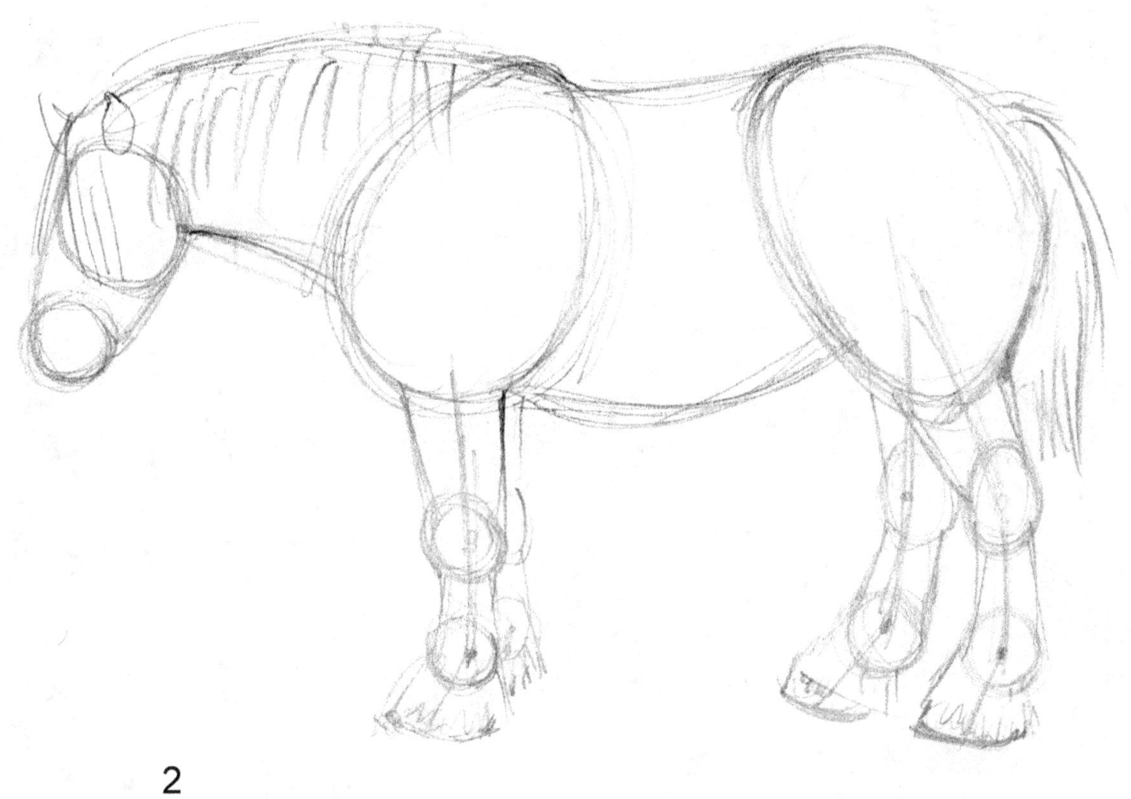

2

Her eye is completely hidden by her long forelock, so I am leaving it out.

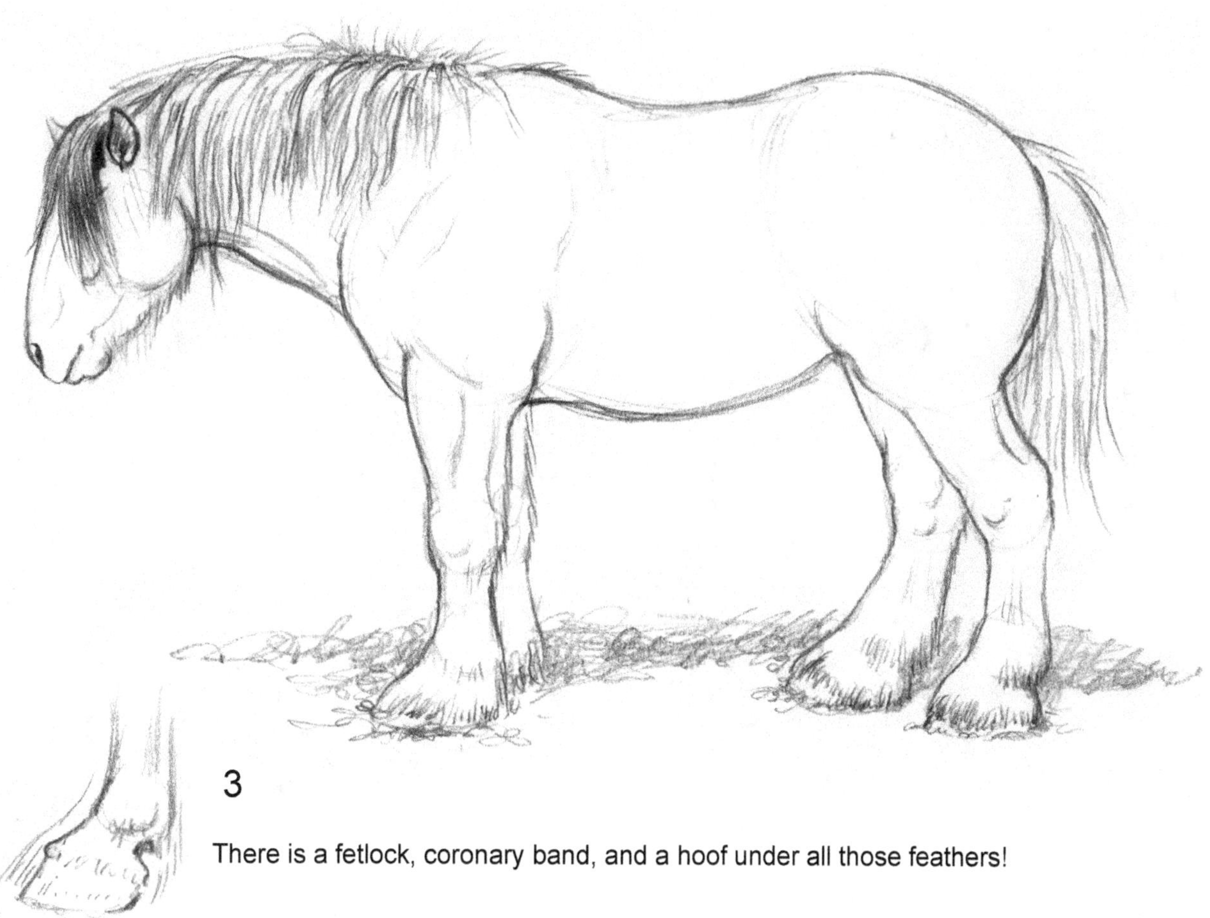

3

There is a fetlock, coronary band, and a hoof under all those feathers!

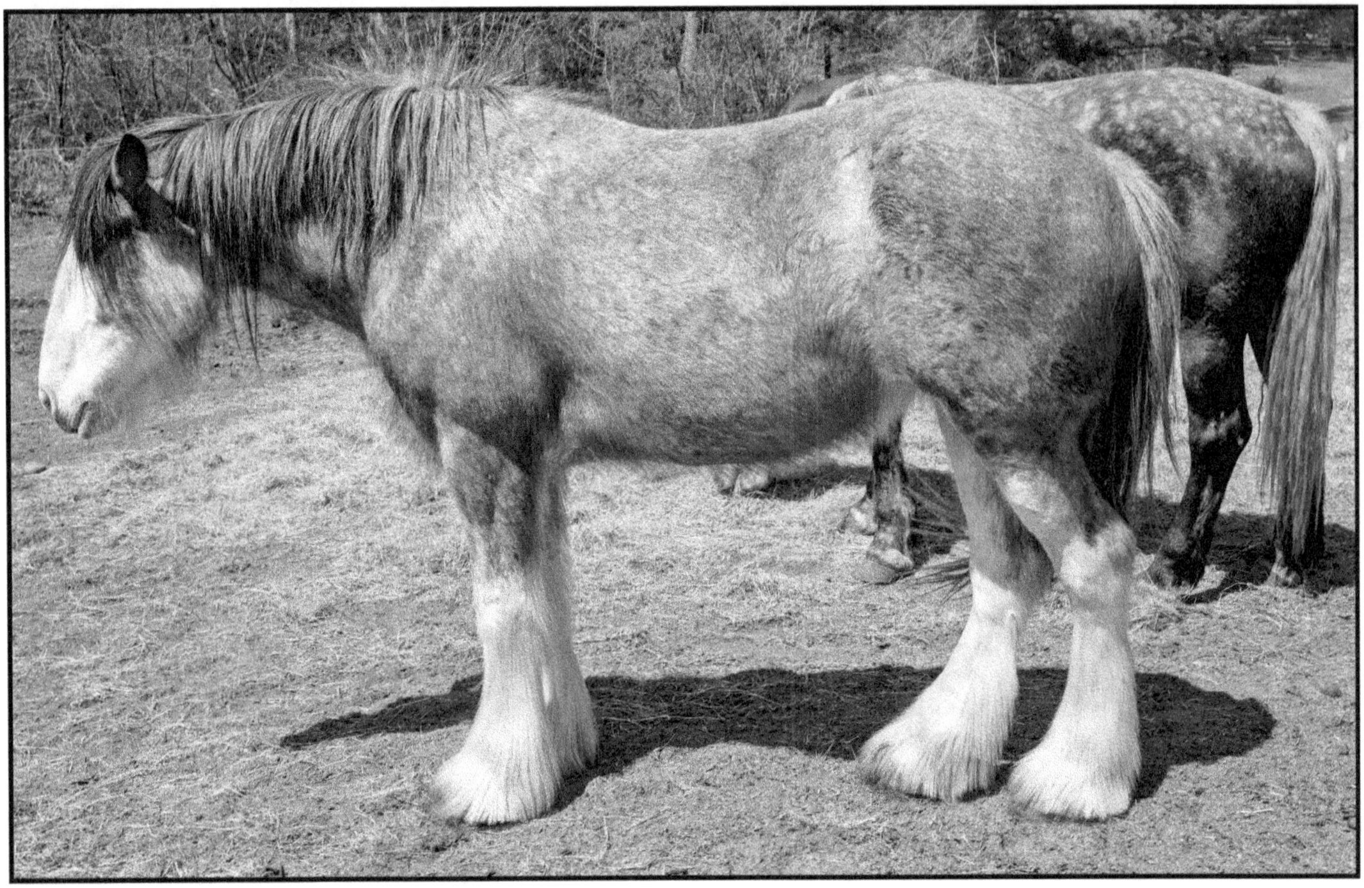

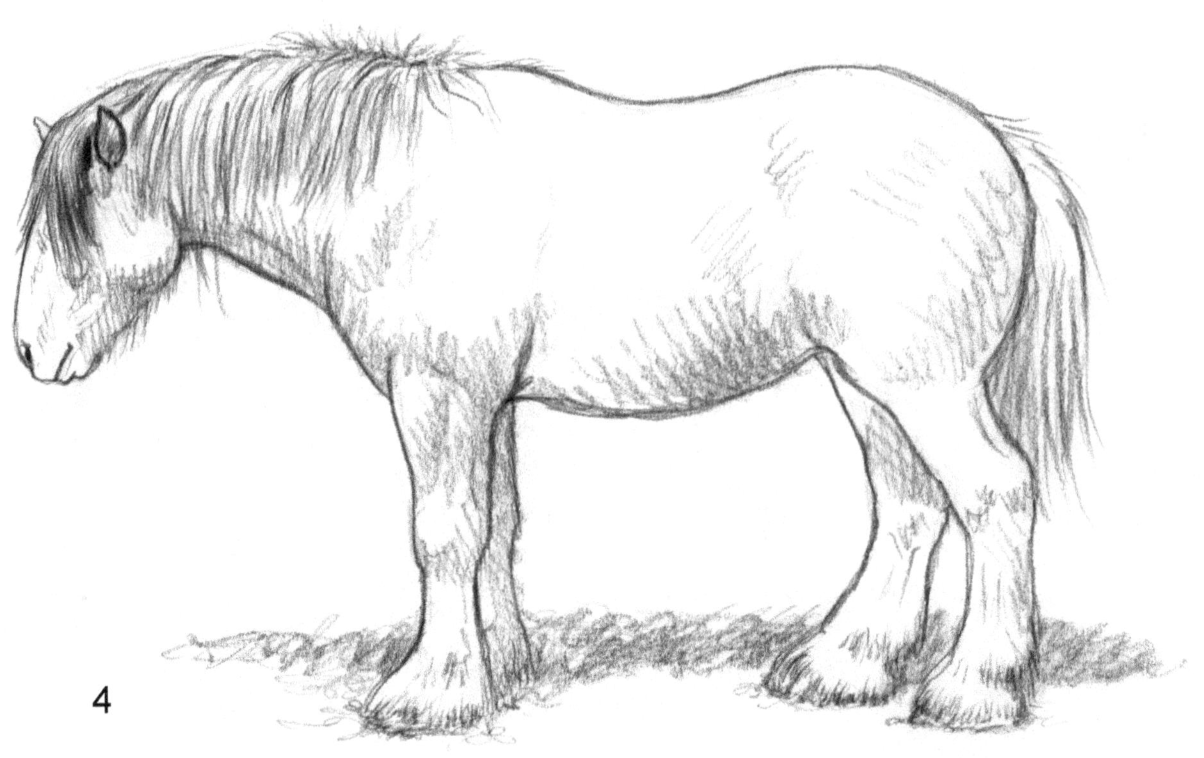

4

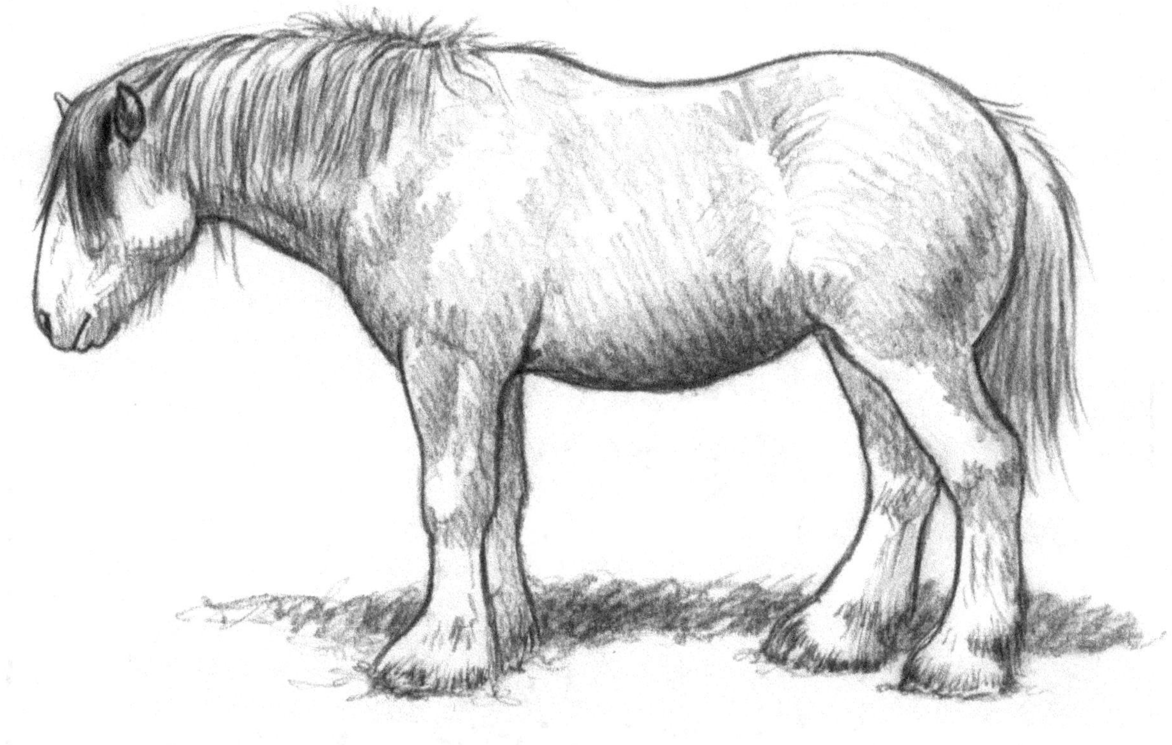

5

For this furry lady I decided to create her coat with lots of little strokes in the direction of the fur. Look carefully at the photo and you will see how the fur grows. I won't use the blending stump on this one.

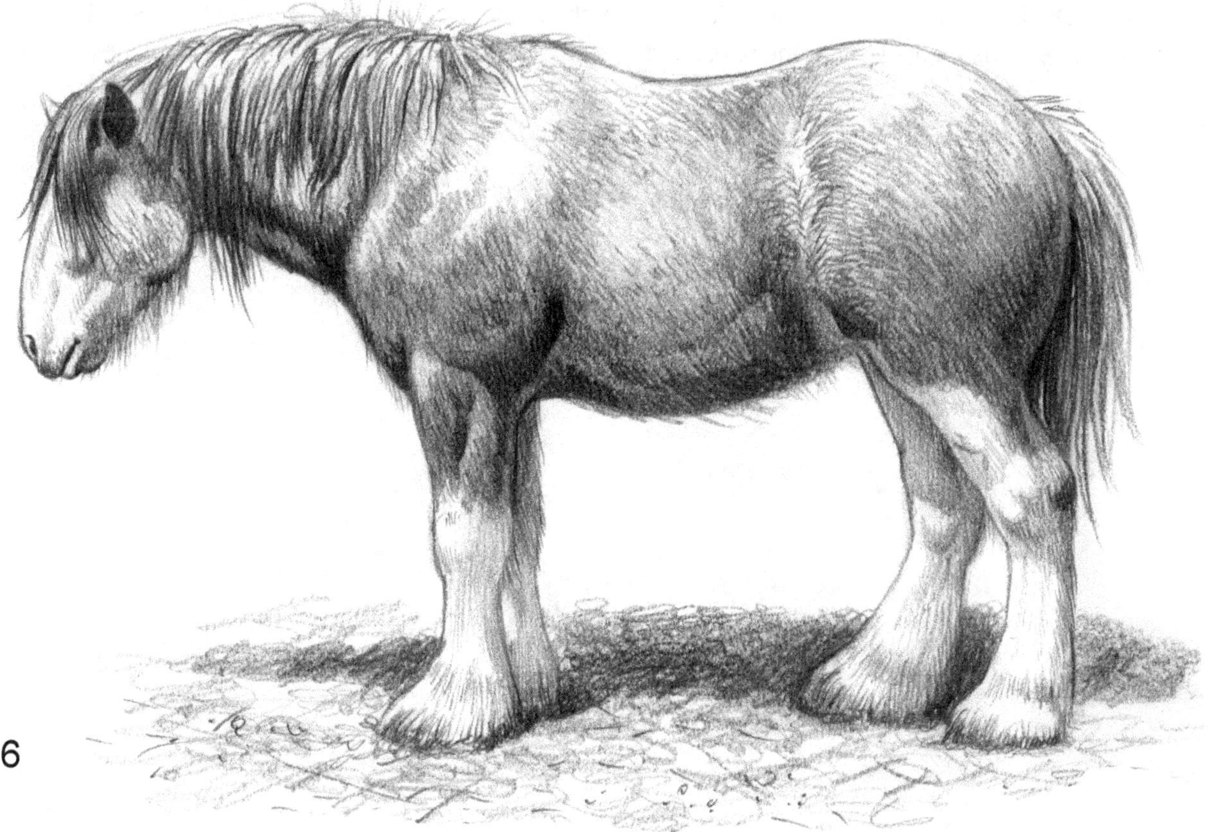

6

Note that the shadow on white areas are not as dark as on the main part of her body. As you get more drawing experience you will be able to identify values and where they fall on the value scale. (p.21)

SHETLAND PONY

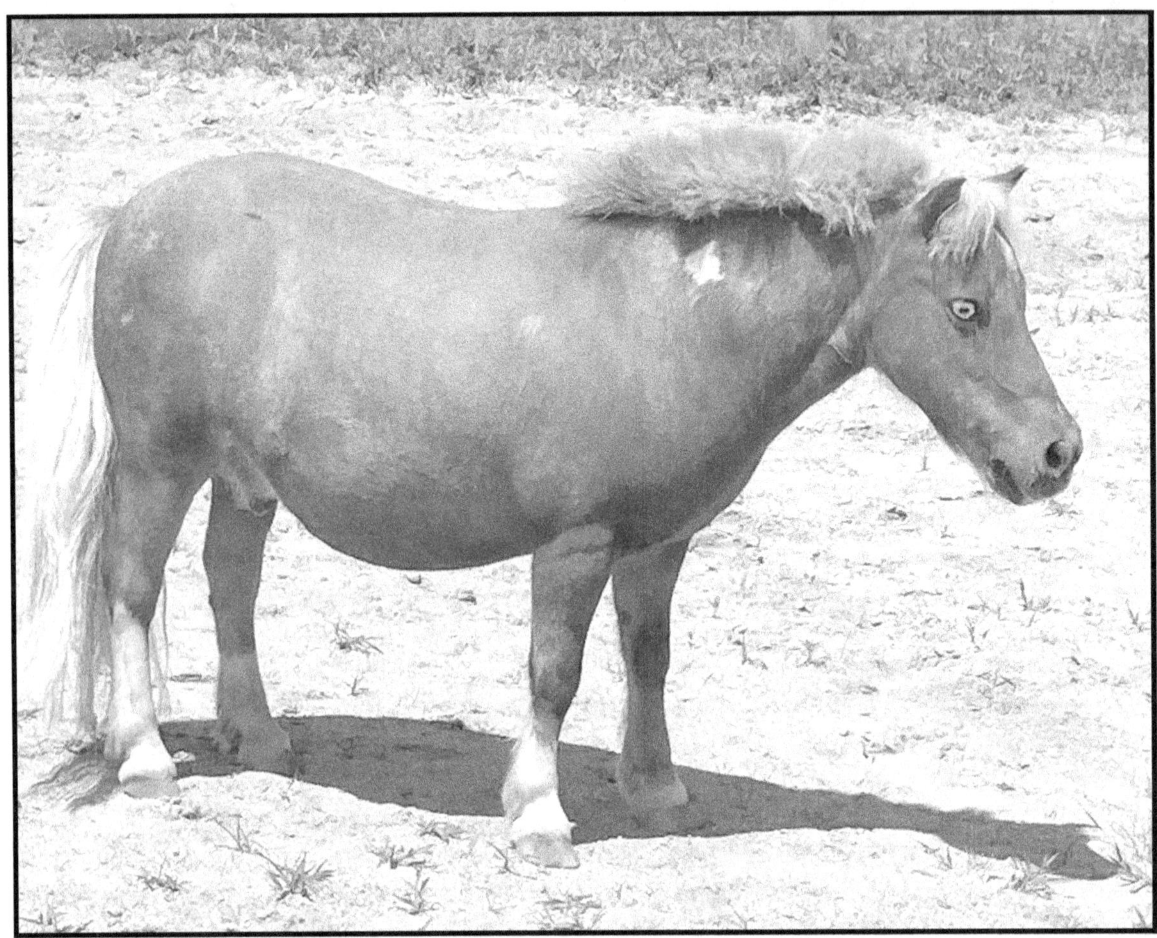

It is easy to see a ball shape in this pony with the sun almost directly overhead. Ponies have short little legs. If you are unsure, measure the head in the photo and set that against his front legs. It is just about the same length.

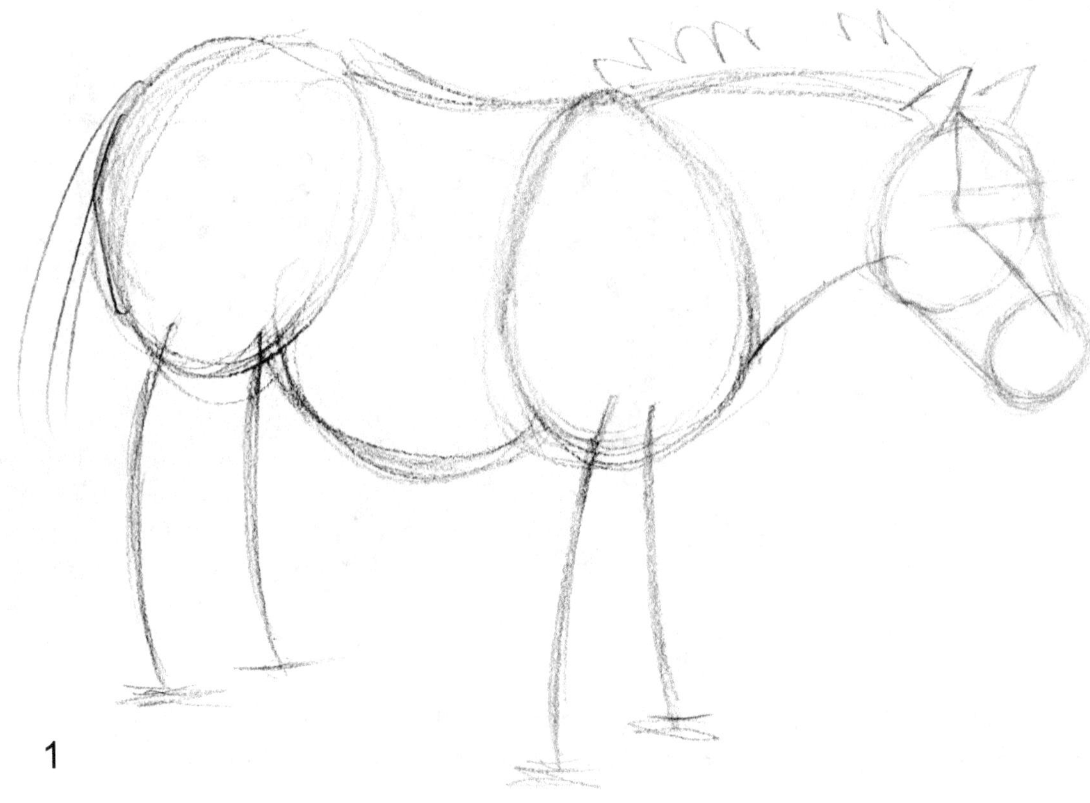

1

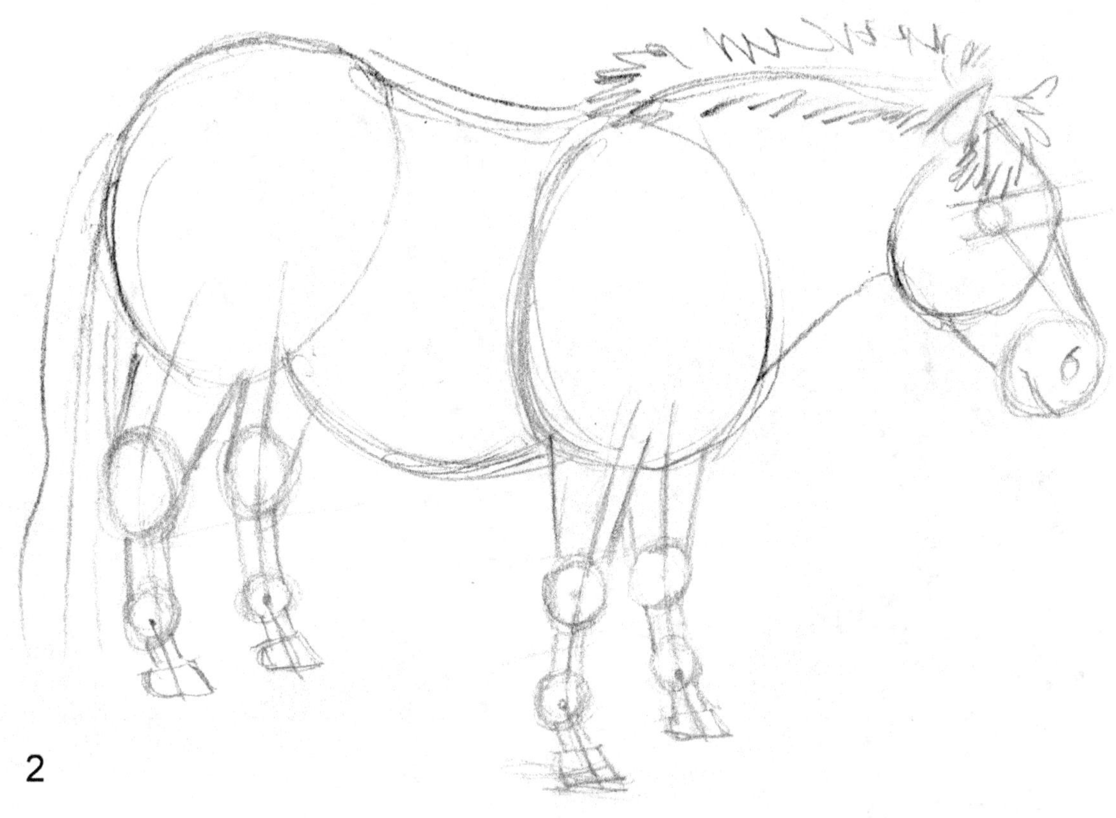

2

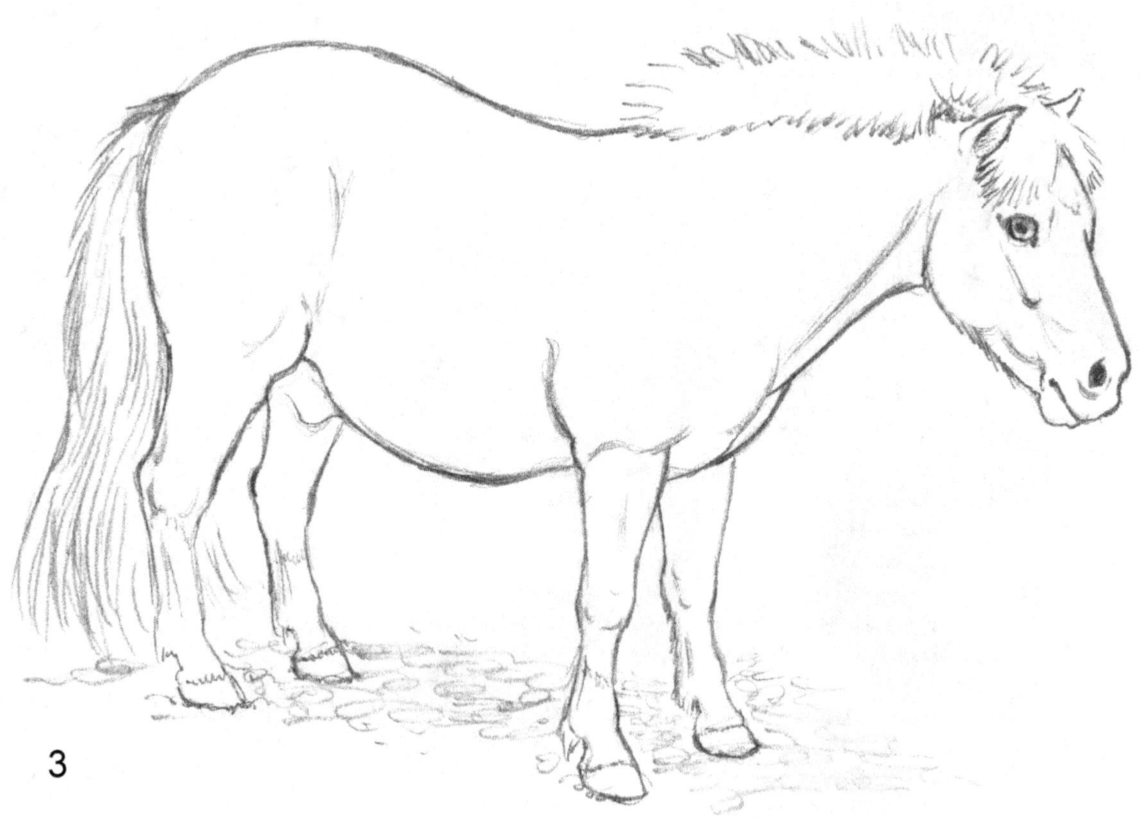

3

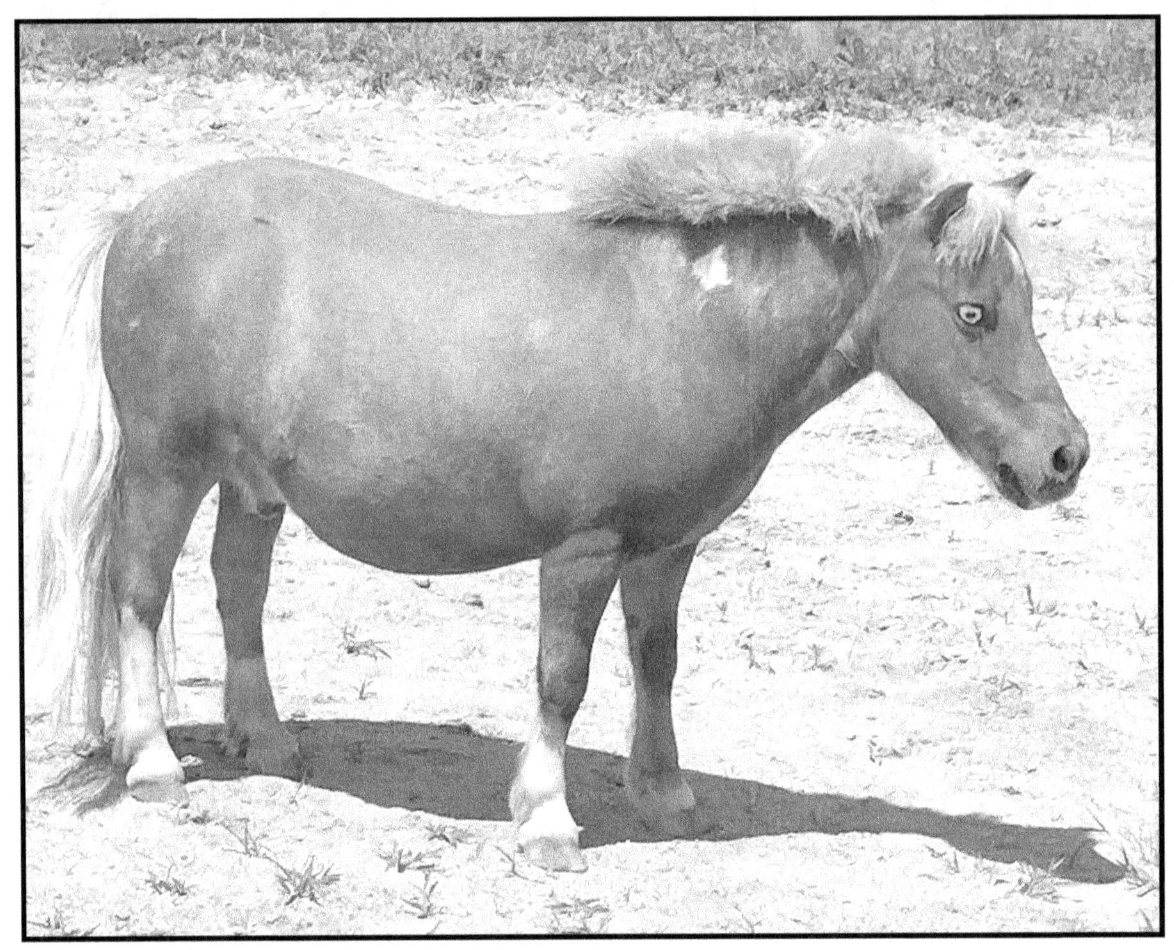

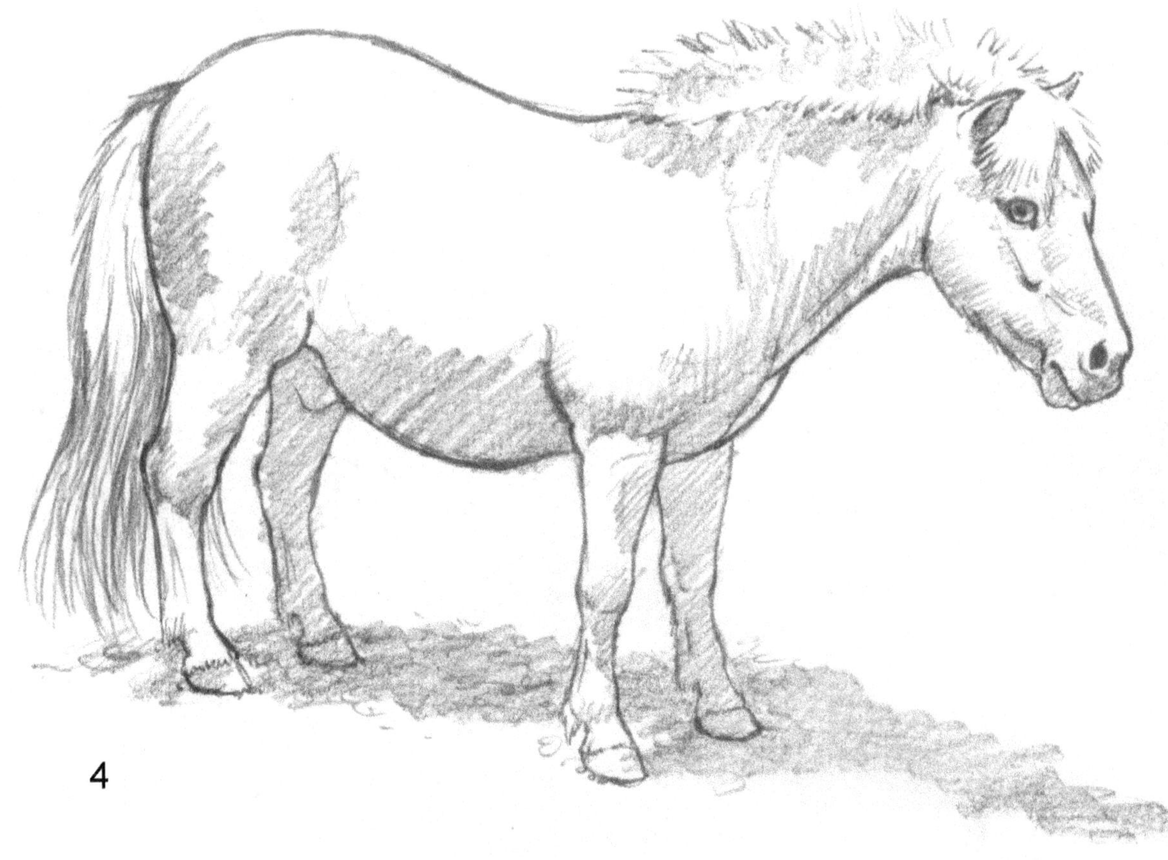

4

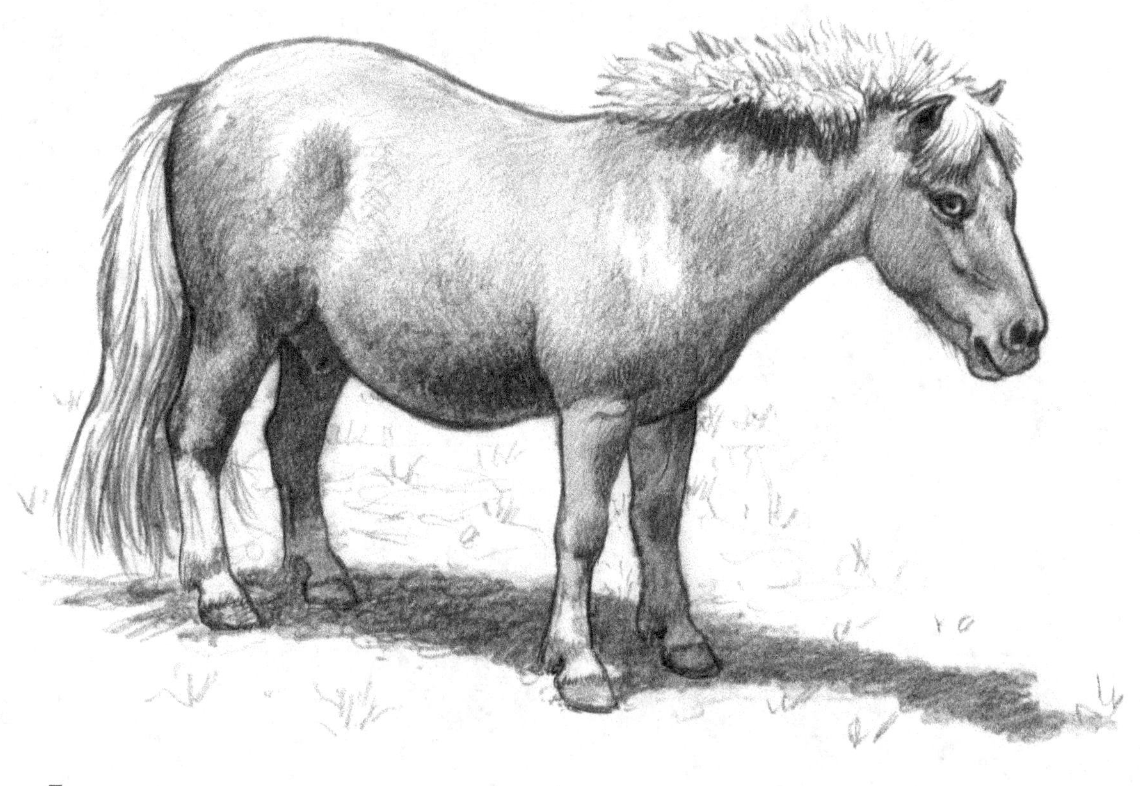

5

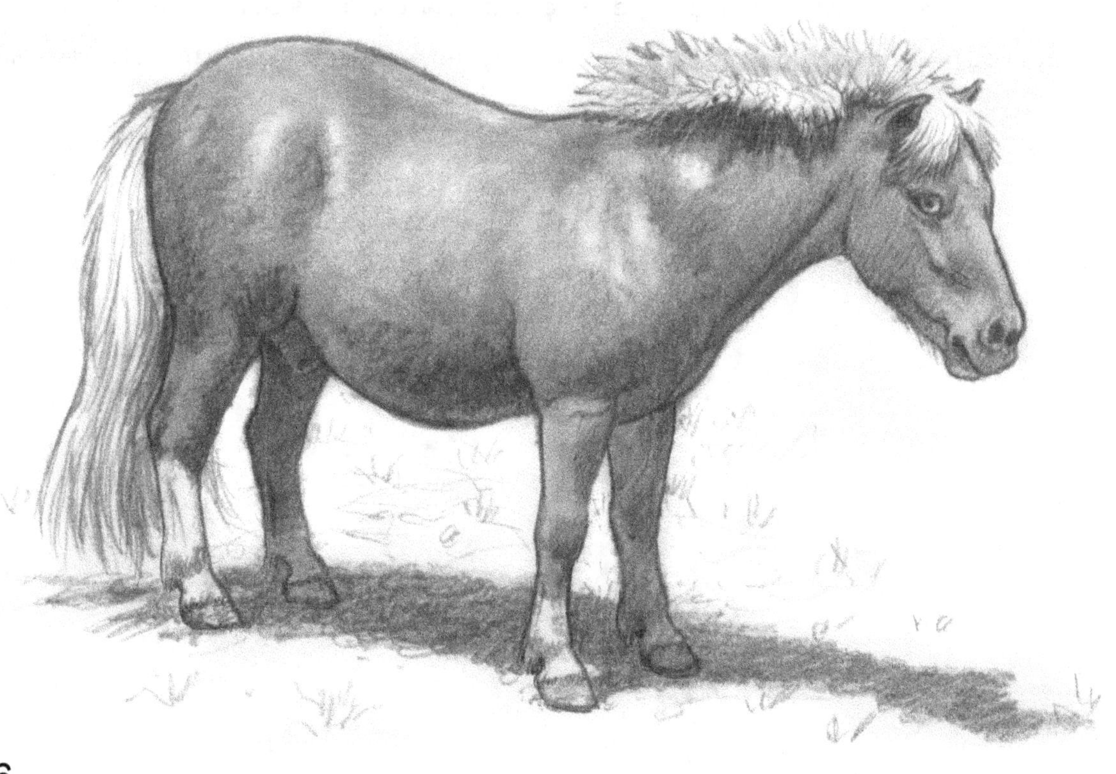

6

I decided to use a blending stump after I added more tone on his body, for a smooth look. You can experiment with the blending stump, or you can also just use your finger to blend. It can get a bit messy, though.

ARABIAN-SADDLEBRED CROSS

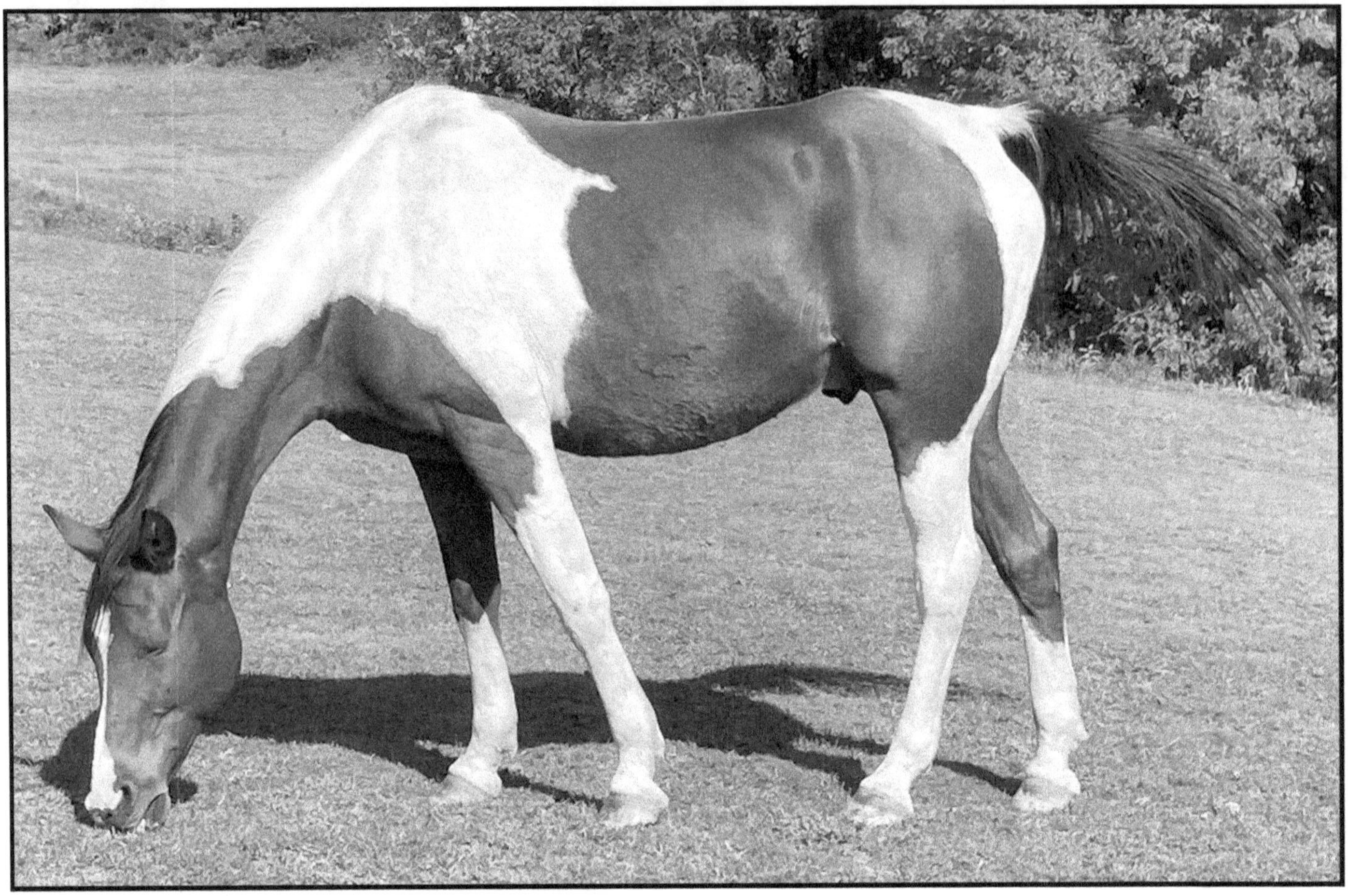

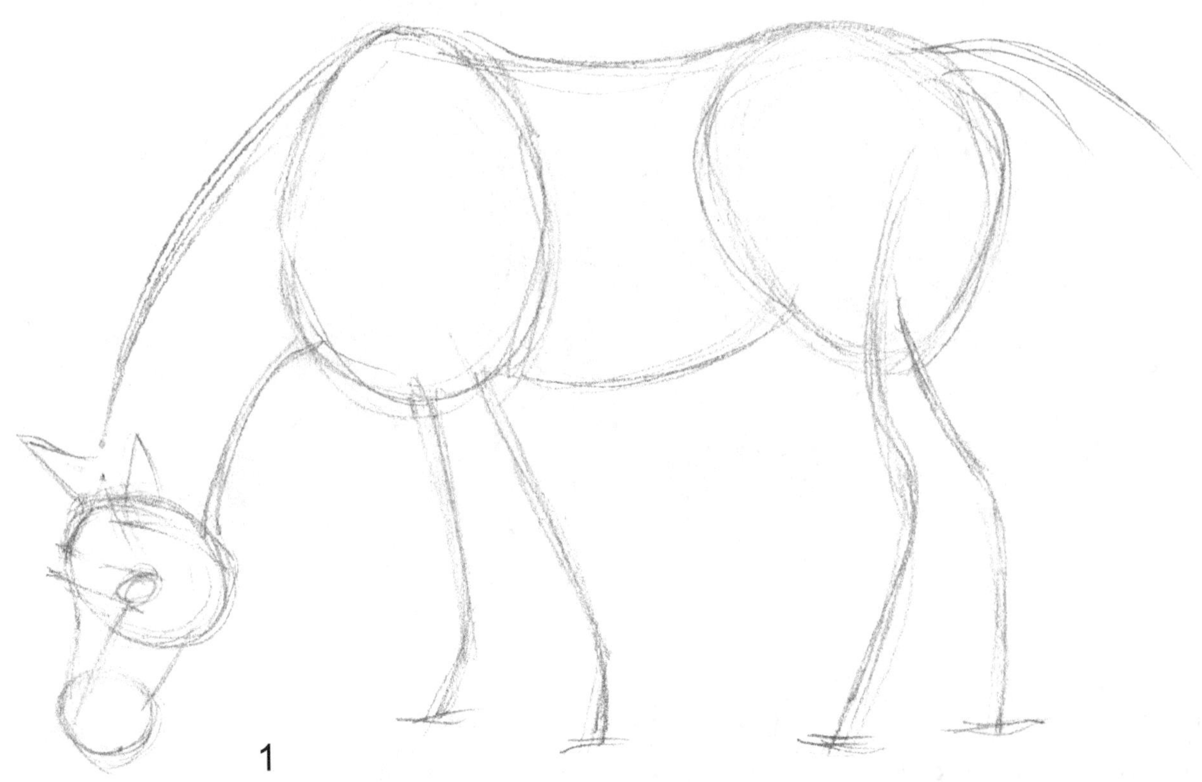

Reminder: Always draw lightly at first, since you'll be erasing your initial guidelines/shapes. I have actually darkened the contrast of my initial pencil lines for this book, so they can be more easily seen. I draw much lighter at first.

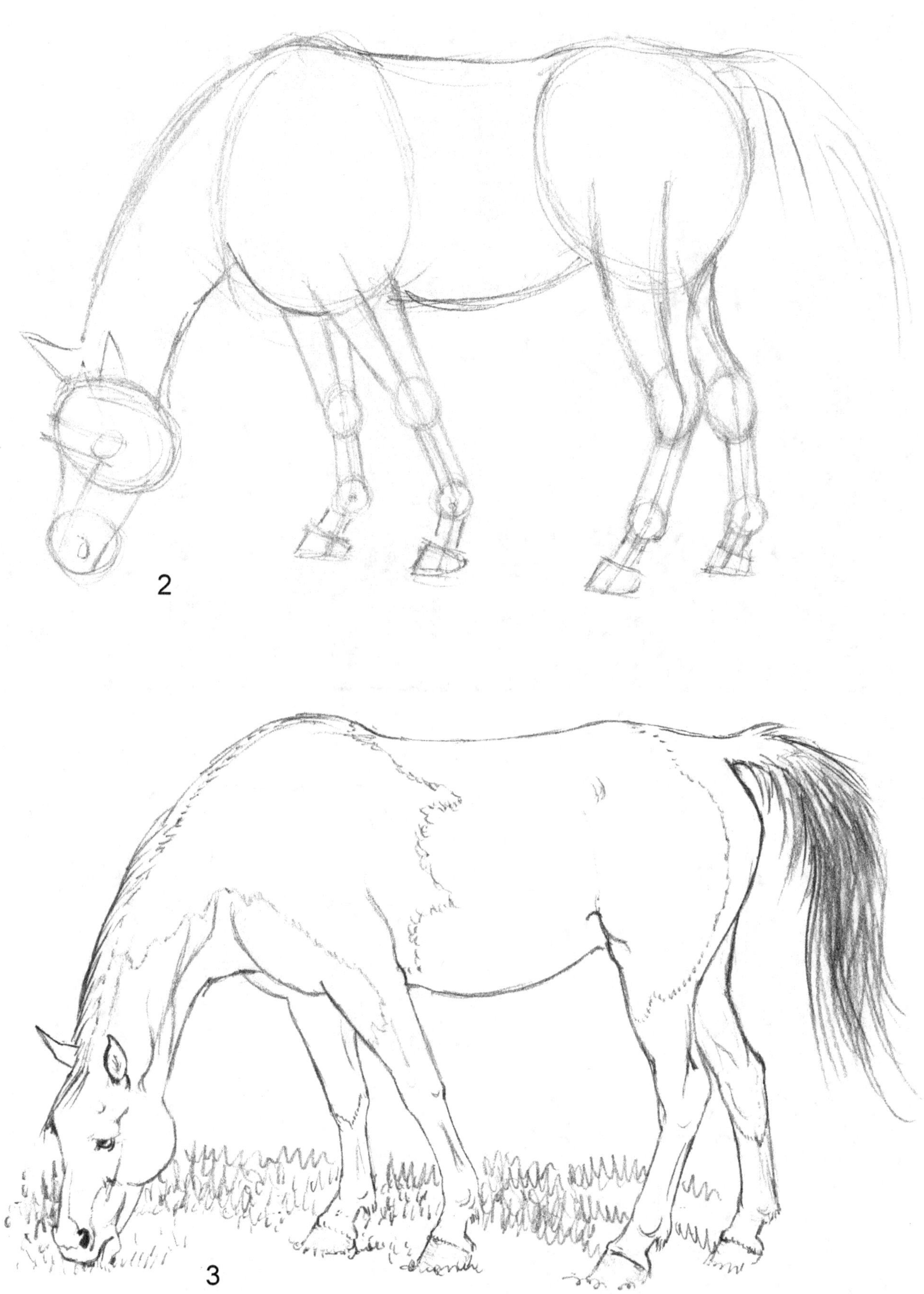

At the outline stage on a pinto horse, I lightly draw the outline of the color pattern on his coat. I didn't like the tail position in the photo, so I created a new pose for it, a "pony tail" shape.

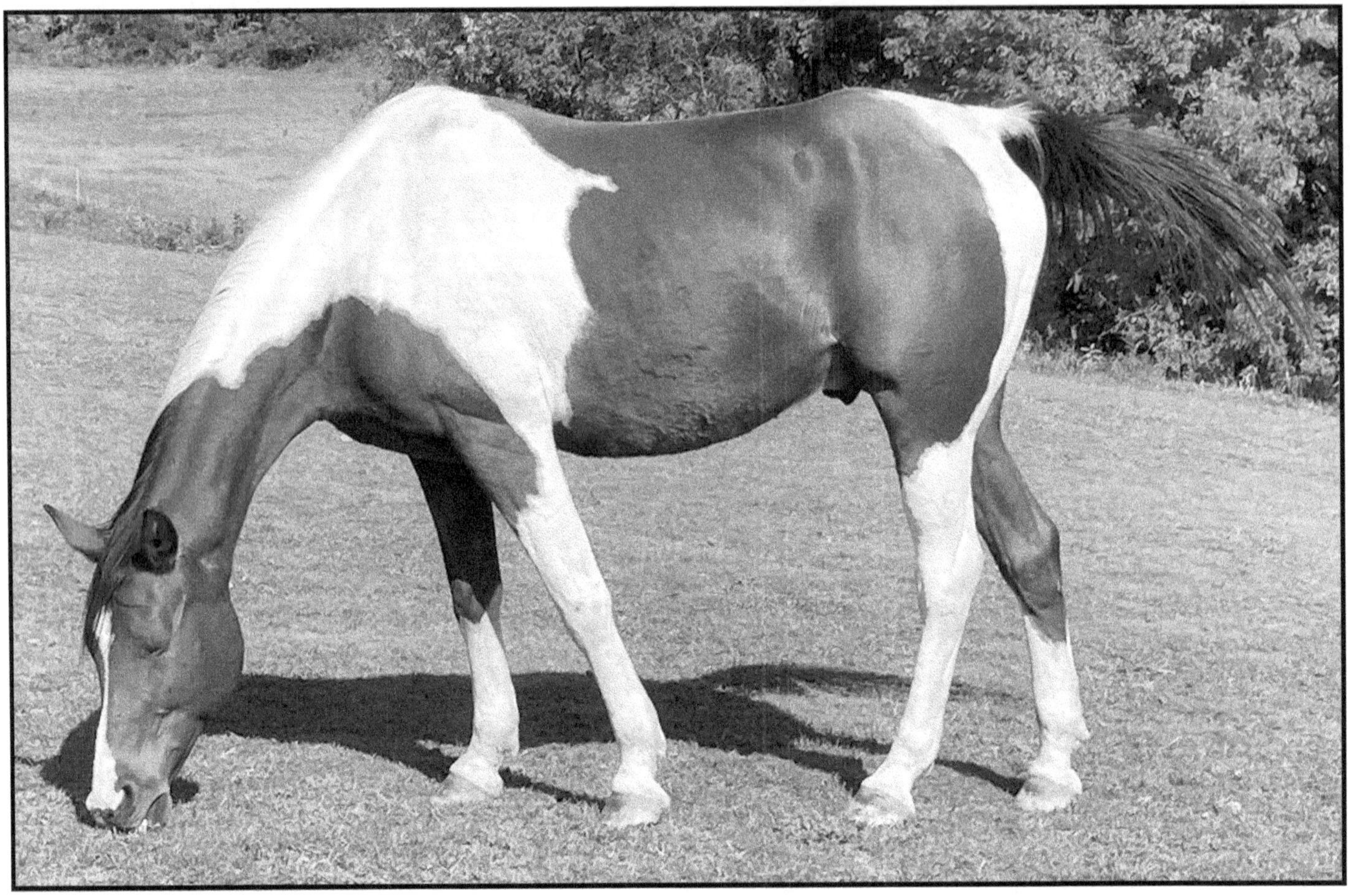

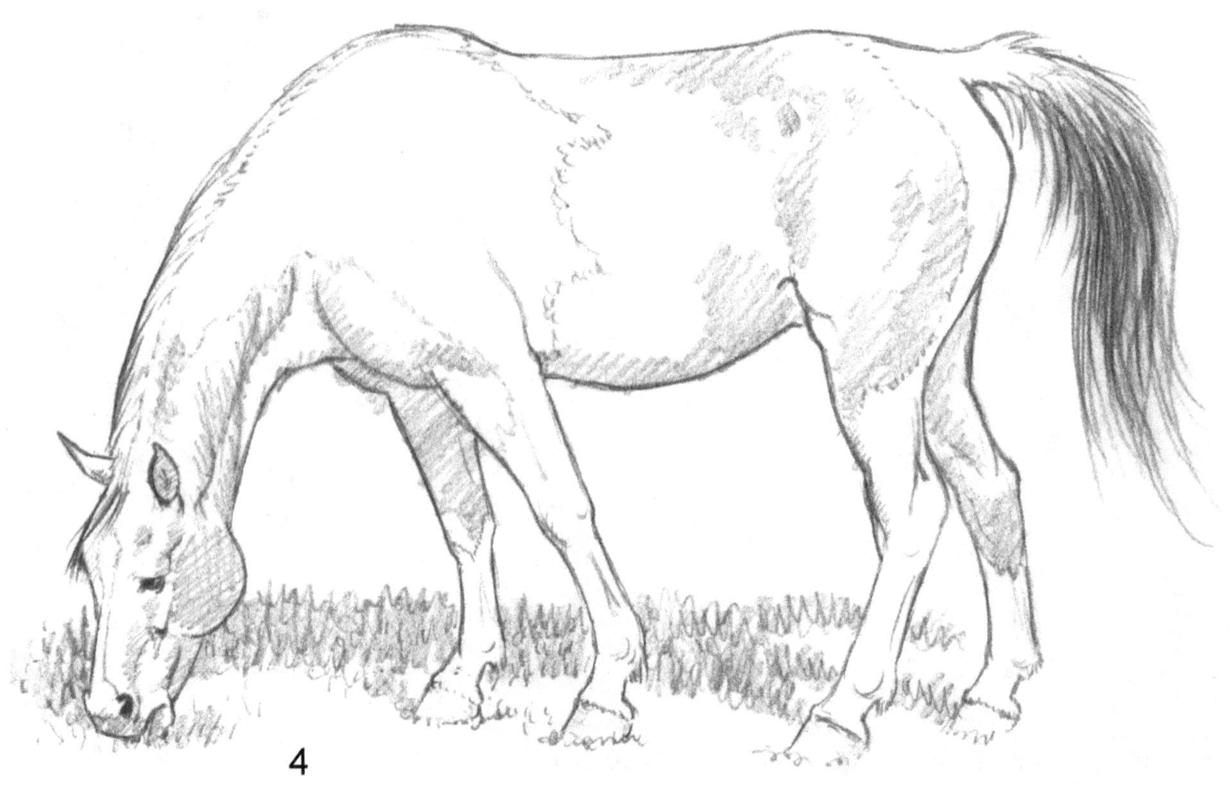

4

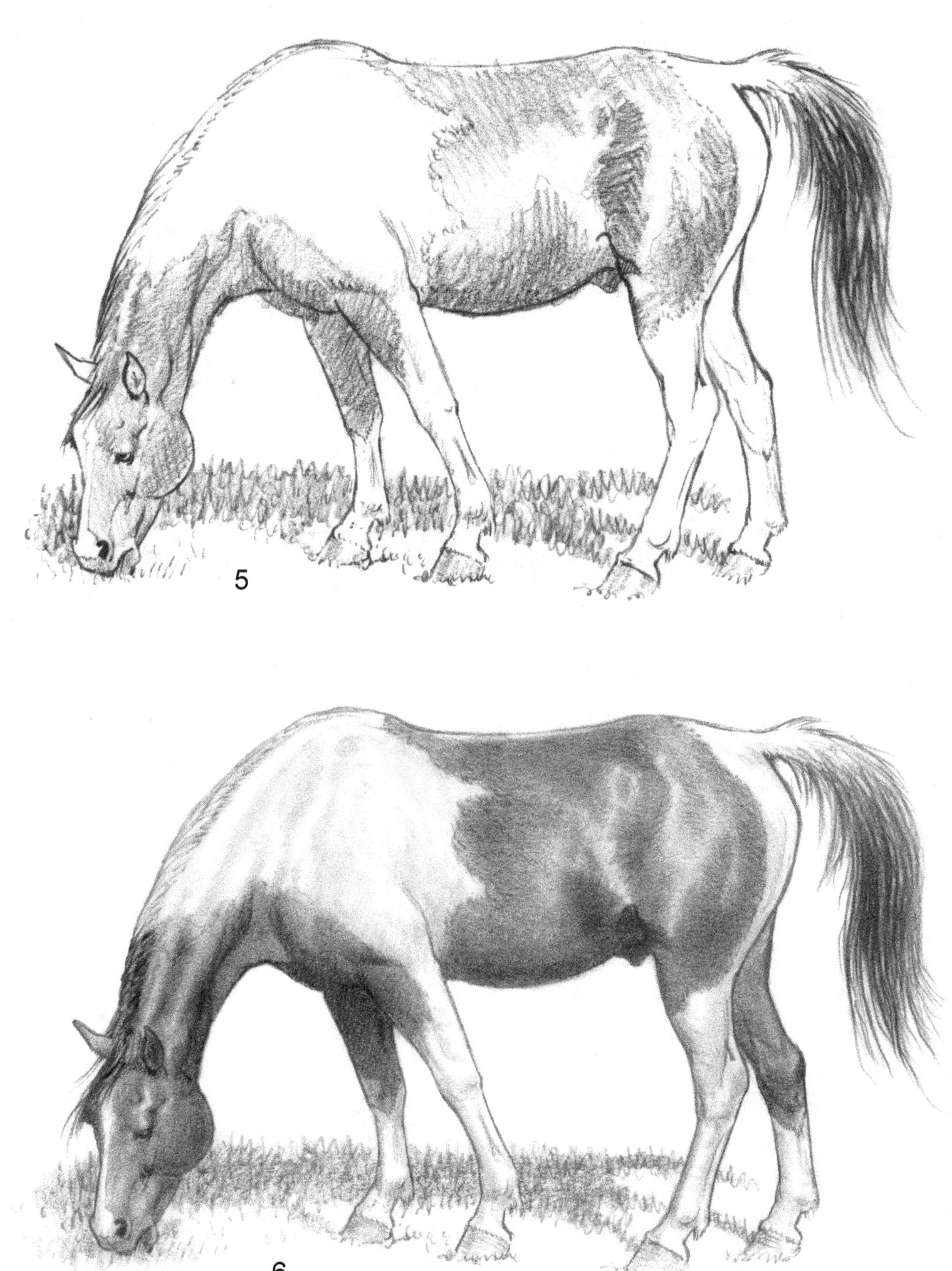

5

6

This horse is black and white, so I went quite dark with his black side. The darker the horse, the longer it takes to build up those darker tones.The shiny parts are not pure white, they are a light gray tone.

HORSES in MOTION

The three main "gaits" of the horse are the walk, the trot, and the canter. A gallop is basically a fast canter. There are breeds with extra gaits, but these are the ones they all have. As you become familiar with how they look at various stages, you should be able to tell from looking at a photo which gait a horse is doing.

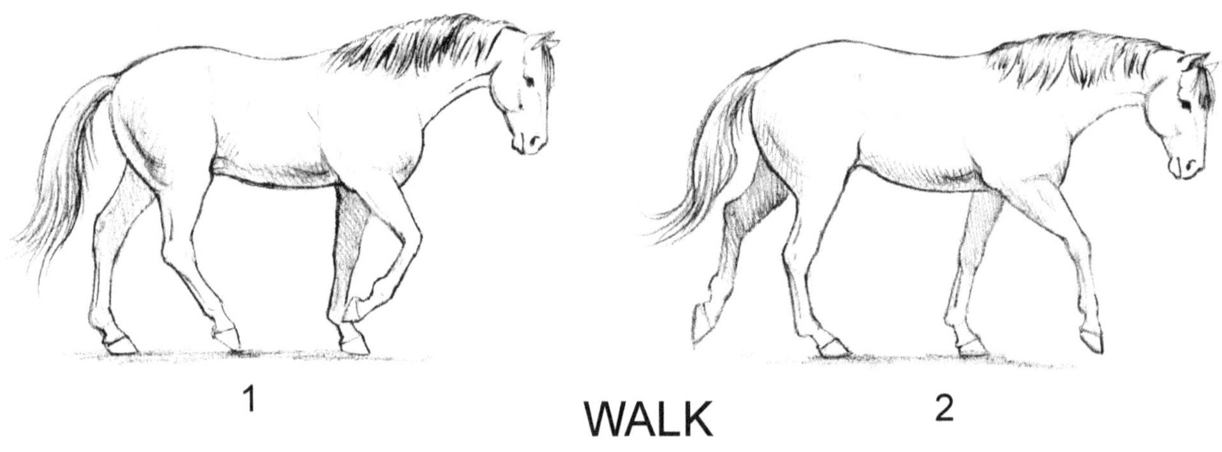

1   **WALK**   2

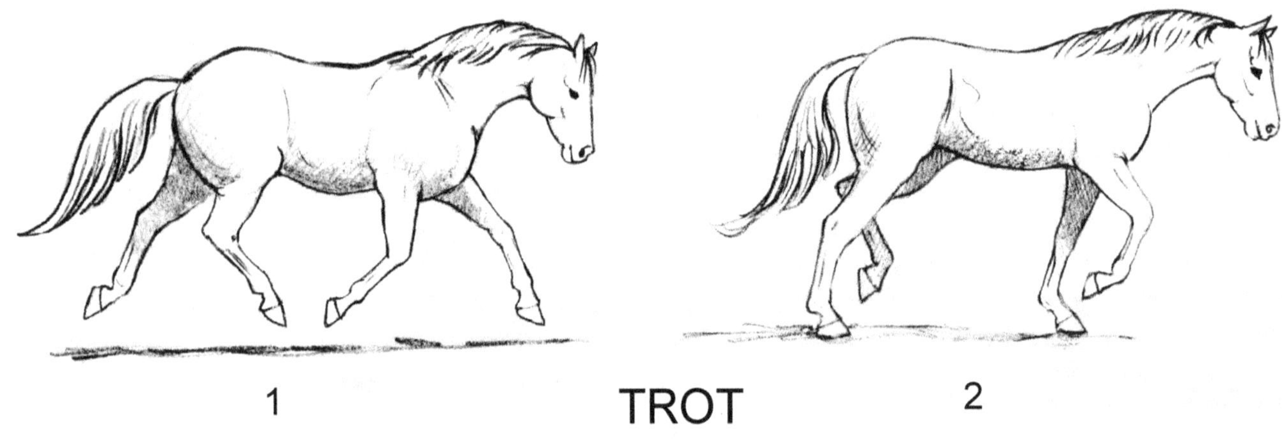

1   **TROT**   2

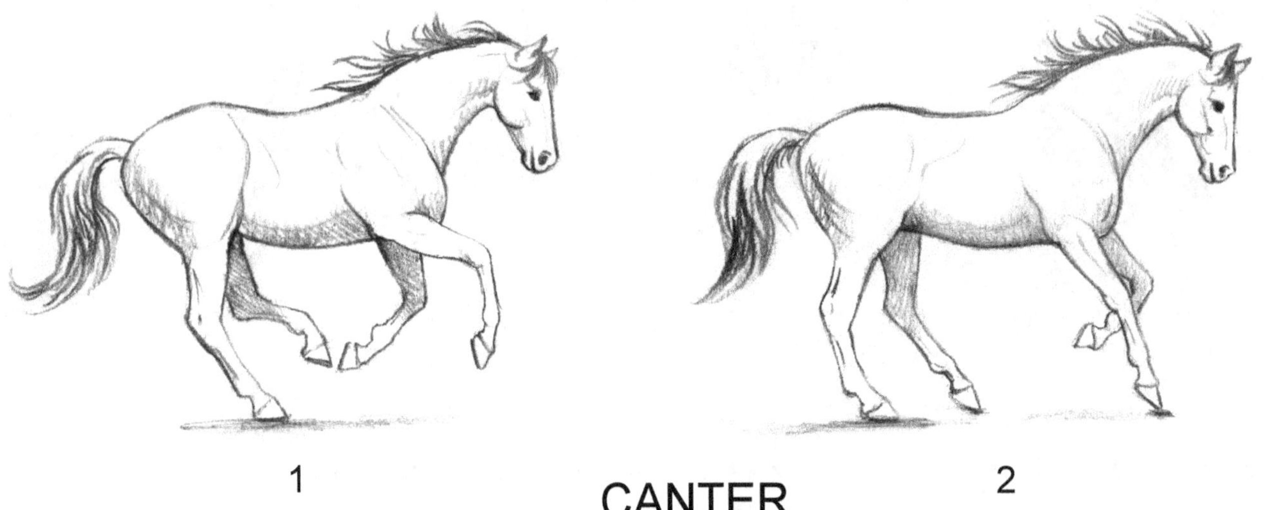

1   **CANTER**   2

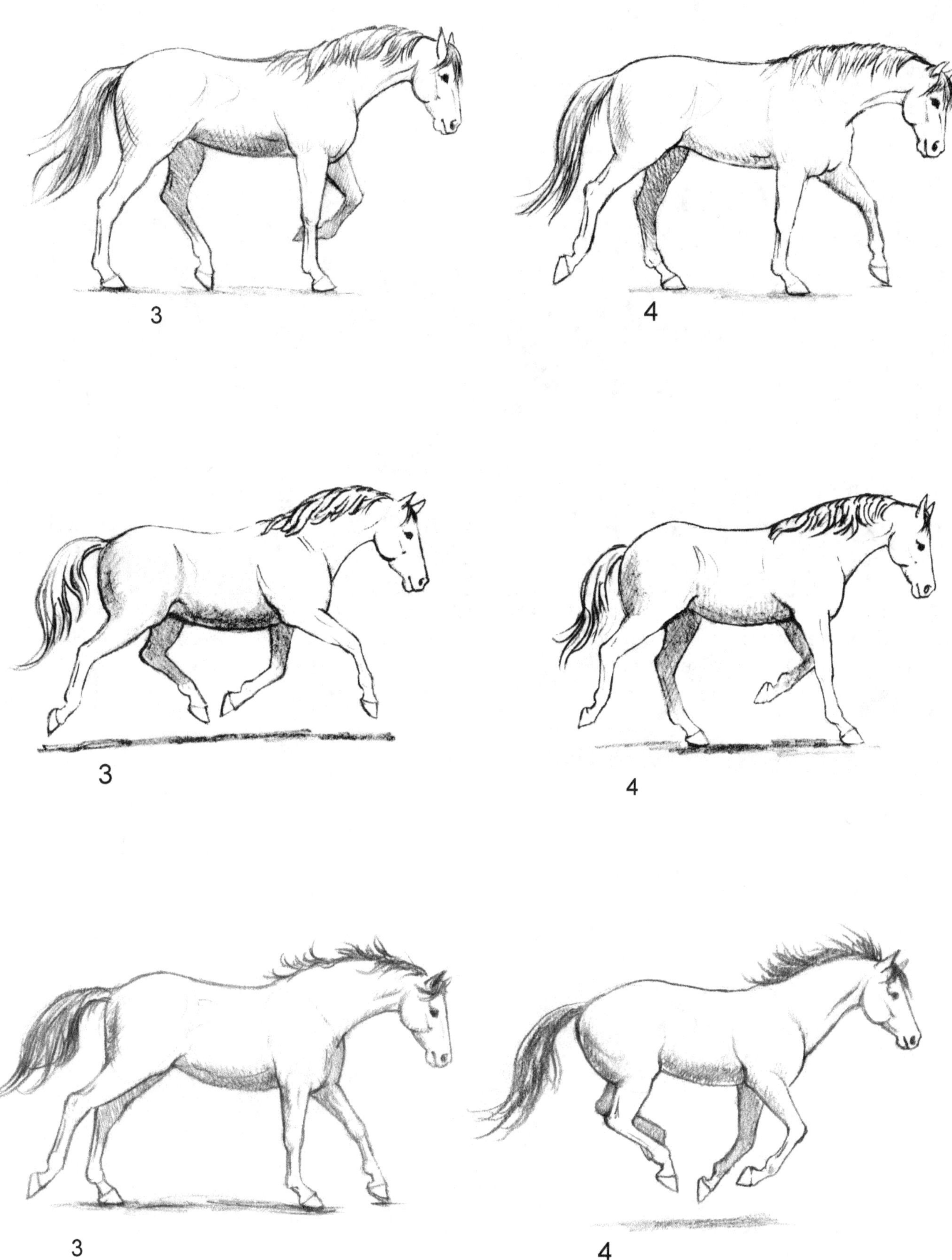

3
4
3
4
3
4

QUARTER HORSE Walking

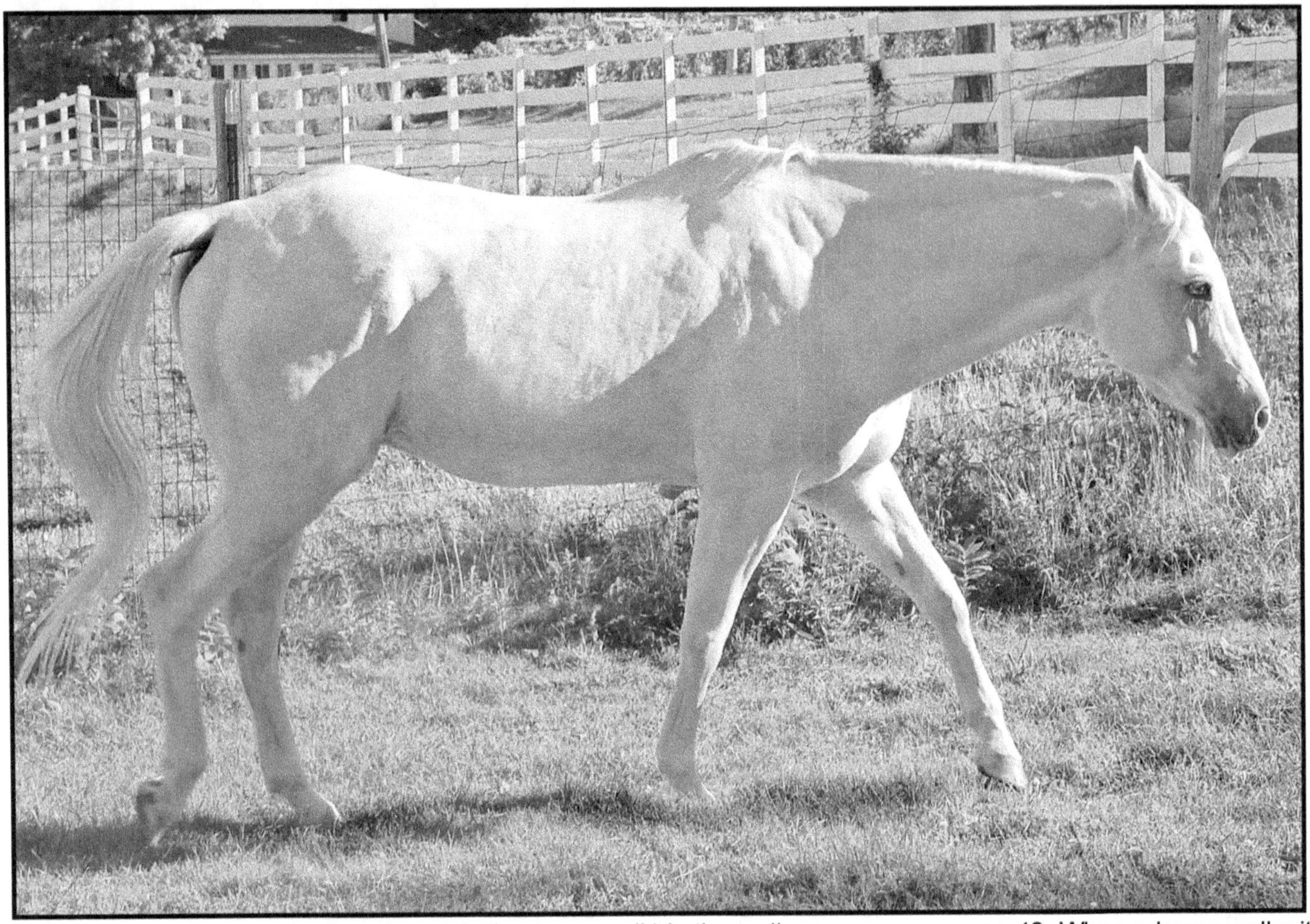

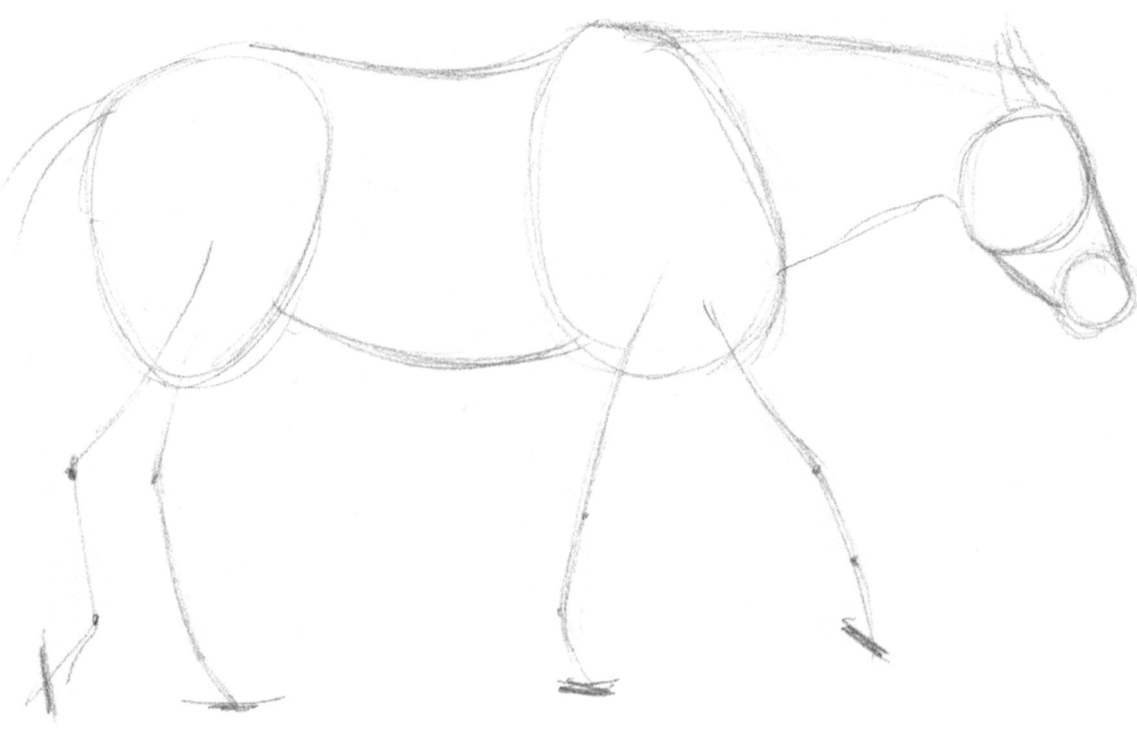

Notice how this pose is almost exactly the same as #4 in the walk sequence on page 42. When a horse walks it always has two or three feet touching the ground. The front lighting here is really dramatic, showing sharply defined muscles, typical of the Quarter Horse breed.

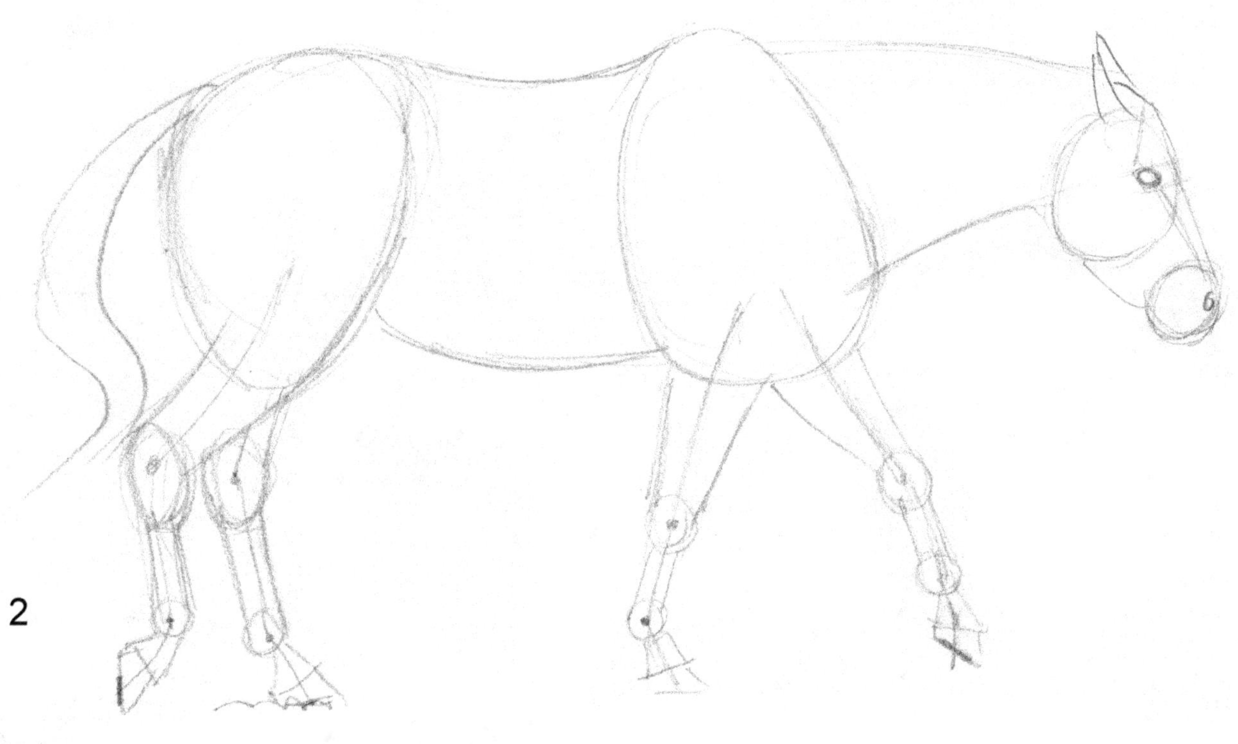

2

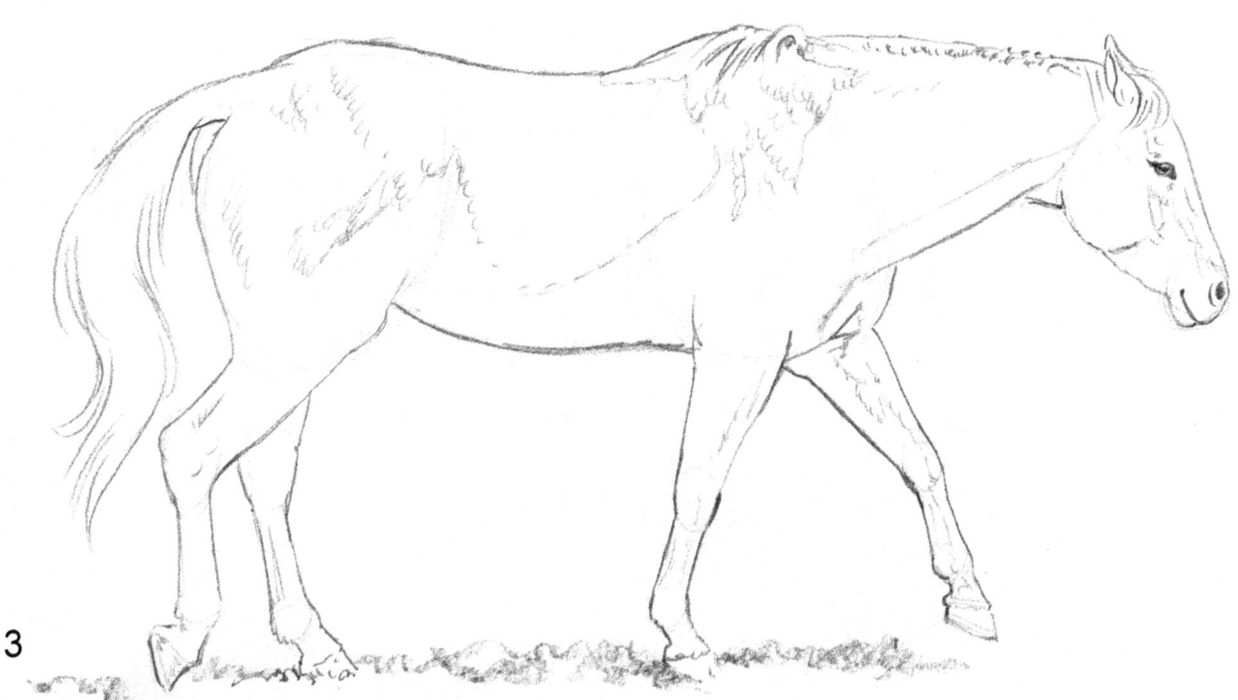

3

Because the shadows are so clearly defined on this photo, I decided to draw them in at the outline stage.

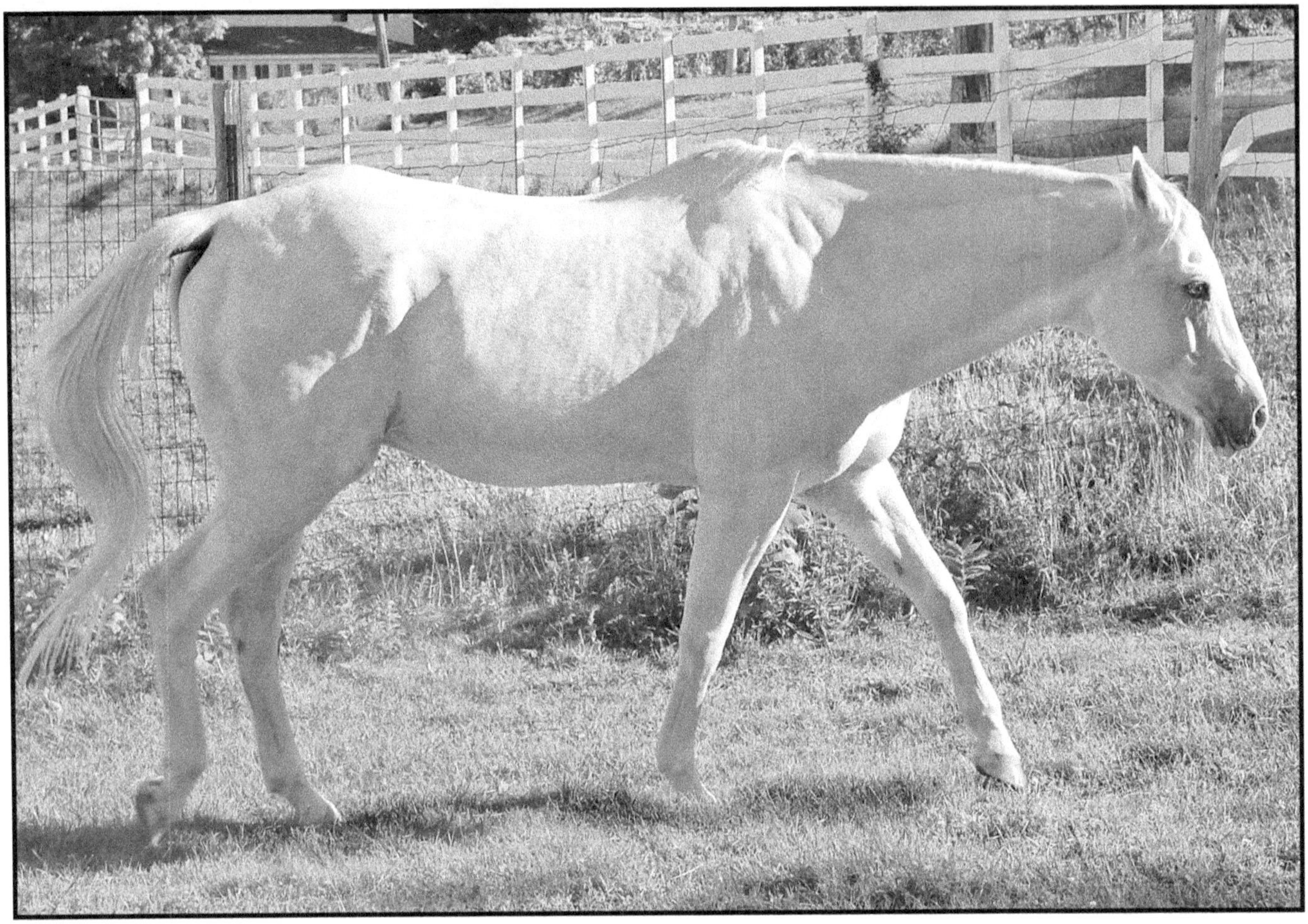

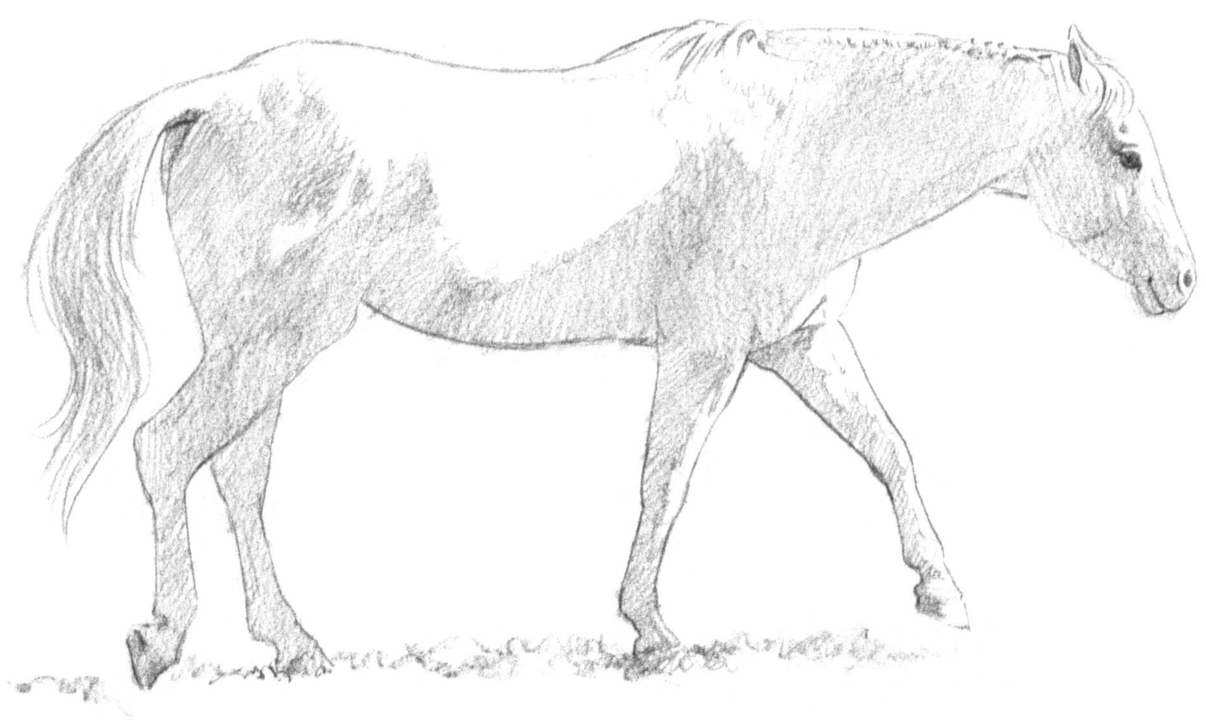

4

Notice how in this stage I used one simple tone for all shadow areas. I always go from the simple to the complex.

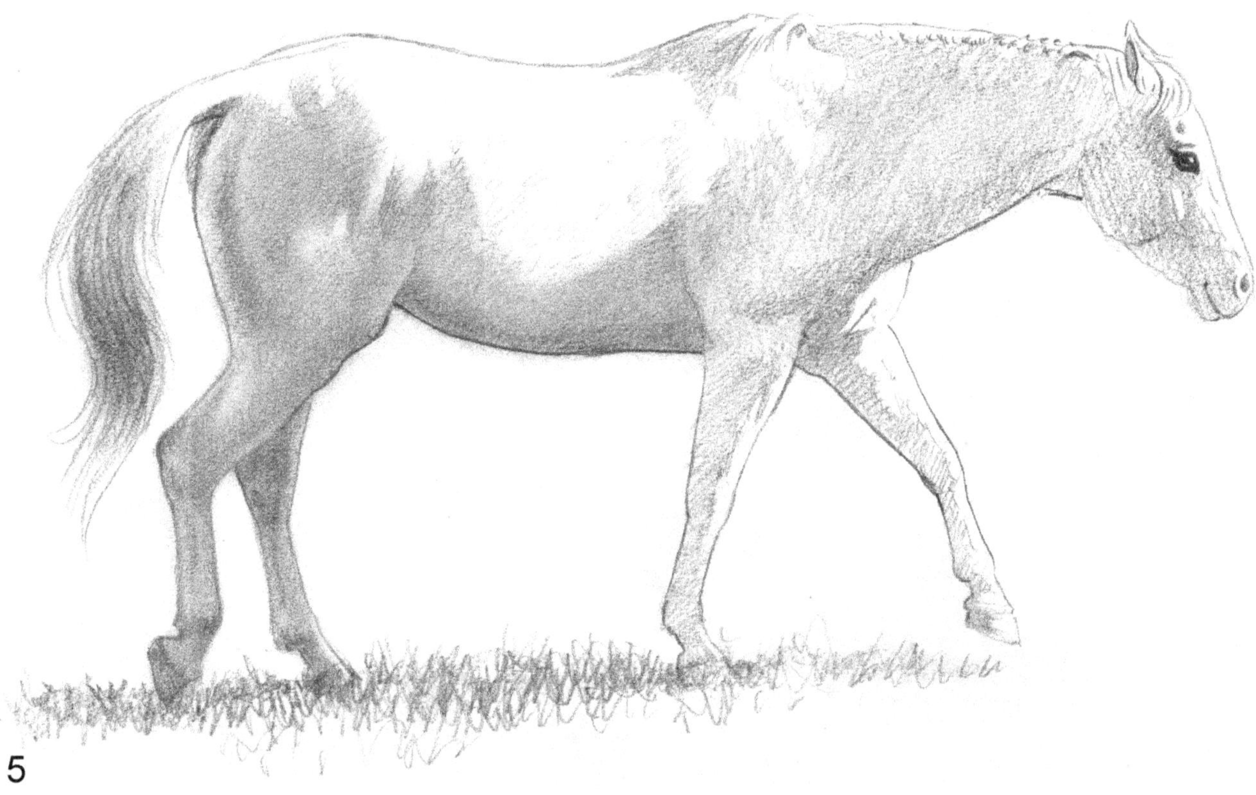

5

Sometimes at this stage I start on the left and finish as I go. The shadow area is done on his back half. Look carefully at the photo to see the cast shadows that have a sharp edge, and the shadows that have a slightly blurred edge going into the light. If you can see and draw that transition you are well on your way to realistic shading.

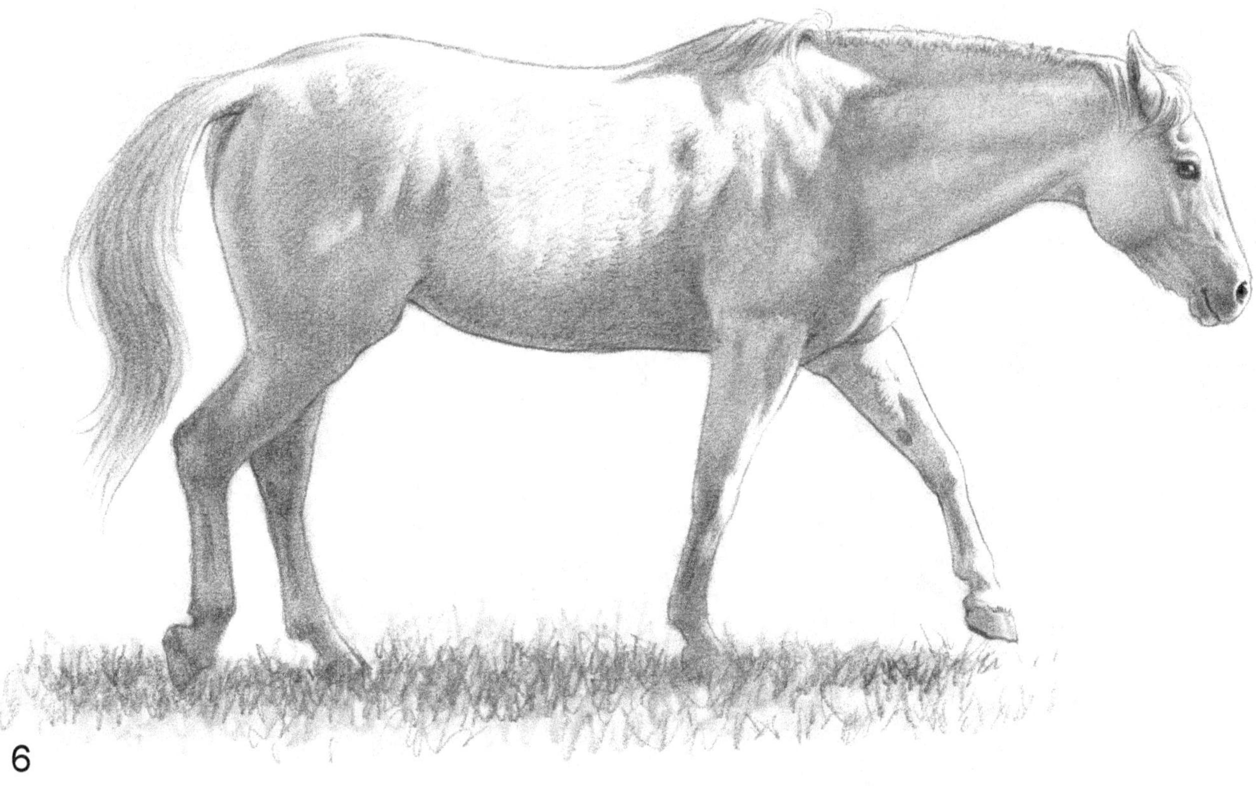

6

After finishing all the main shadow areas I went into the light side and added some subtle shading into his coat.

To make sure he looked like a white horse, I kept to medium tones, not dark tones, in the shadows.

Advanced Lesson: Colored Pencil on Toned Paper

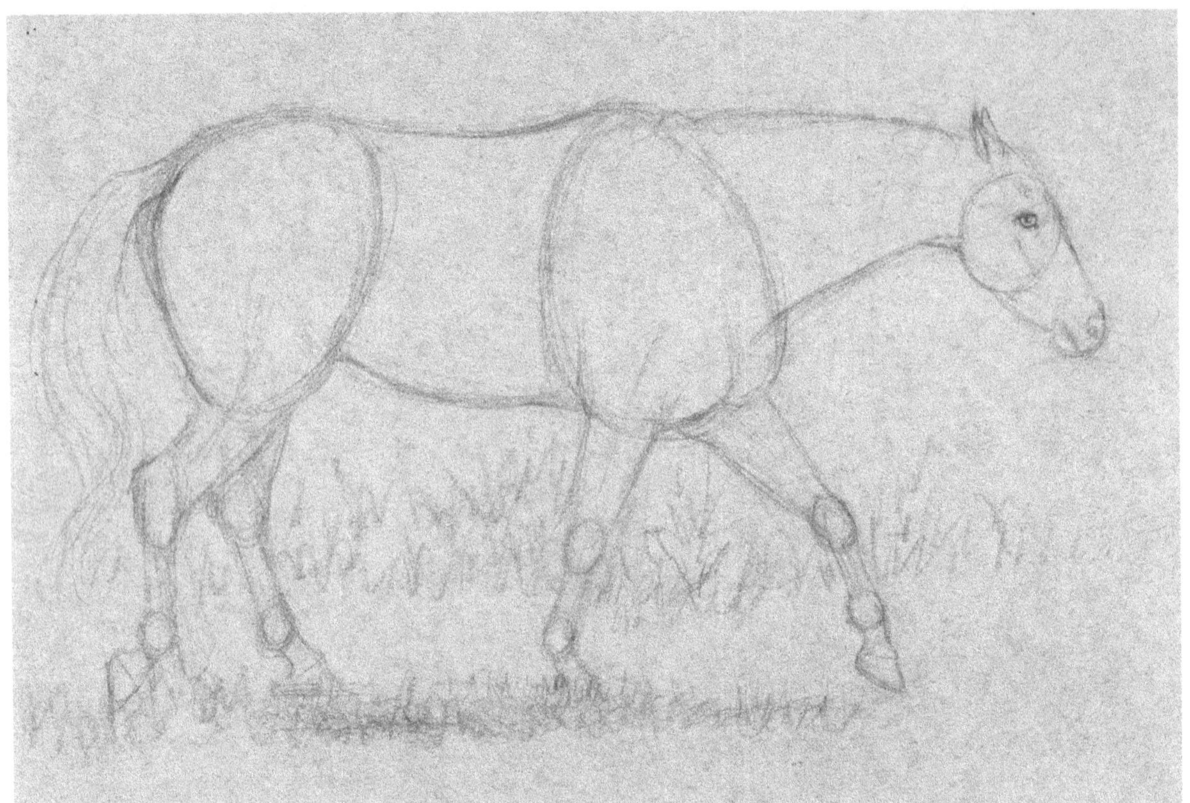

1. Use the horse photo from the previous lesson. You can use a Col-erase black pencil or charcoal pencil. I like the control of a sharp colored pencil, but regular colored pencils ar hard to erase. Lightly block in the horse with steps similar to the ones for graphite pencil drawing. Start to indicate the grassy shadows.

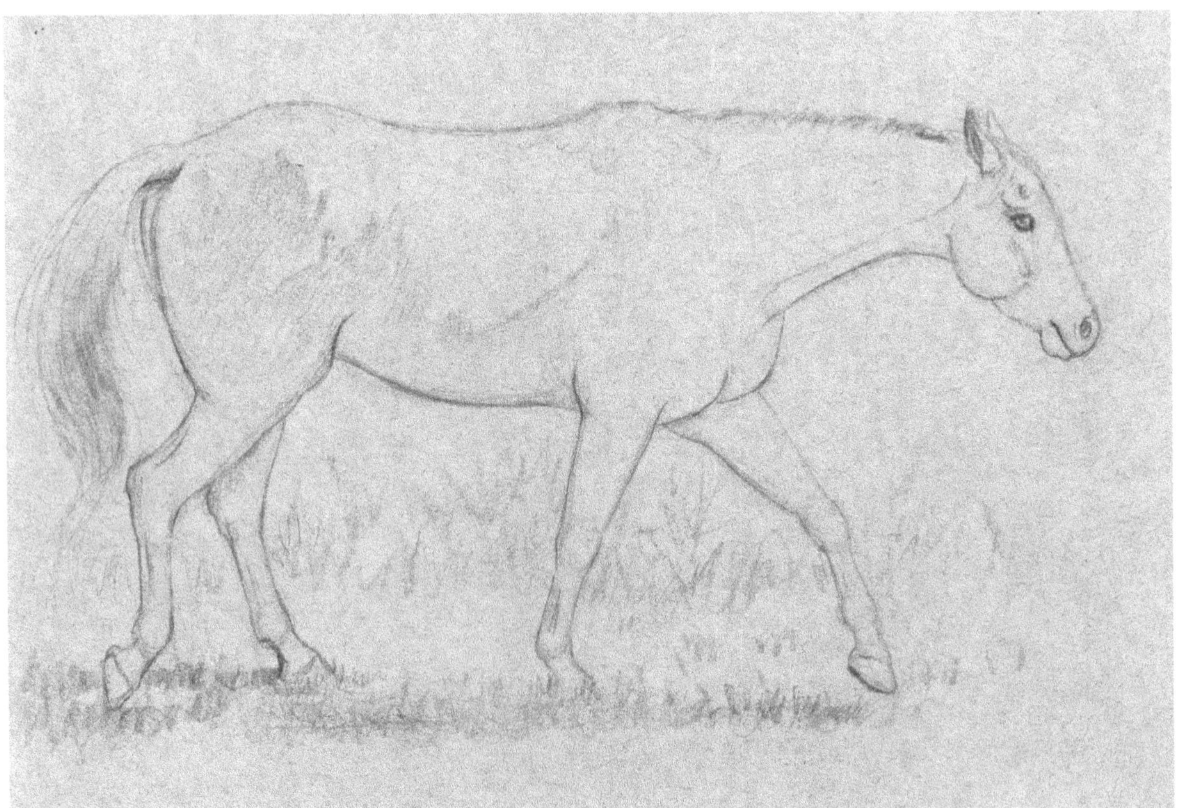

2. Look carefully at the photo and refine the outline. Like the graphite drawing, I am marking the edges of the shadows. Lightly add tone in places with the black pencil, but plan to leave some gray unmarked, to do a lot of the "work" of creating the shadow side of his body. I will erase the back line and make it white.

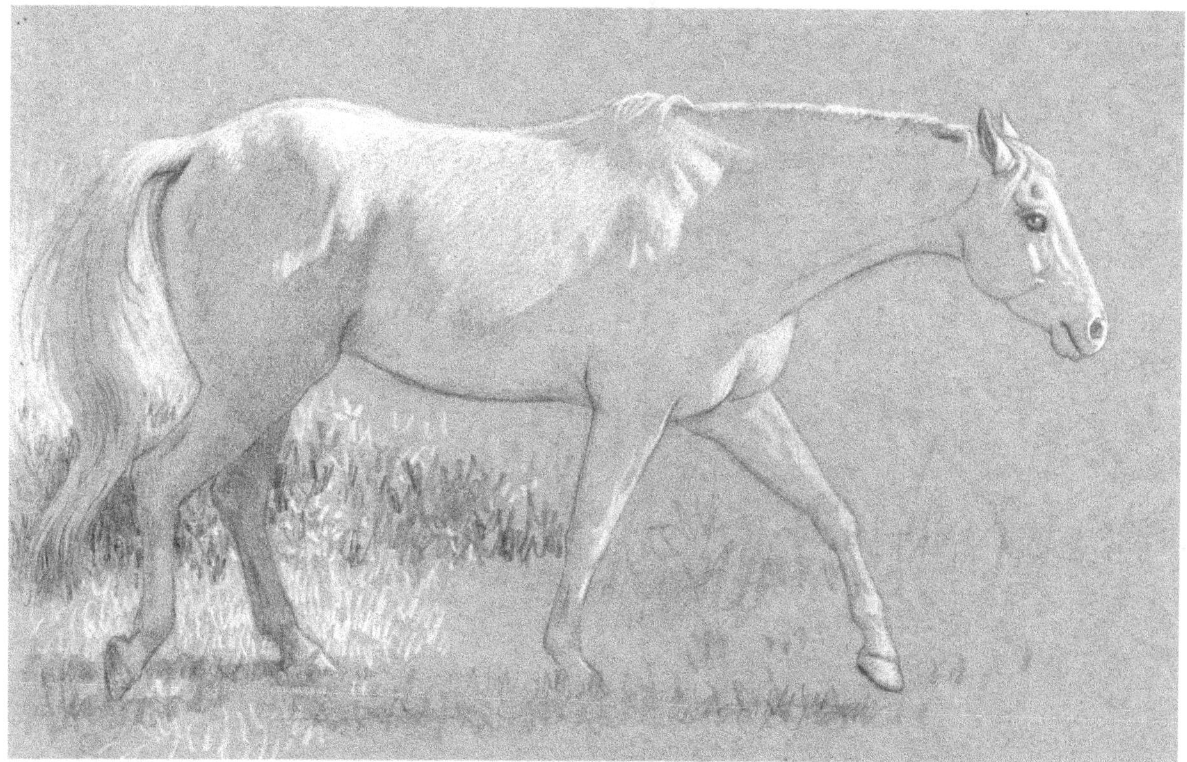

3. Start adding light tones with the white pencil on the light side of his body. I added light grass behind the upper part of his tail, and dark grass in the bottom third of his tail, which is mostly the gray of the paper. I love playing with light areas against dark ones and dark areas against light ones. This is one of the most important ways to make things stand out in a full scene with a background.

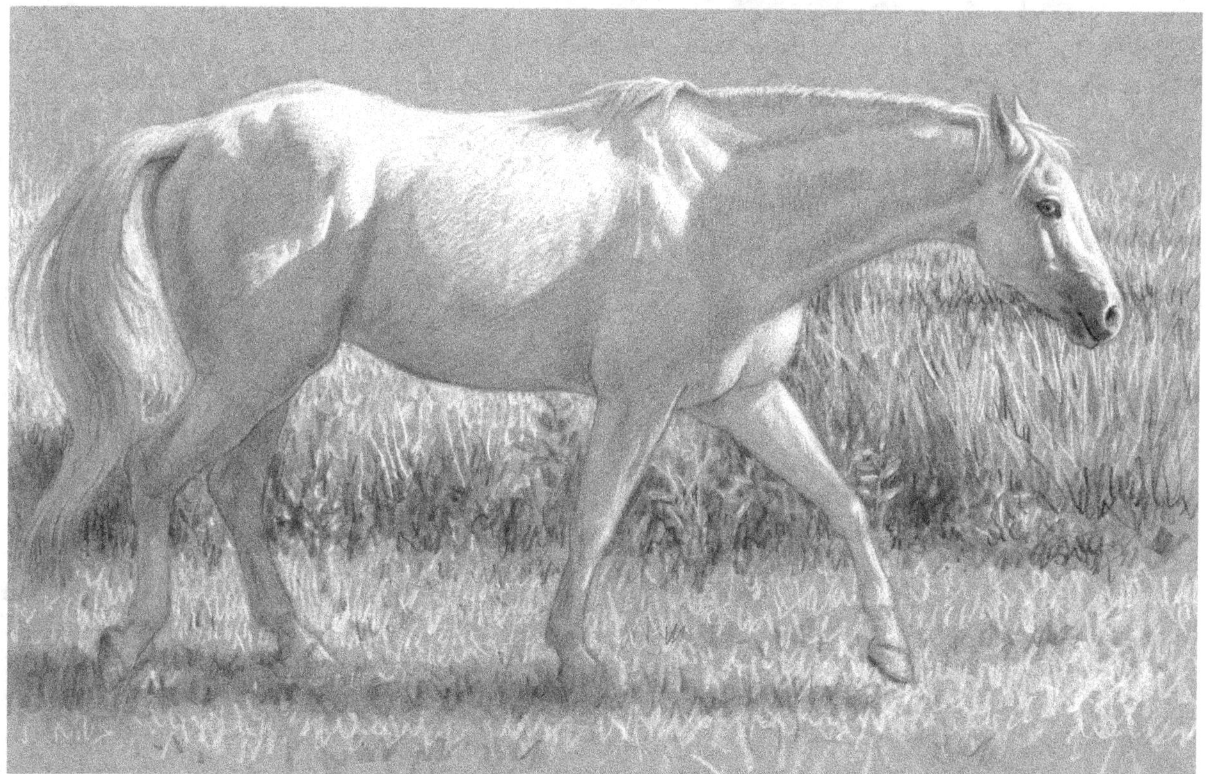

4. I built up the light areas, adding more and more light strokes with the white pencil, pressing harder for areas I want to be close to pure white. I added some soft shading with very light pressure with the black pencil to the shadows, but left a lot of the gray paper unmarked, as the gray looks like a perfect shadow tone. I used the same system of "light against dark" and "dark against light" on many parts of the picture to make the horse stand out against the background. Once you get the hang of it, you might get hooked on toned paper!

AMERICAN PAINT HORSE Walking

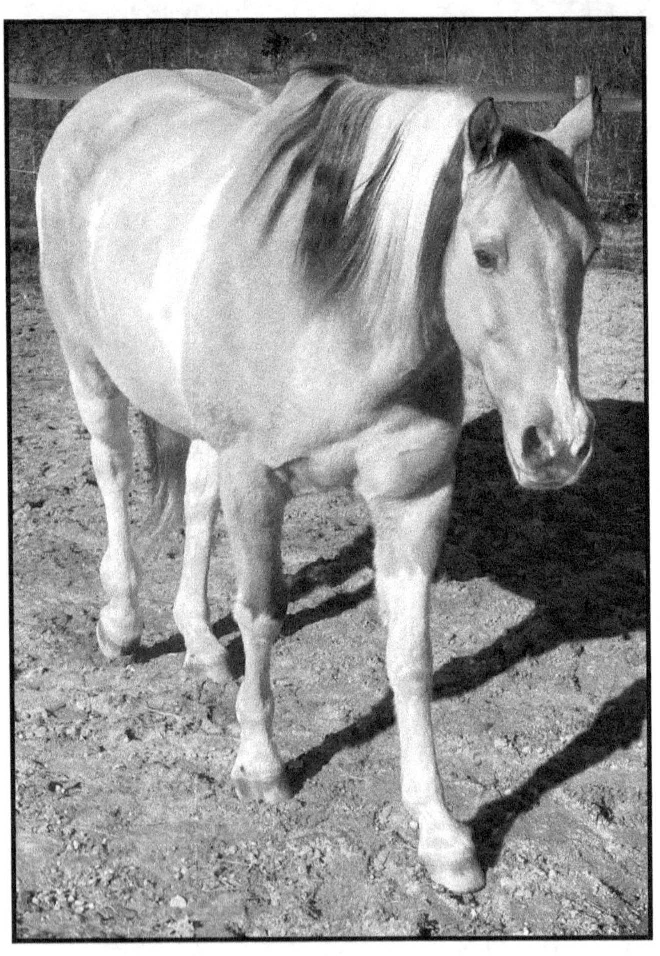

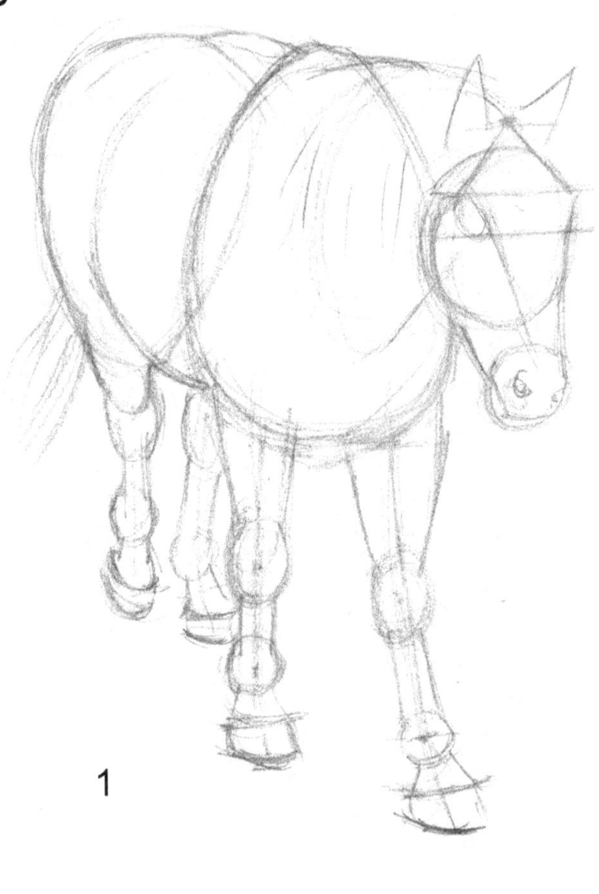

1

I did need to use Photoshop to correct the distortion in this pose, so that his head is not too big in proportion to his body and legs. His back legs are maybe still just a bit too short, but I feel the proportions are acceptable.

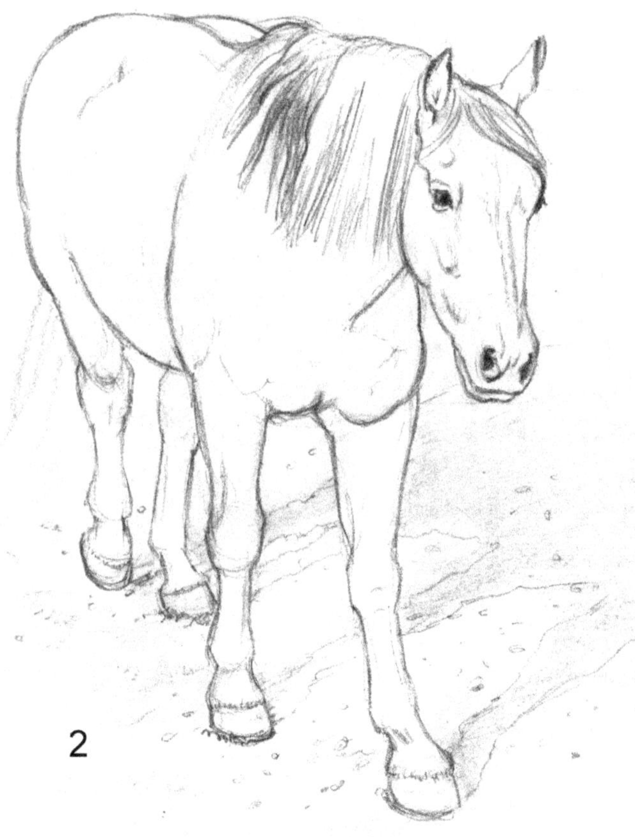

2

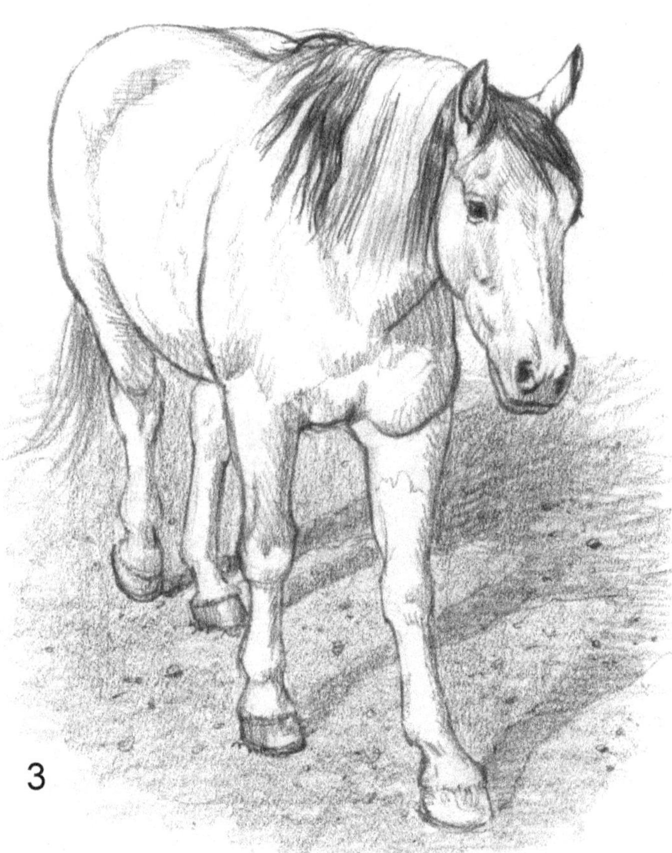

3

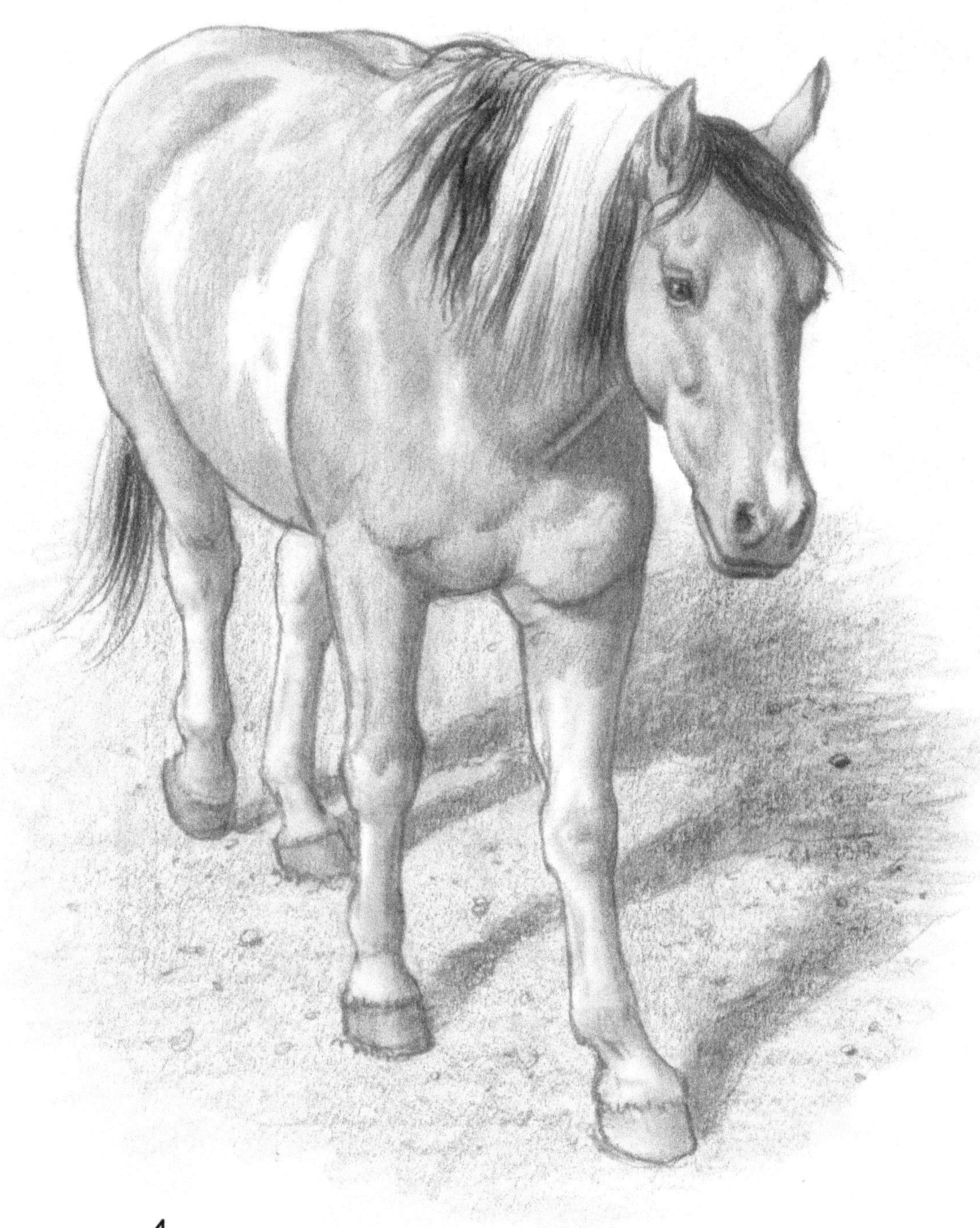

4

The markings on this horse are really striking, with a buckskin paint body and a black and white mane. Notice how I have kept the shading on his body in lighter tones. It helps to squint at a photo and then at your drawing in order to better match the tones from light to dark. For this drawing I wanted his black and white mane to stand out, so I did not go too dark with the shadow on the ground.

ICELANDIC HORSE Trotting

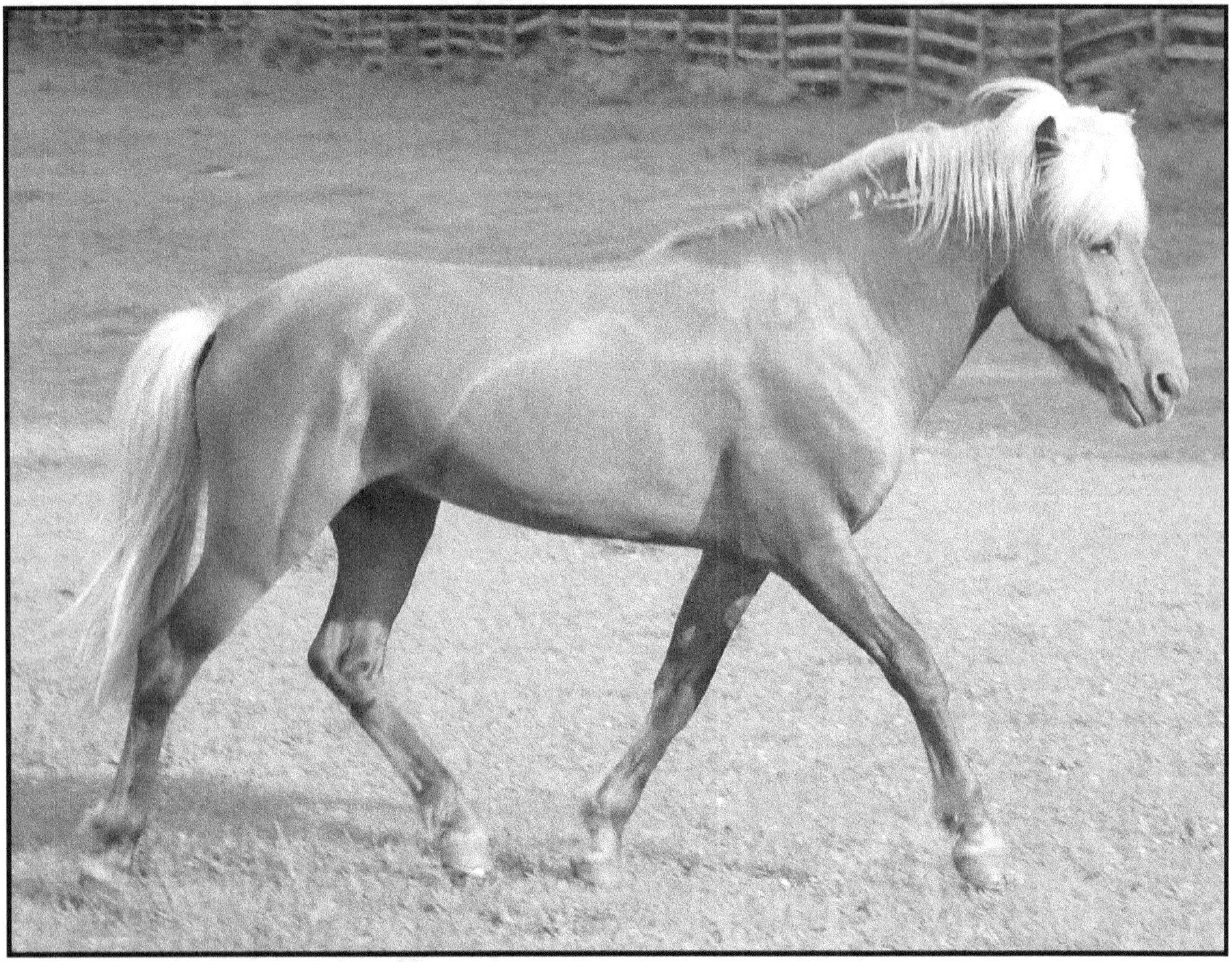

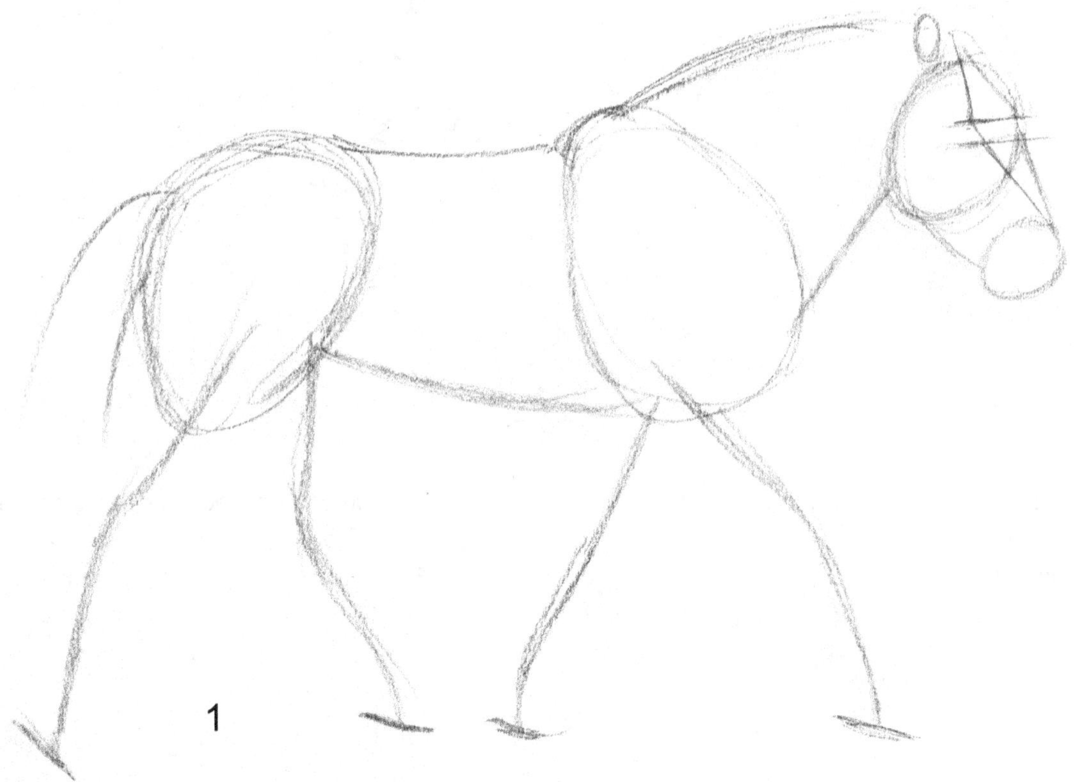

Icelandic horses have more "streamlined" conformation than most horse breeds, and remind me of greyhounds. They usually have really thick manes and tails. These horses have a very fast extra gait, called a "tolt." This photo is a trot. Try to capture the action lines simply at first, and his unique body proportions, as in the sketch below.

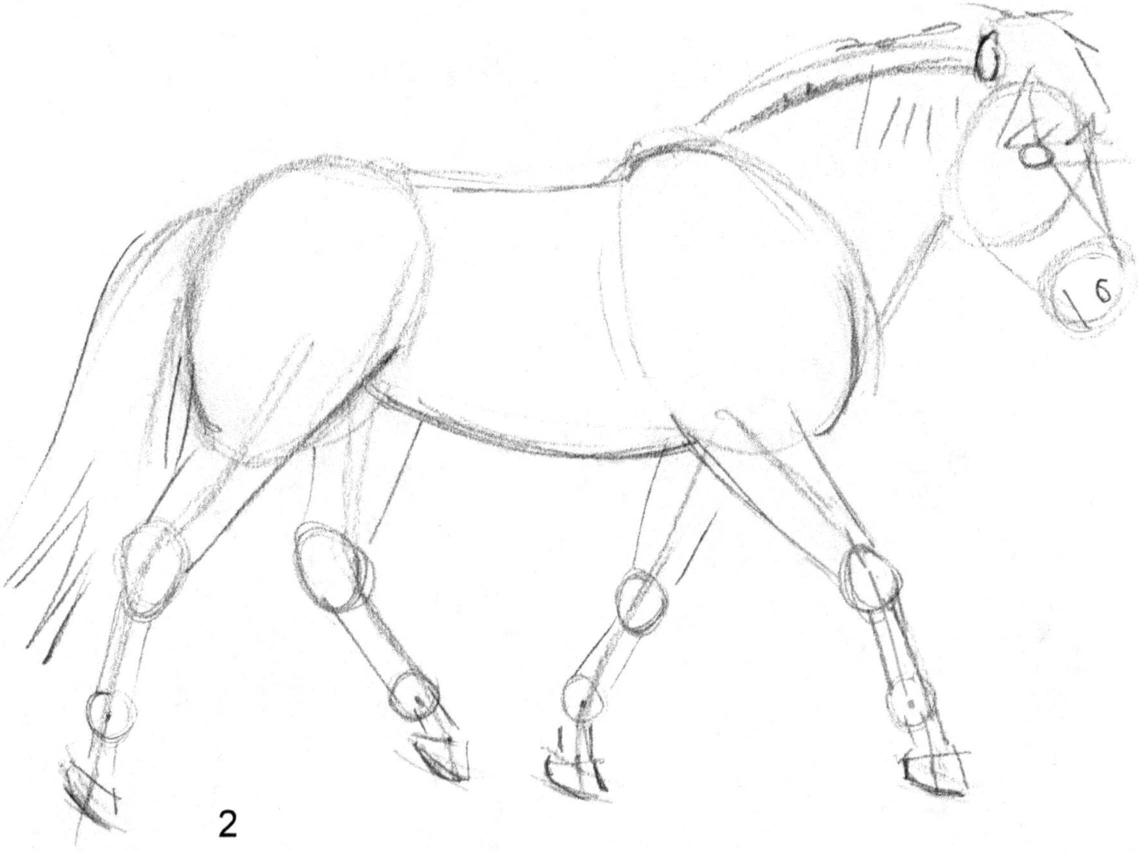

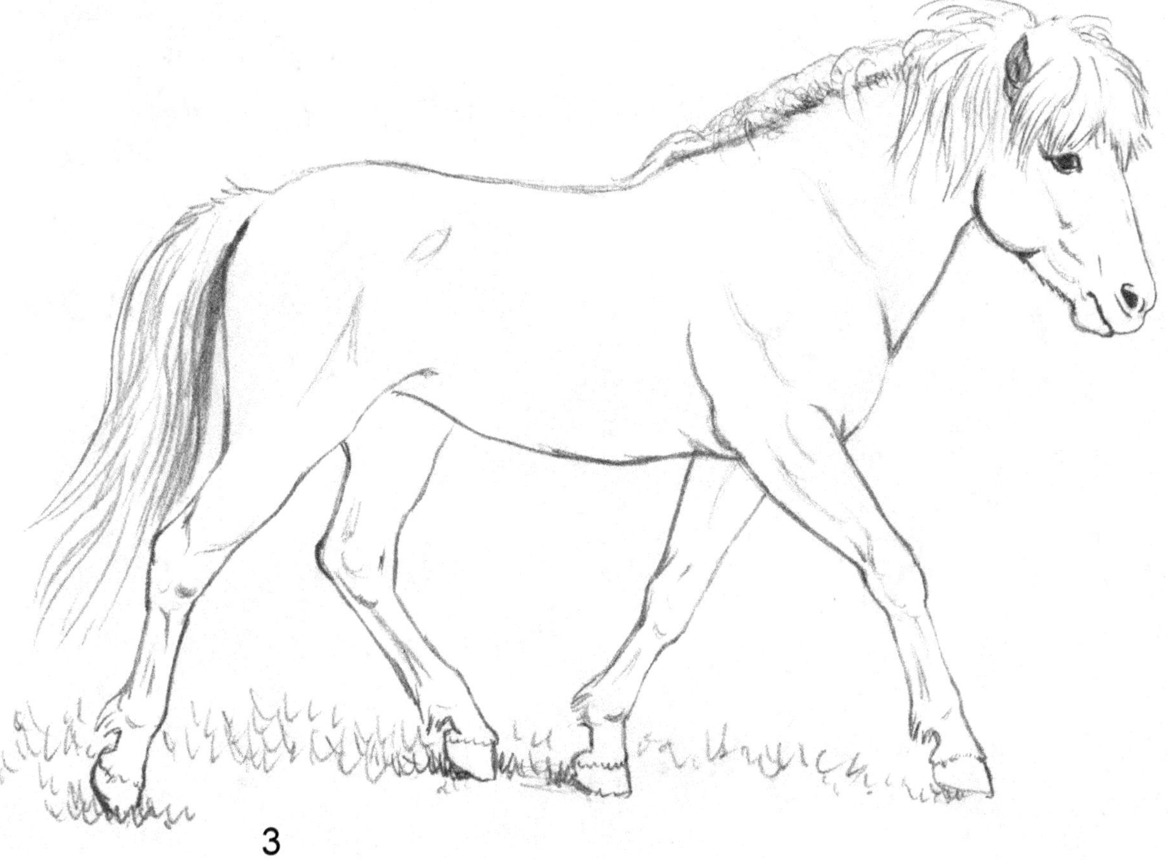

2

3

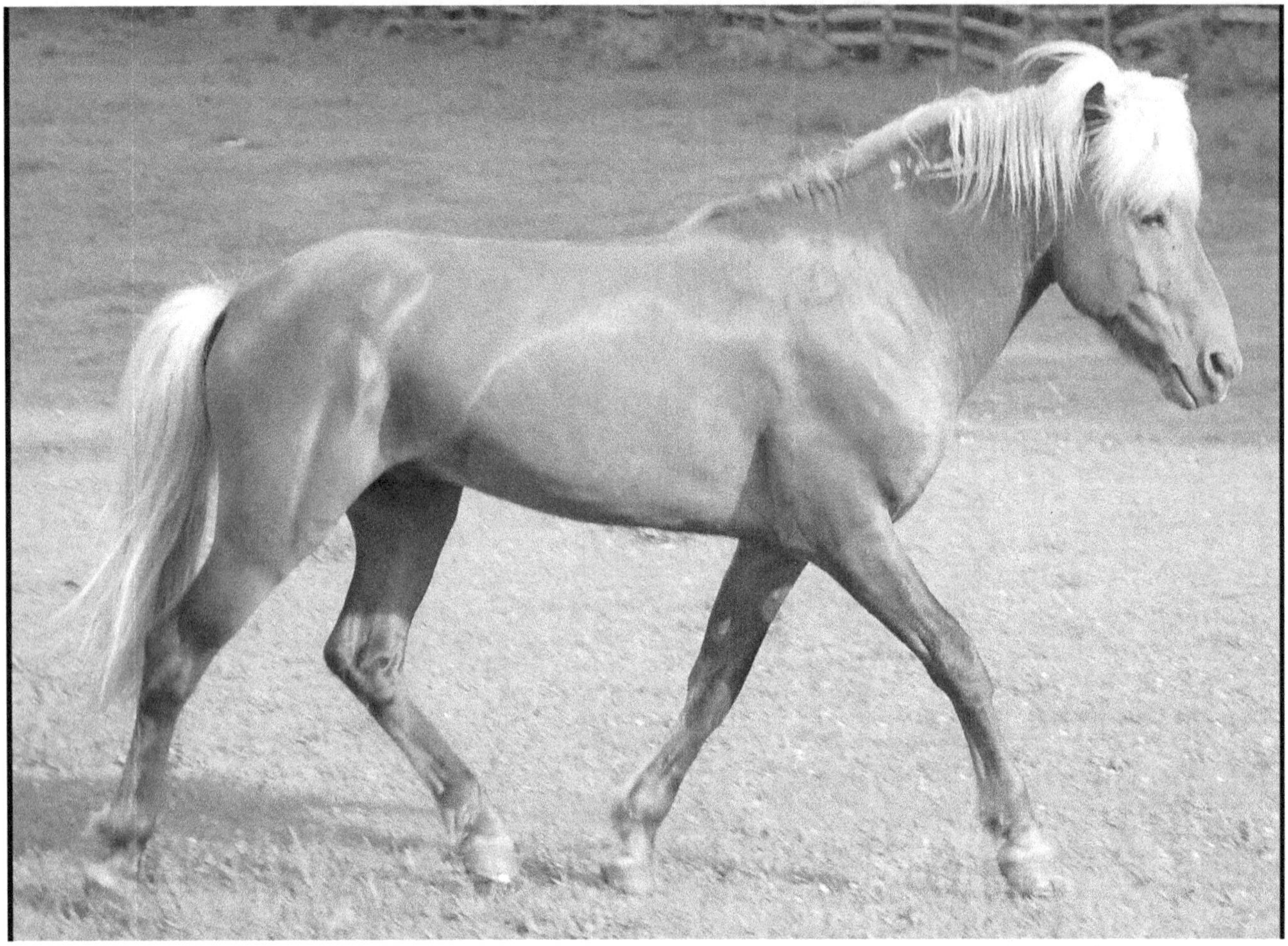

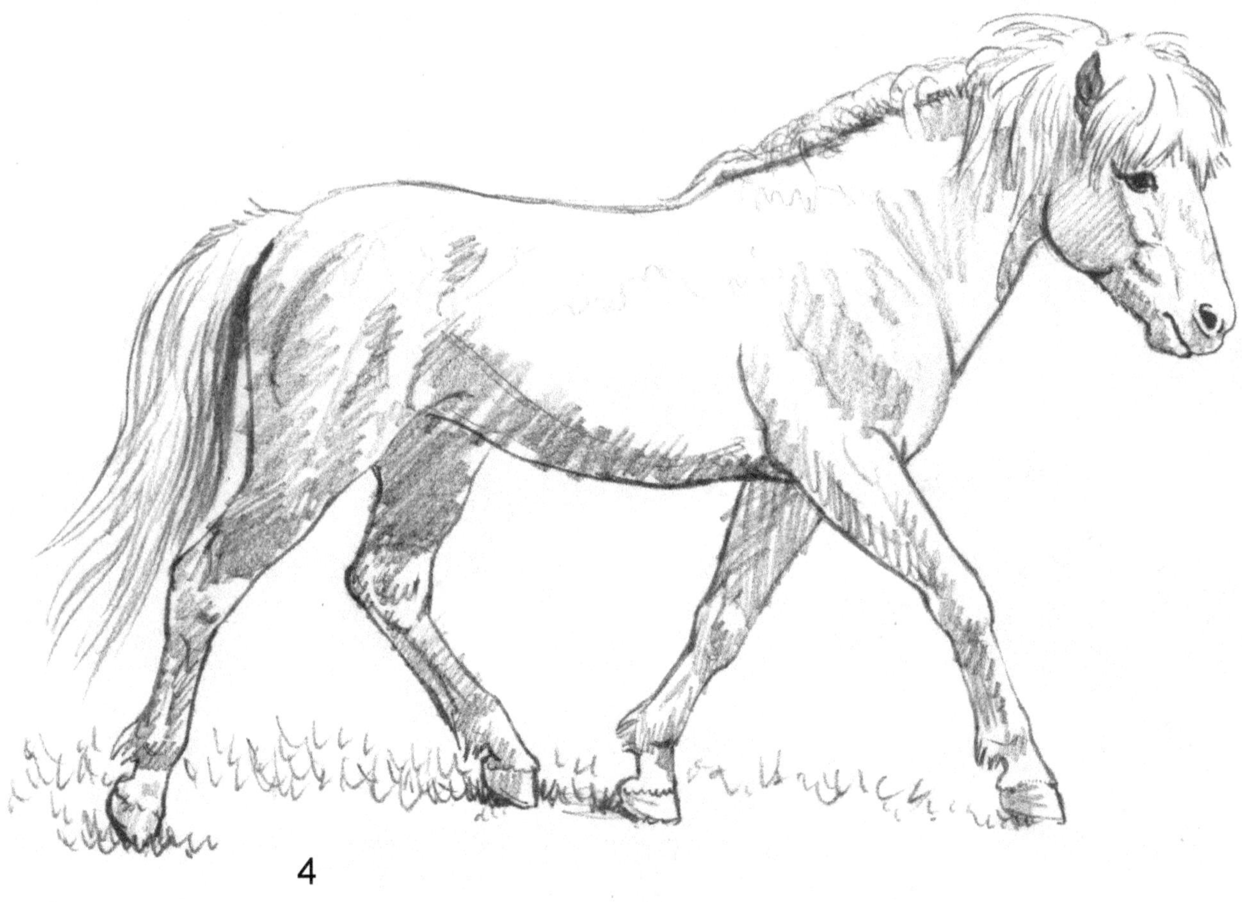

4

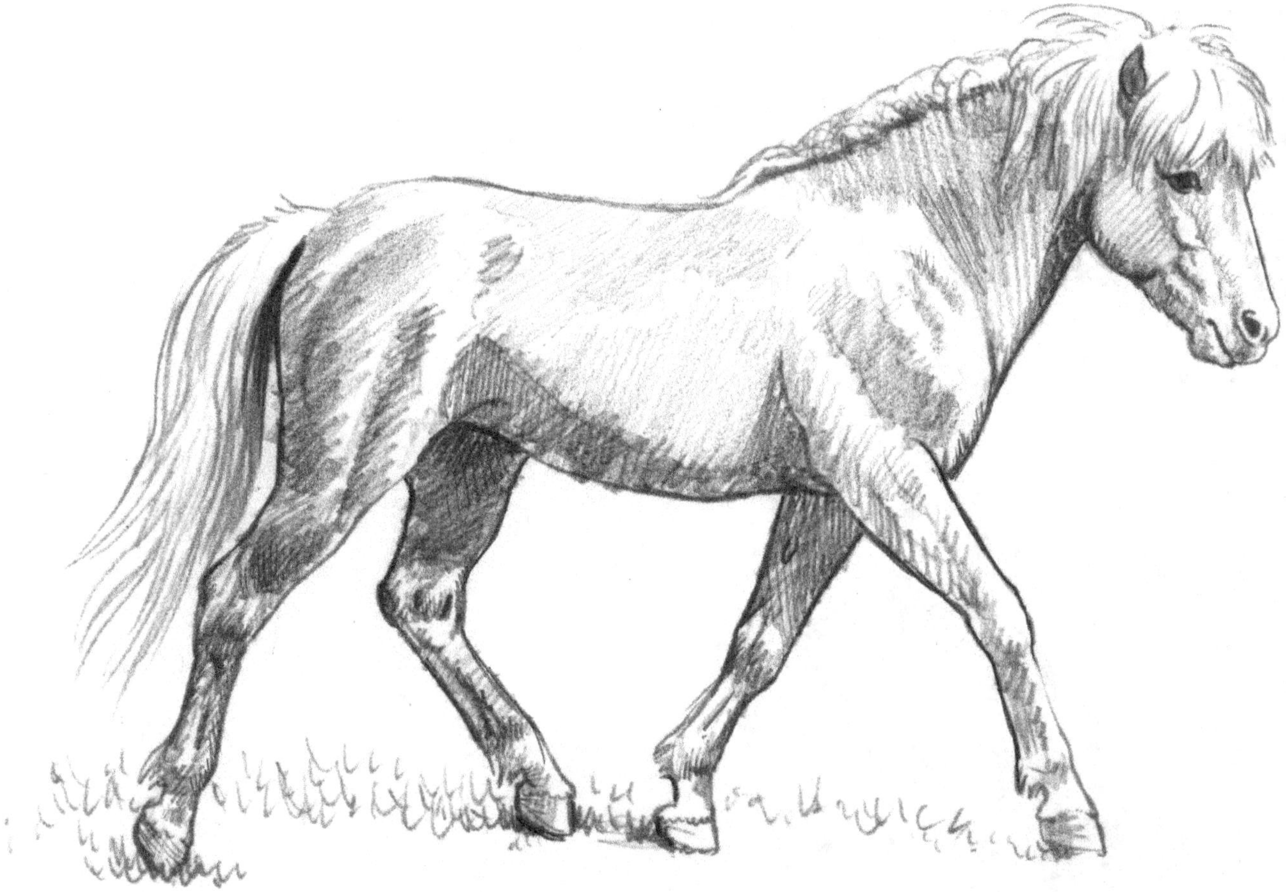

5

6

APPALOOSA-DRAFT HORSE CROSS Trotting

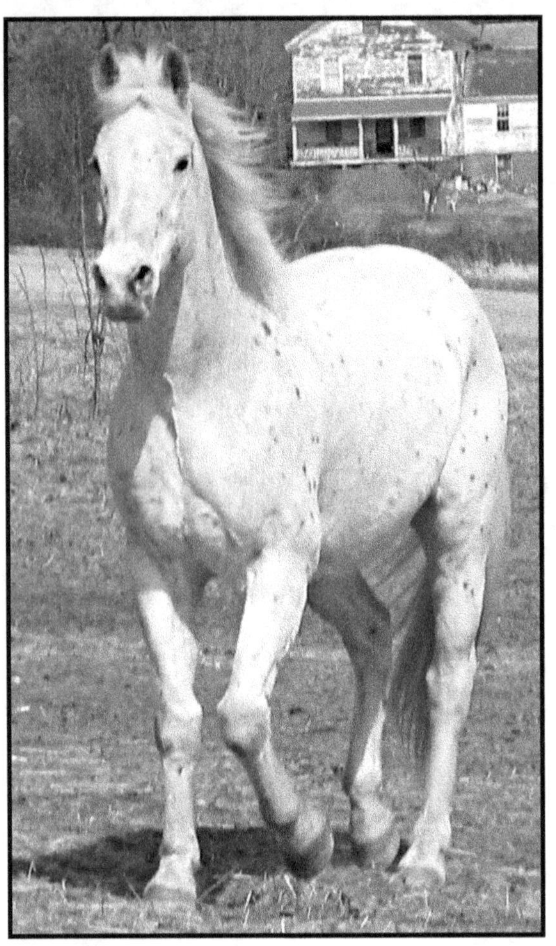

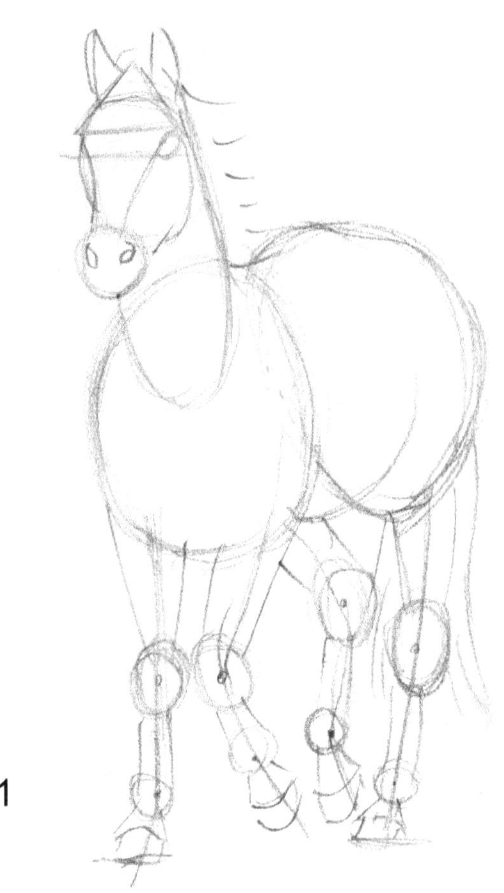

1

For this 3/4 trotting pose, draw the egg shape of his front end first, then the hind end oval and connecting back and stomach lines. Then overlap a long oval for his neck, overlap a big oval for his jaw and a small one for his muzzle. The photo is from a very low angle, so his hind legs are not that far behind the front legs.

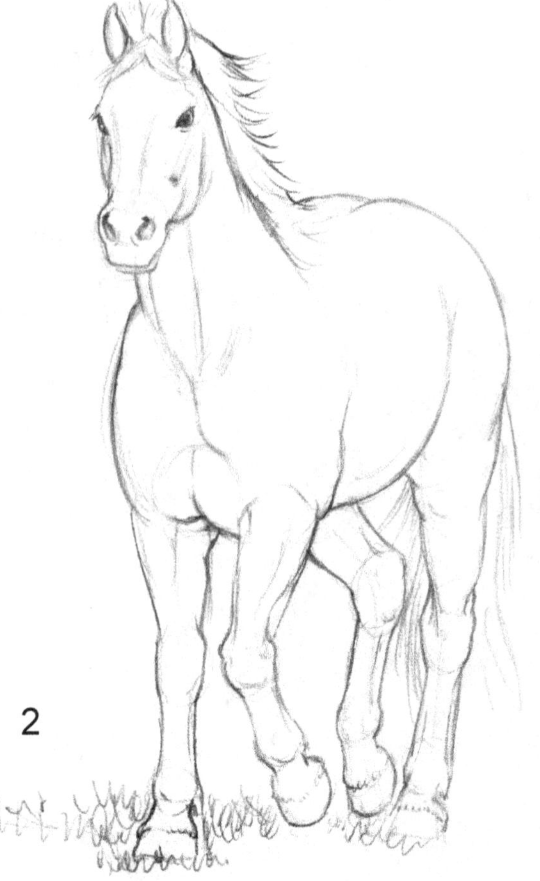

2

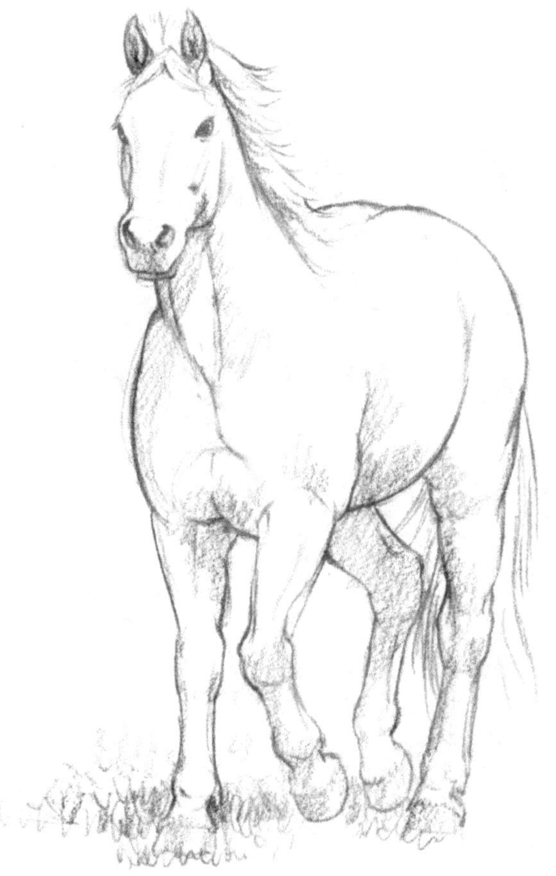

3

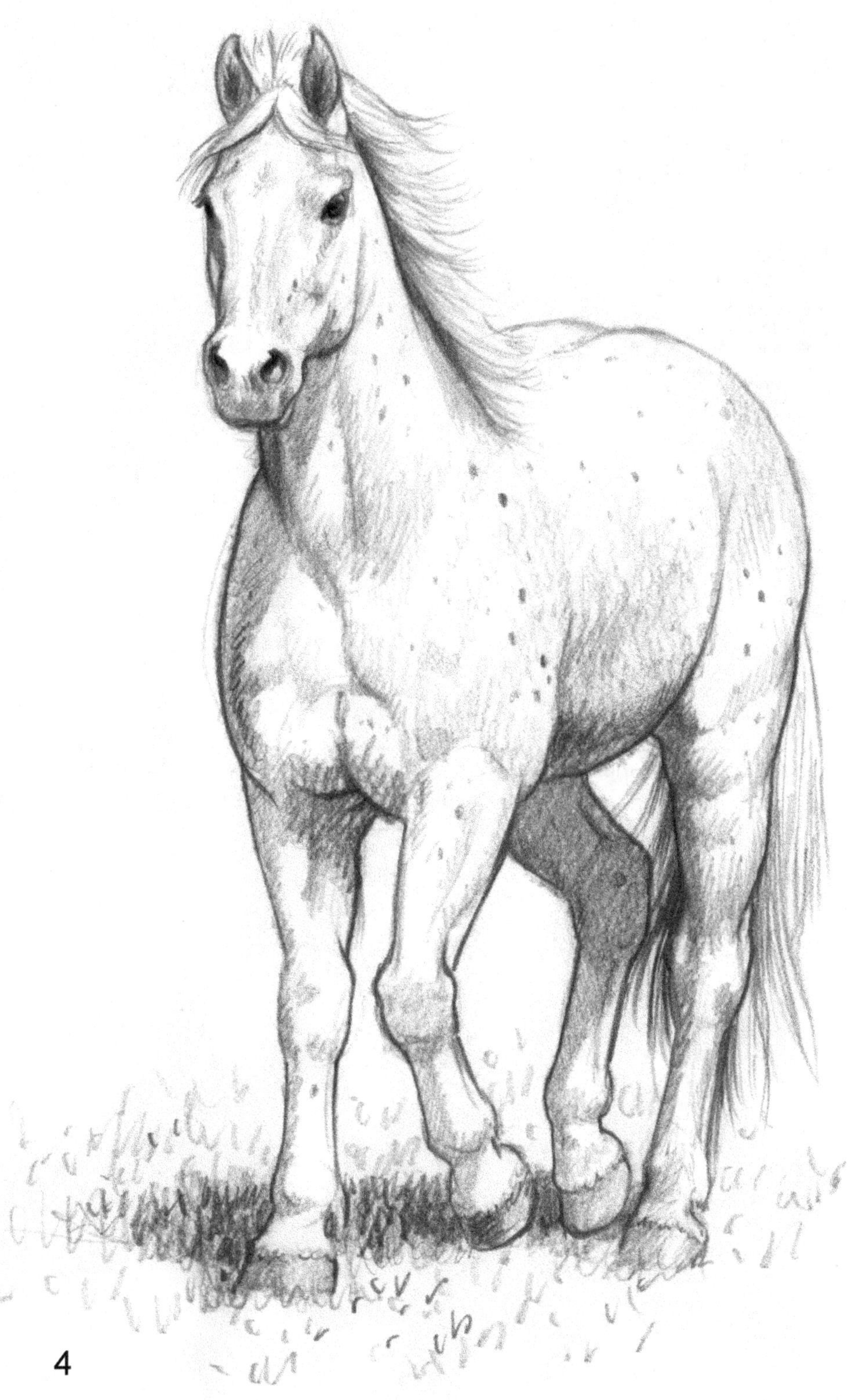

4

Gray horses are easier to shade, since you can leave white paper for much of the light side of their body, and the shadow side is not too dark. I had fun adding some Appaloosa spots. I did not attempt to copy every spot, but do notice that the circles are more oval-shaped in a side view and follow the shape of his body. And like the photo, I made some spots lighter than others. Small details like this will make your drawings look more real.

TENNESSEE WALKER (2) Trotting

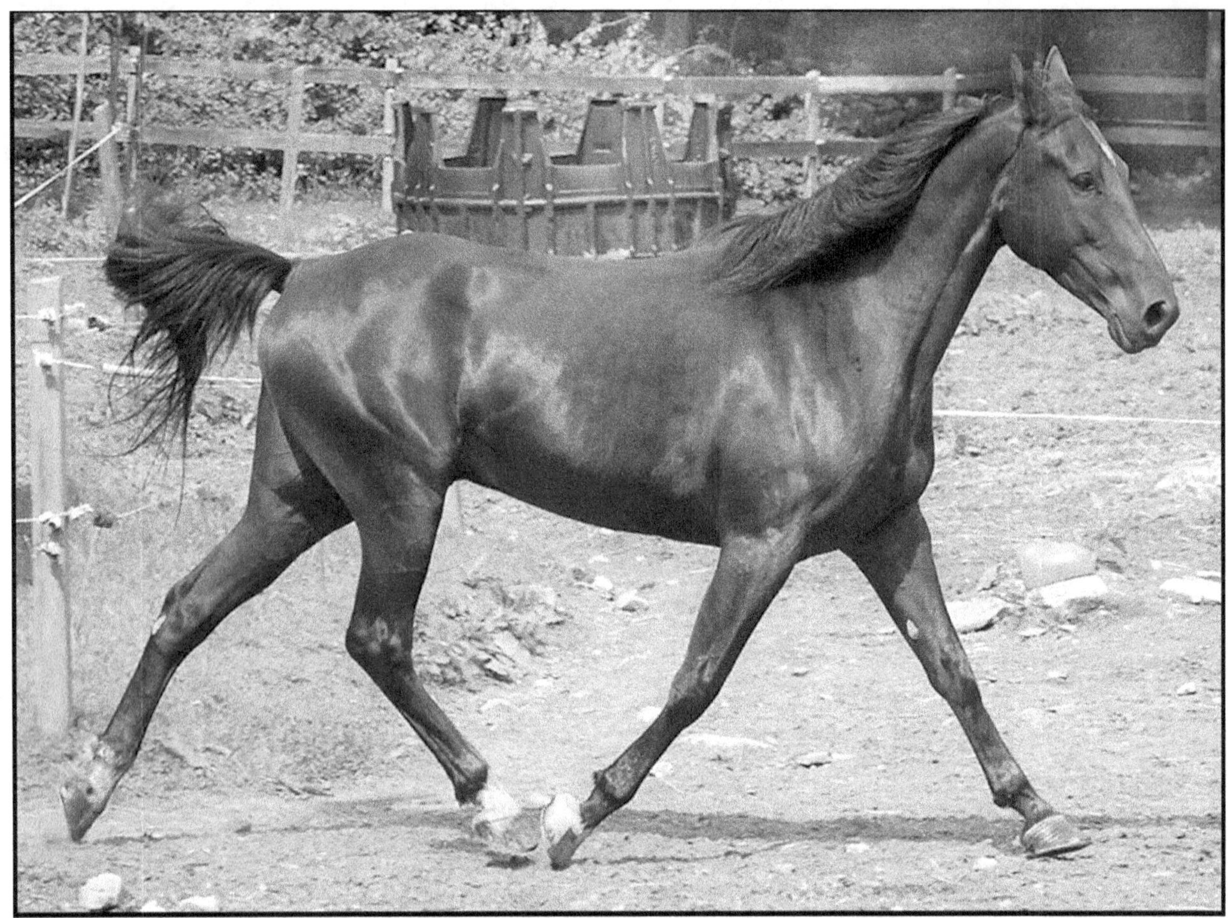

The Tennesse Walker has an extra gait, the "running walk," which makes for a very smooth ride. This pose, I believe, is just a big trot. Dark horses take more time to build up all the darker tones, but the highlights on their shiny coats are fun to draw.

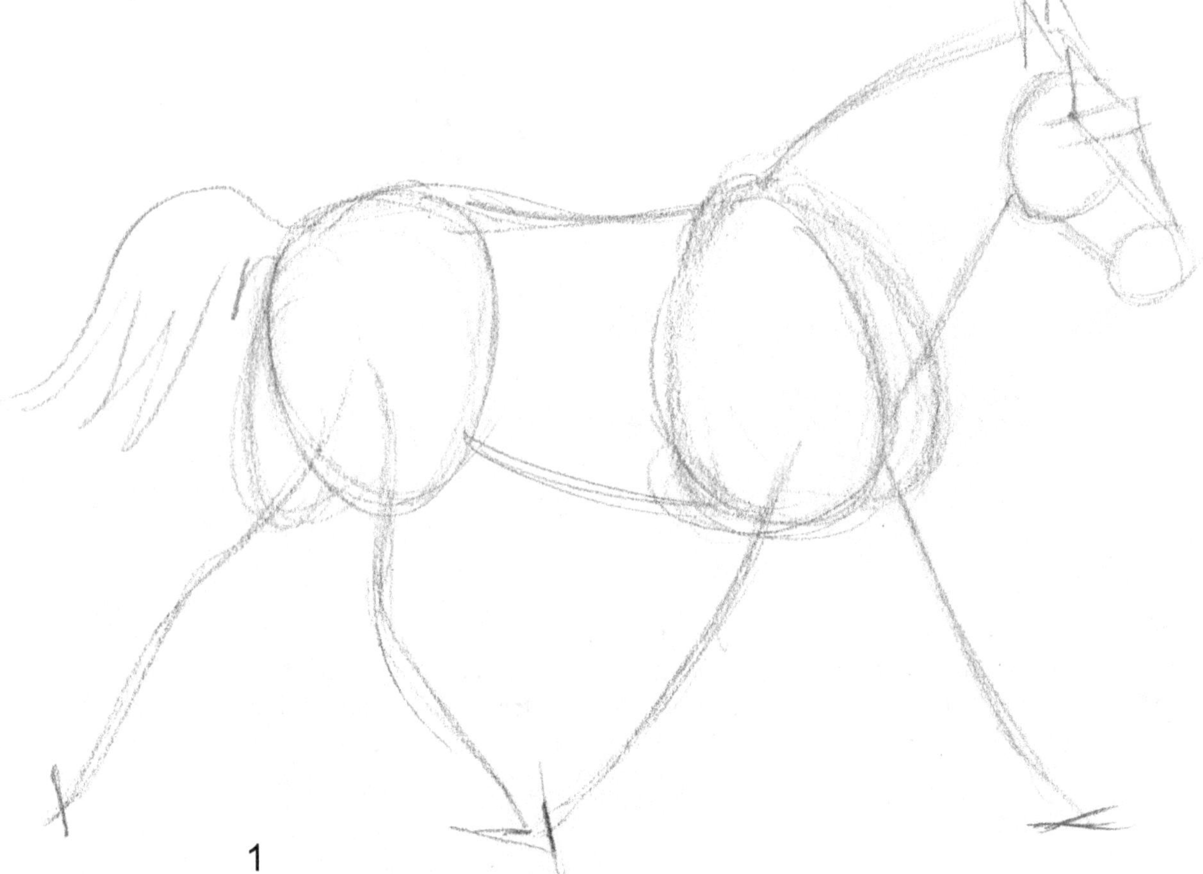

1

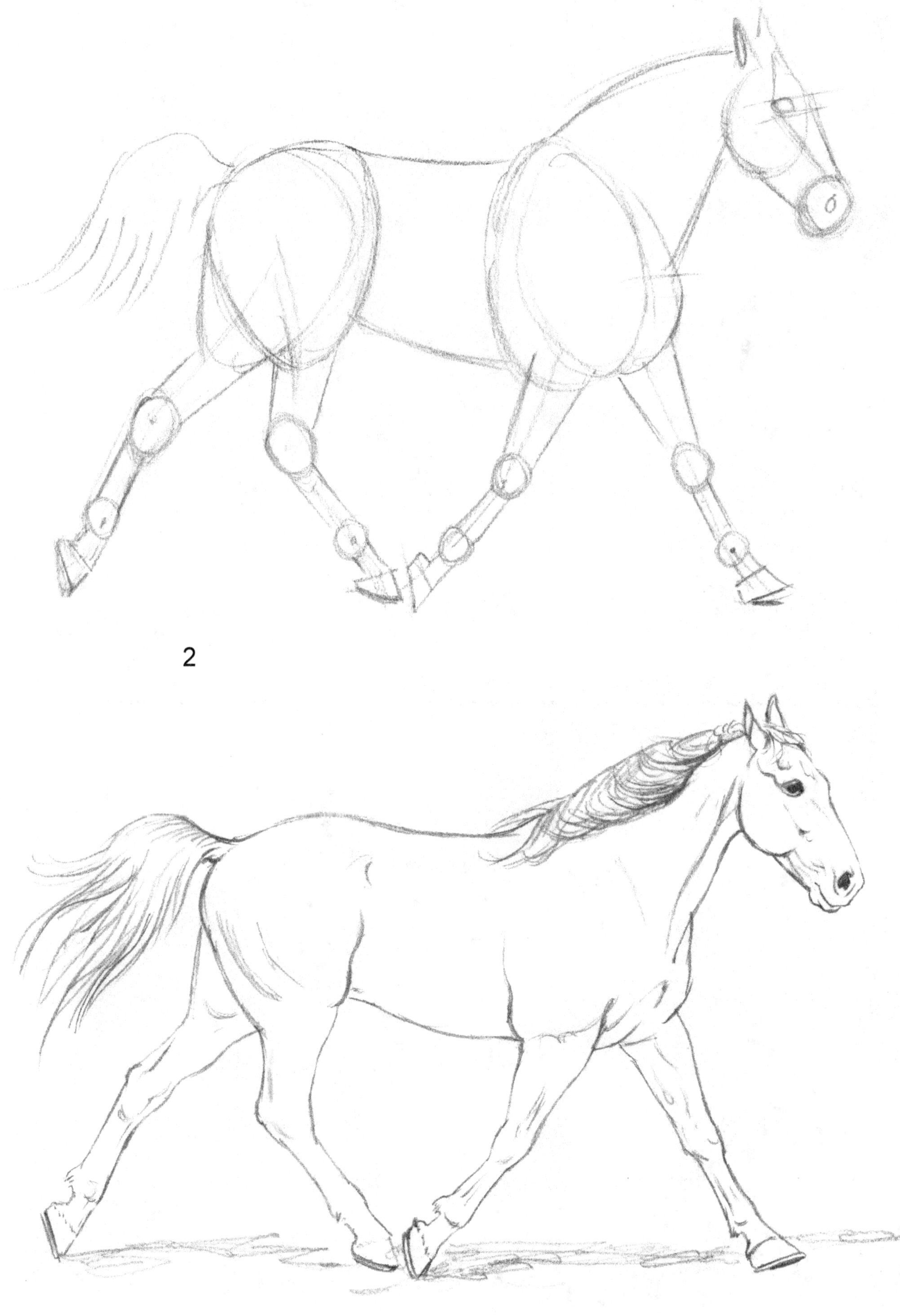

2

3

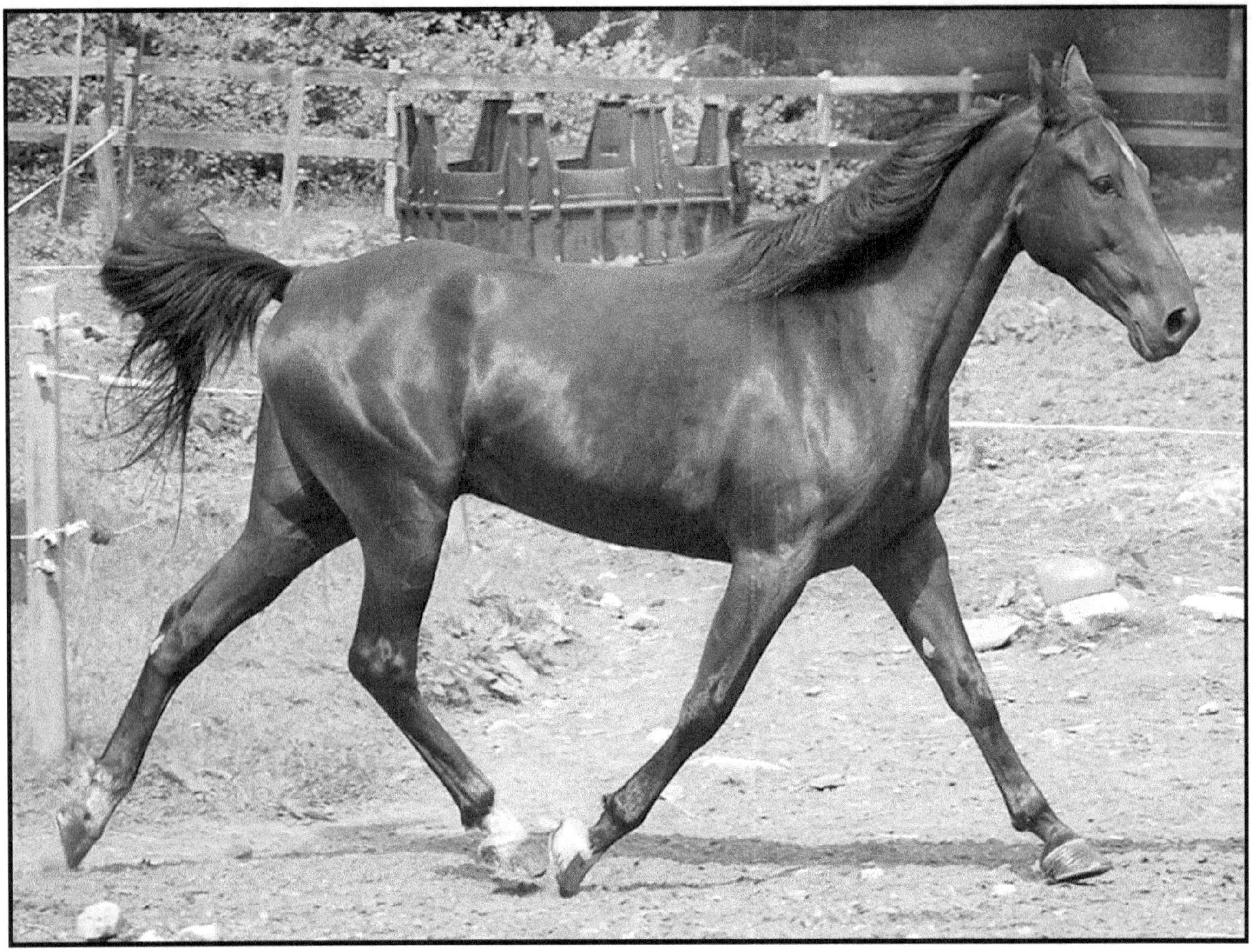

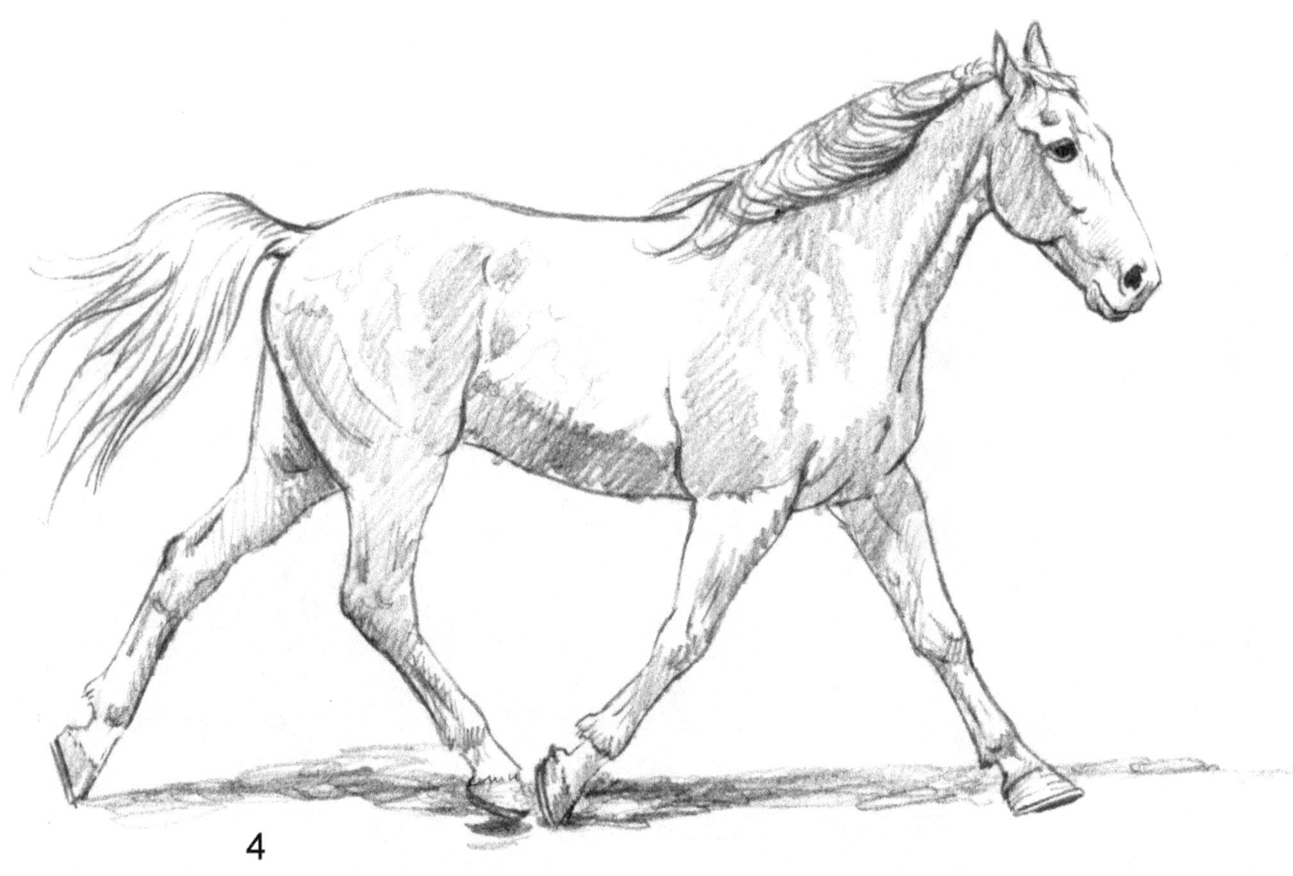

4

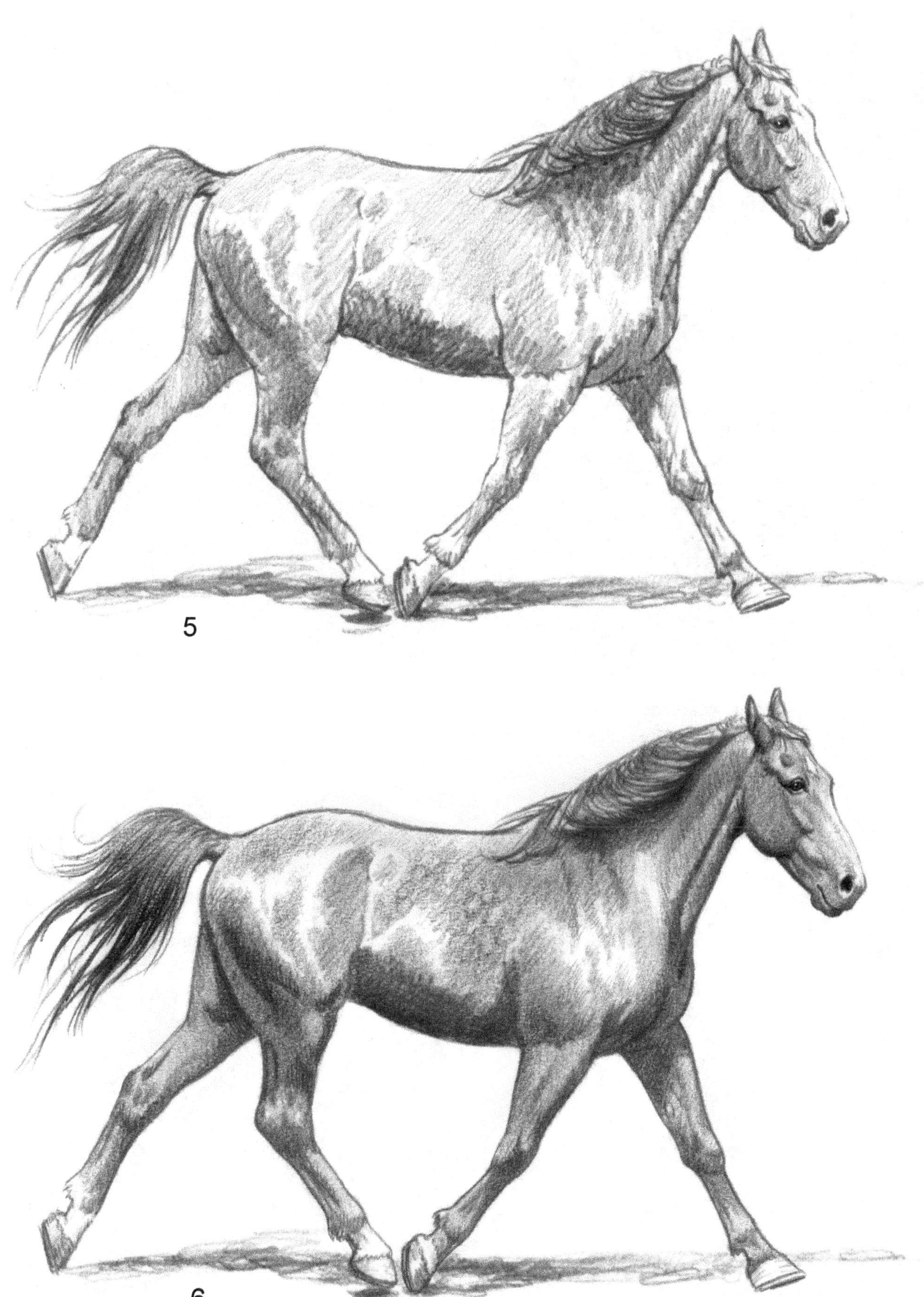

5

6

I chose to pull out the highlights on the coat with the eraser. I used "artistic license"—they are actually a light grey. There are no absolute rules in art. I draw until I think the picture looks pretty good, and then I stop. Some artists prefer a sketchier style, and stop at a looser stage, such as #5 above. Draw in the style that suits you!

BELGIUM DRAFT HORSE Trotting

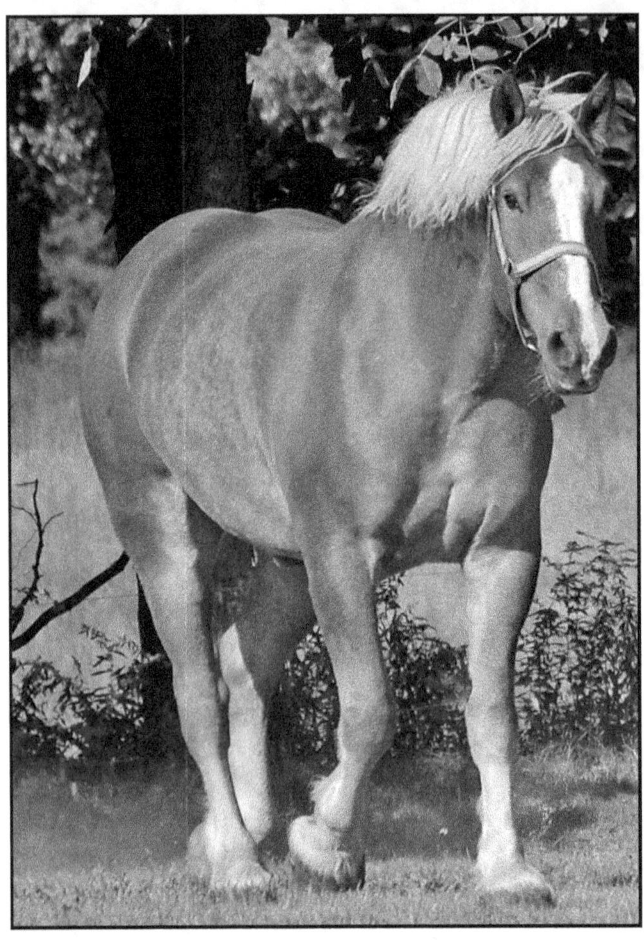

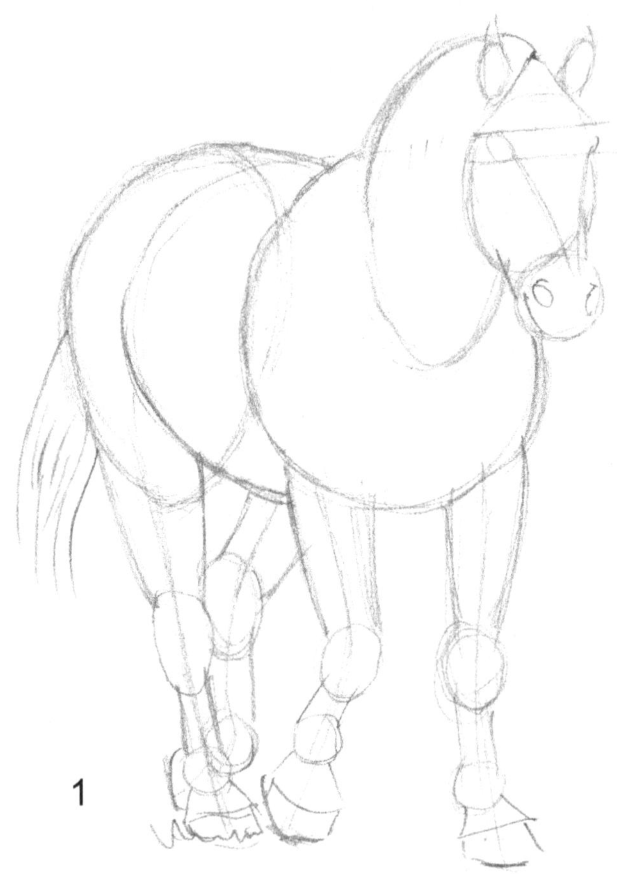

This is a very similar pose to the Appaloosa on p. 55, but reversed. His flaxen chestnut coat shows more highlights, though he is still a light-colored horse. Make him nice and wide.

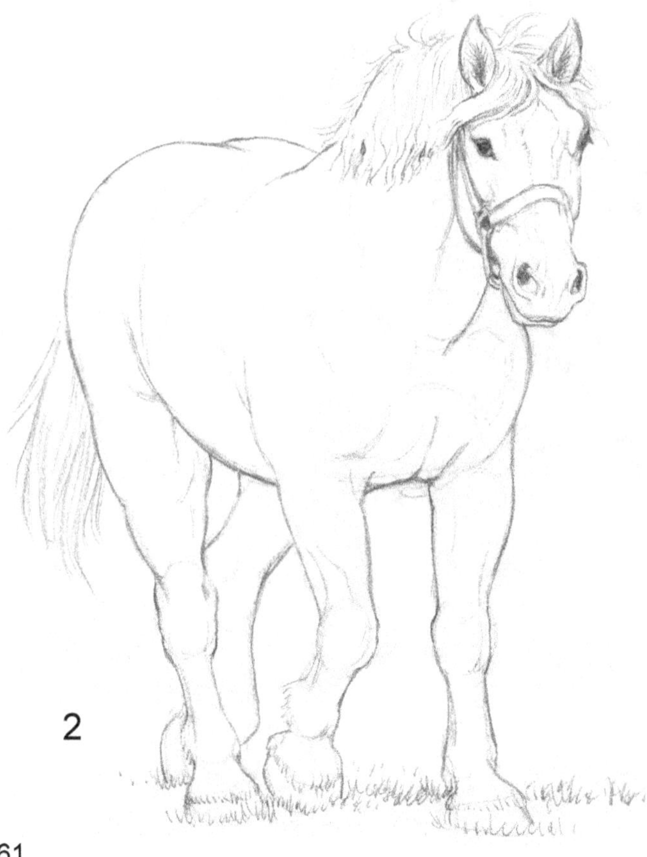

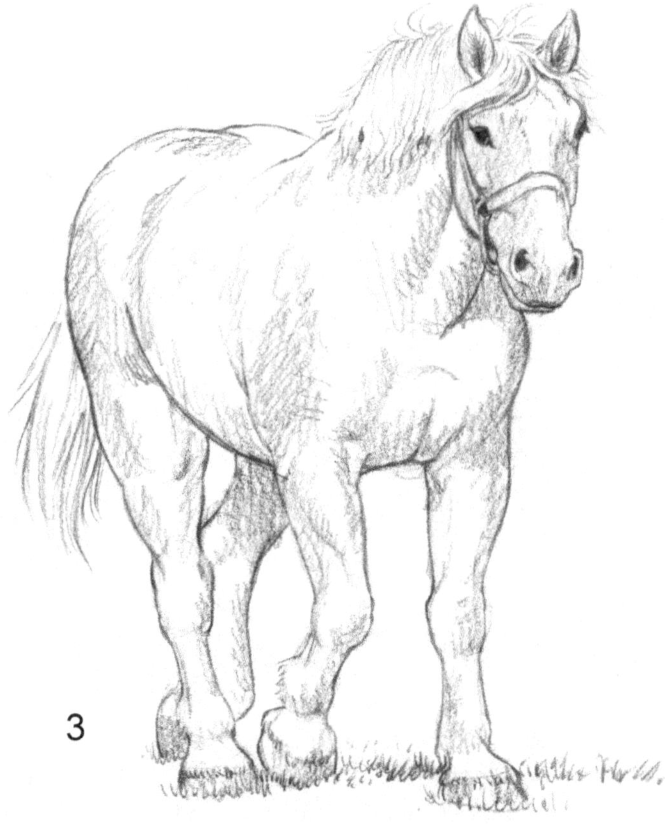

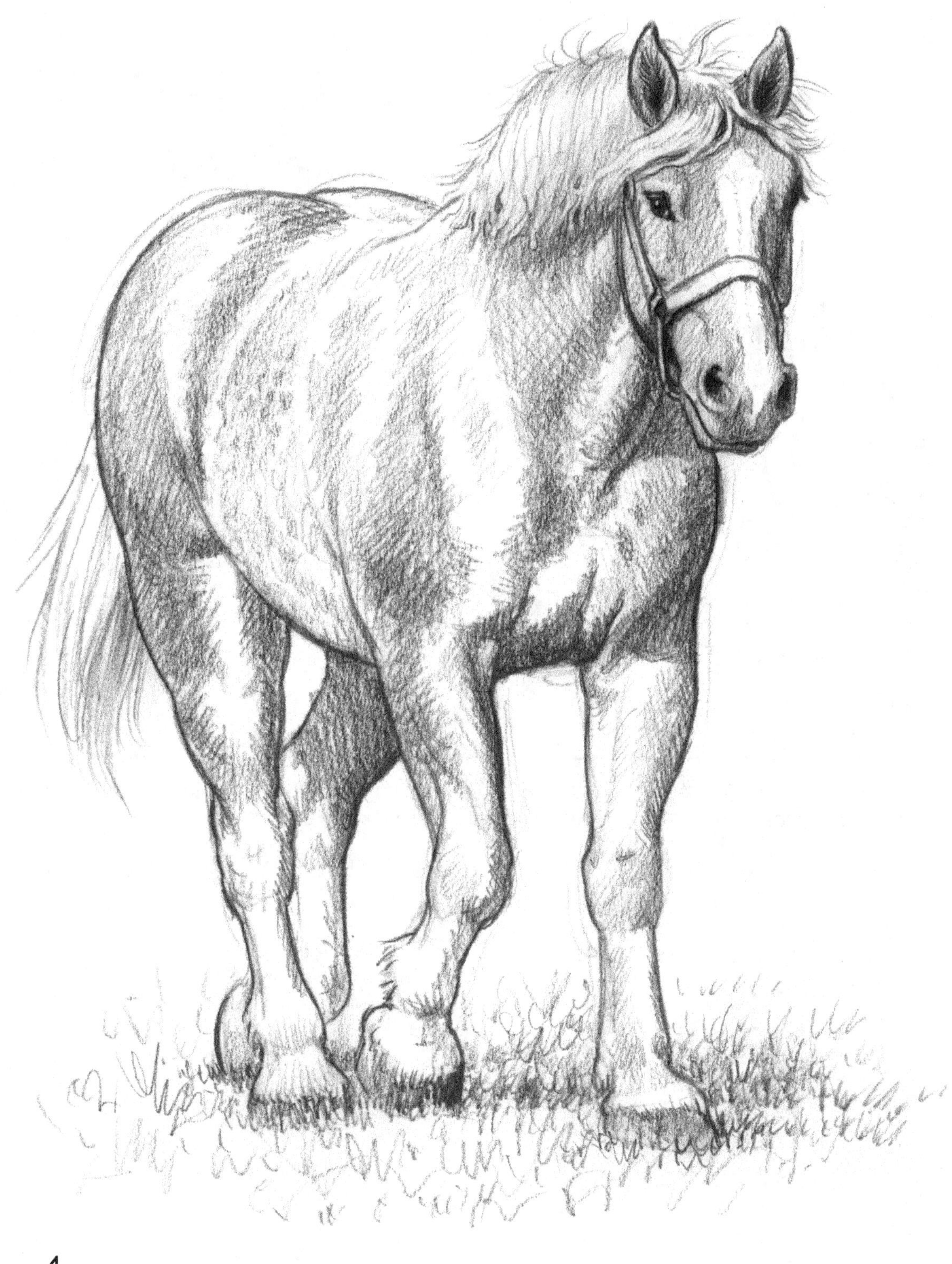

4

For this Belgium Draft horse I decided to go with a looser finish, leaving my pencil strokes and not softening/blurring them with the blending stump. Some artists prefer a "sketchy" look as a finished drawing. It is up to you when to say "done!" as you develop your style of drawing and your personal preferences.

FREISIAN Cantering

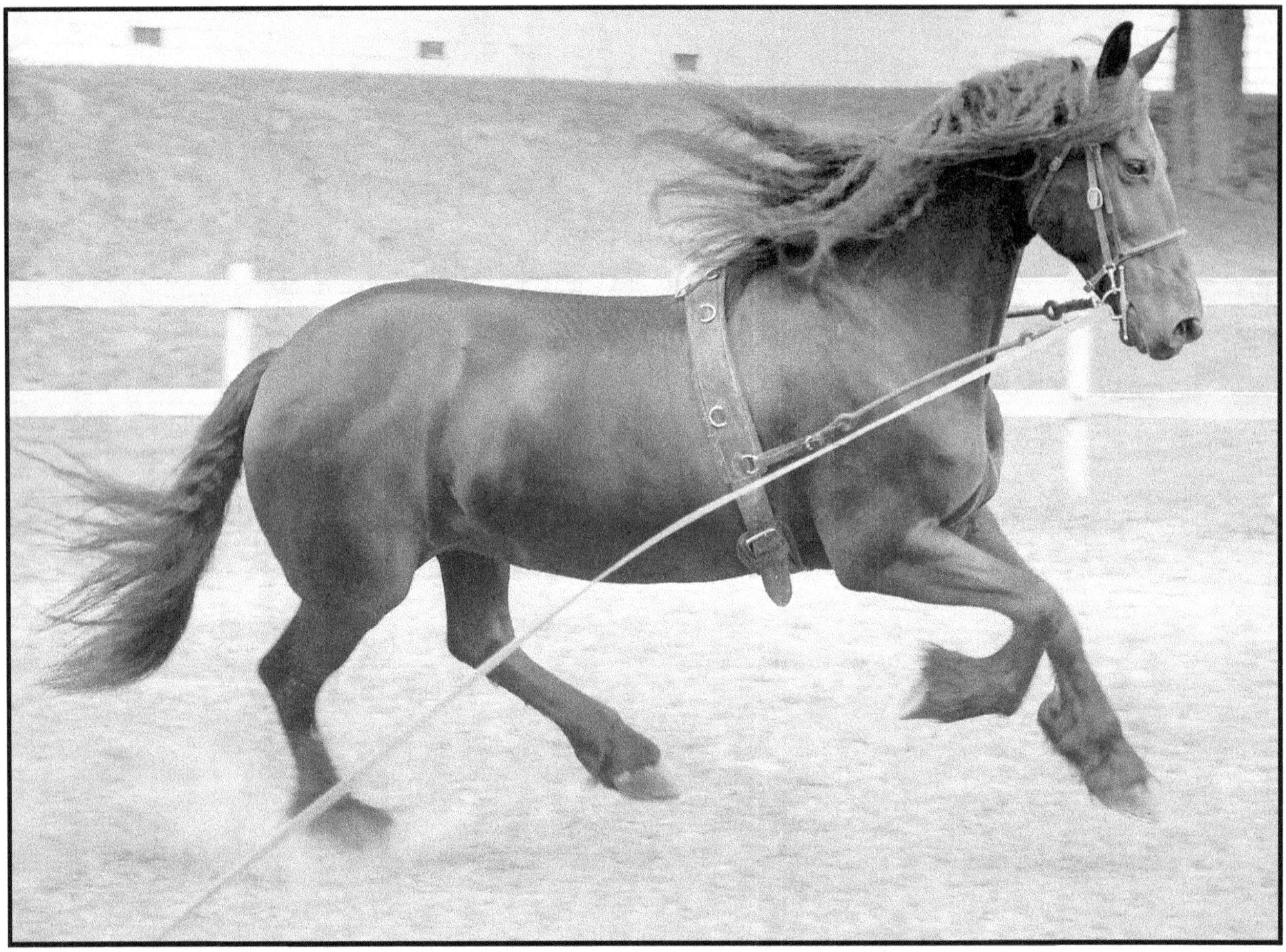

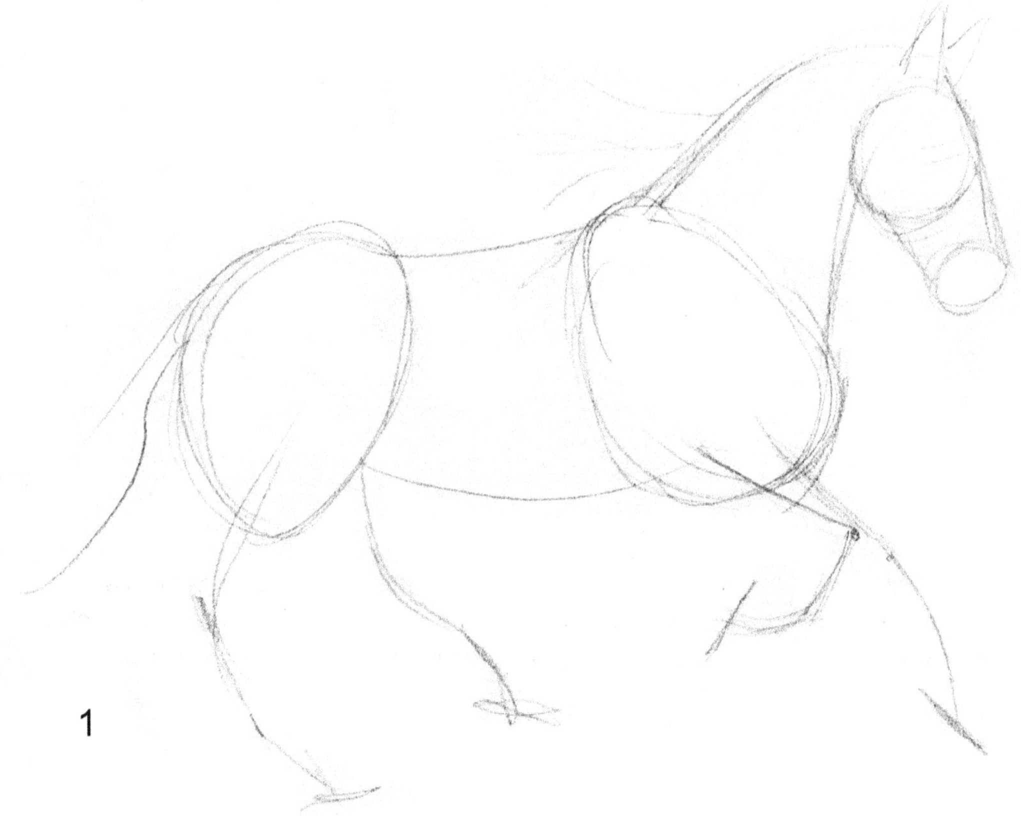

Because of the camera angle, the near back leg of this beautiful Freisian mare is a bit foreshortened. I don't always correct distortions of photos in Photoshop, sometimes I just correct it in my drawing.

1

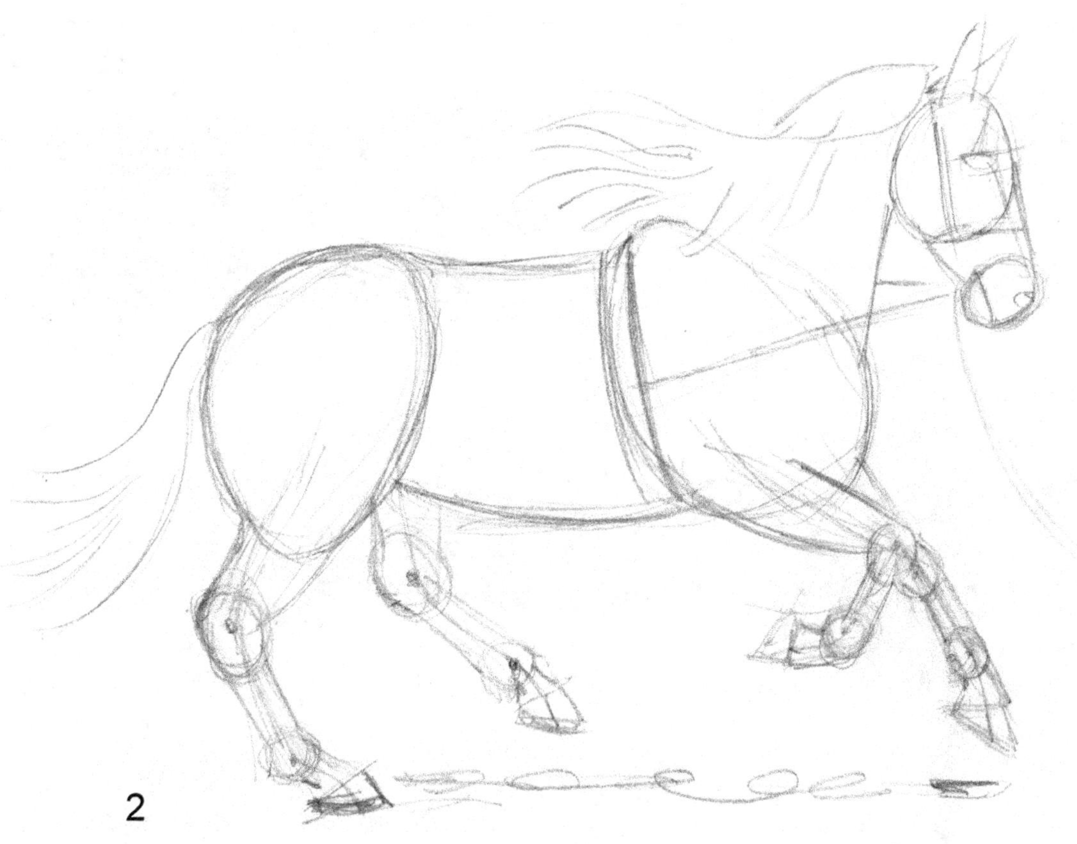

Block in the surcingle loosely at first, trying to get the basic placement correct. I did not like the look of the long longe rope crossing her body, so I moved the angle to the front.

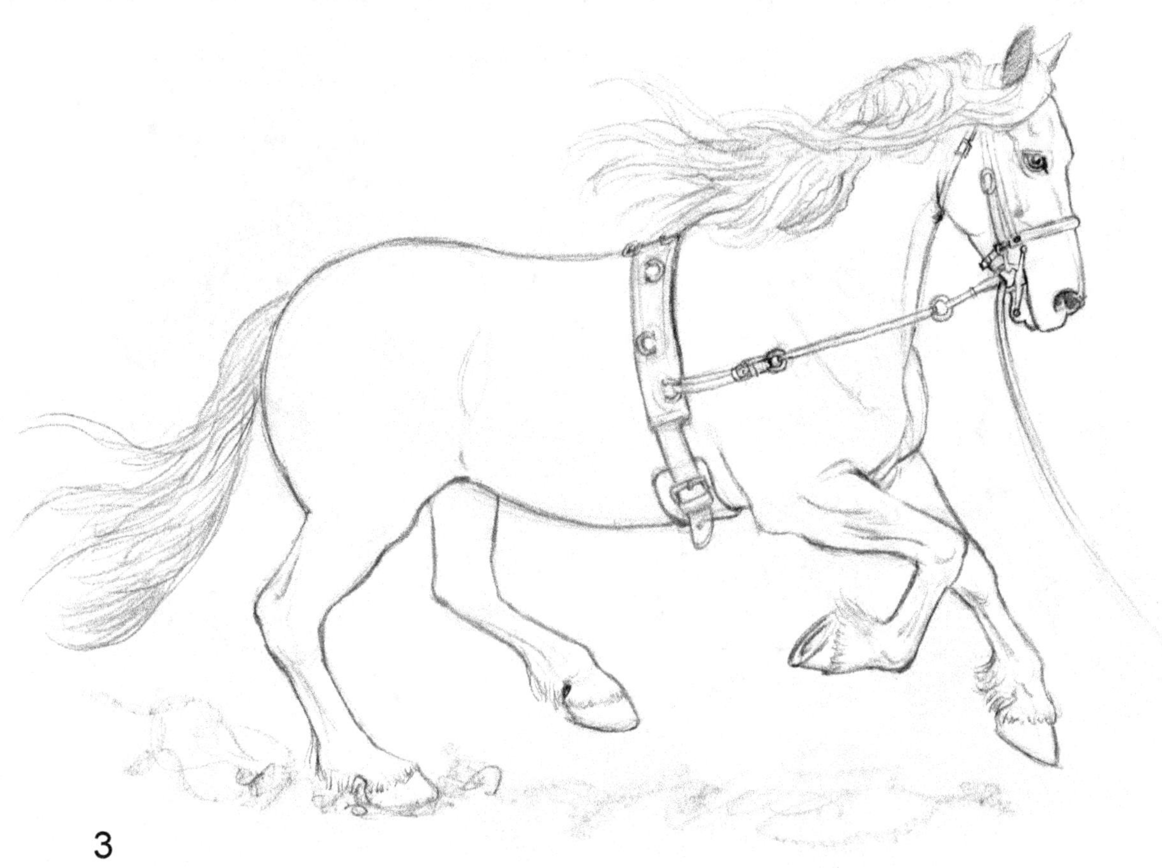

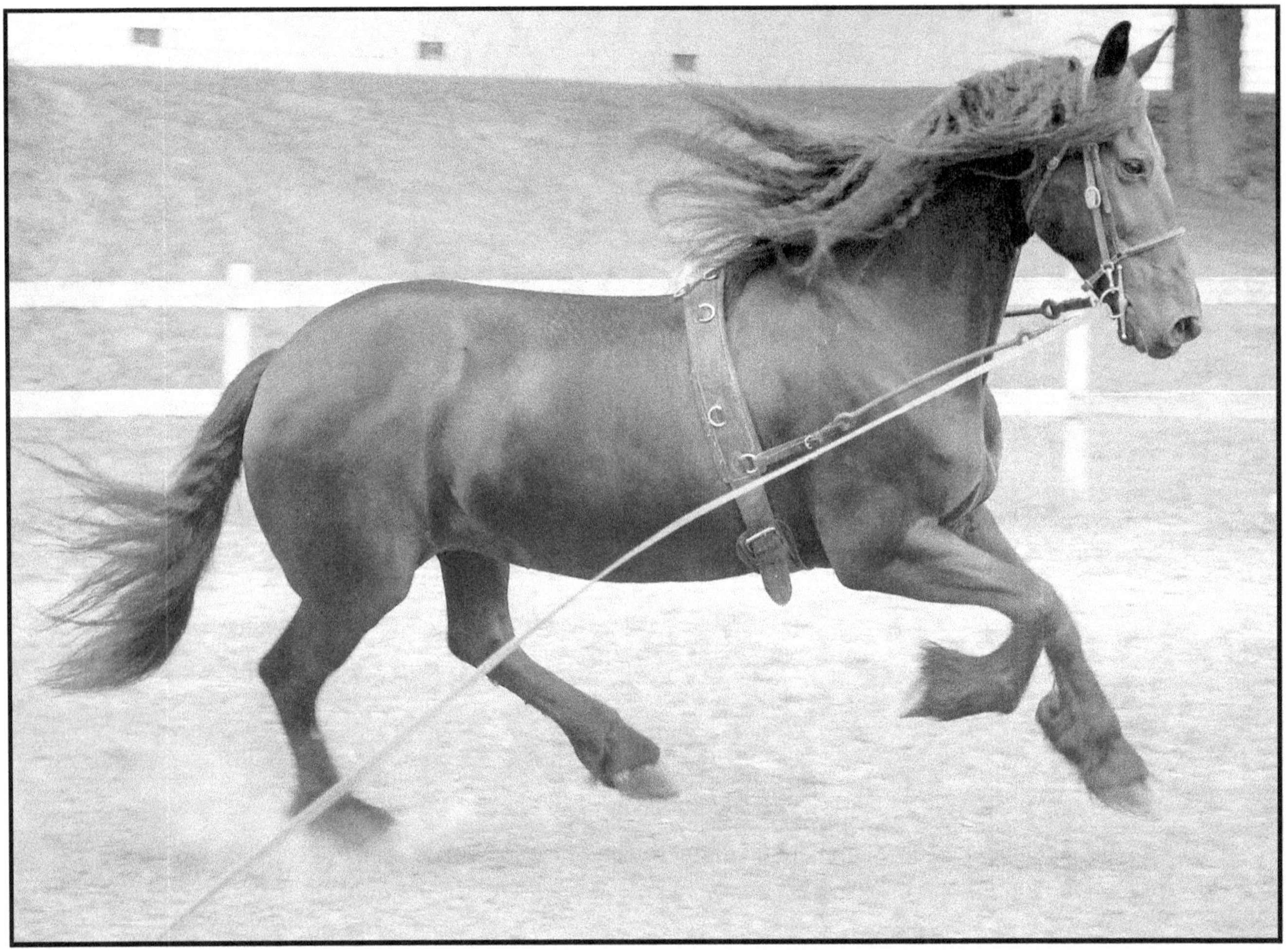

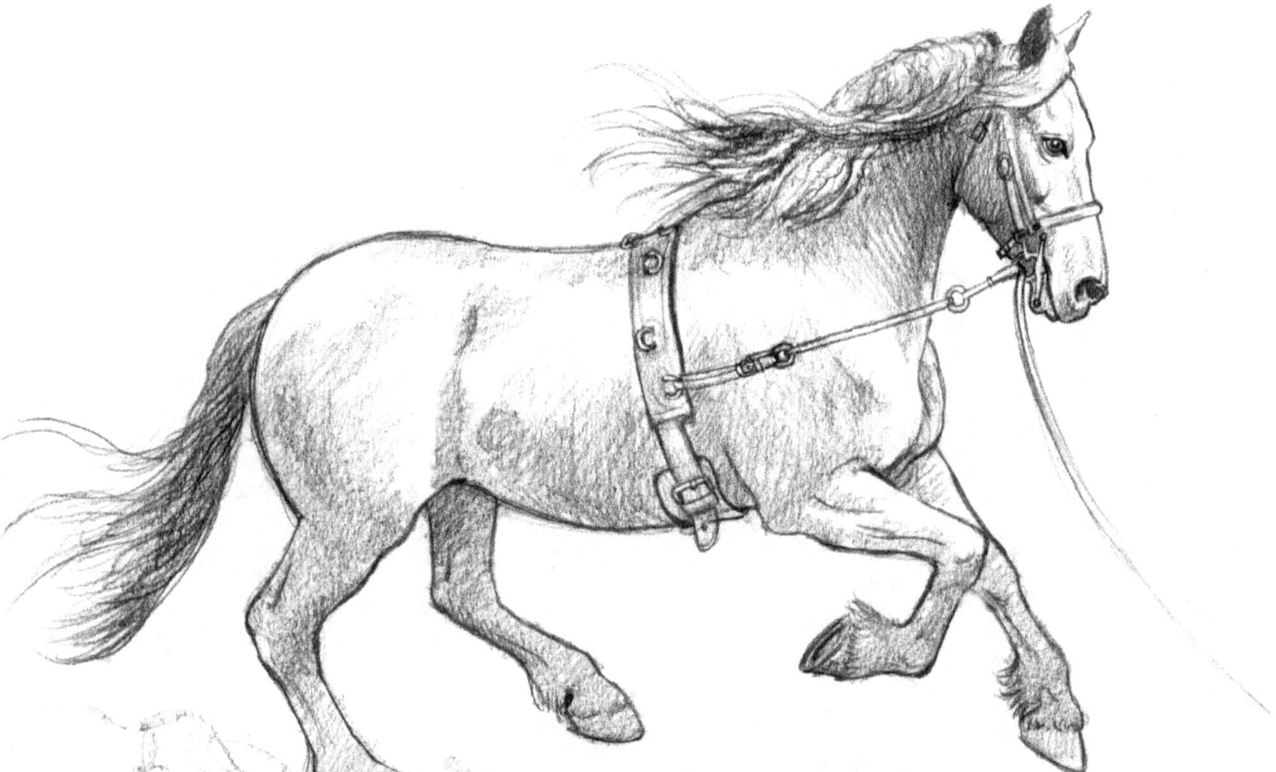

4

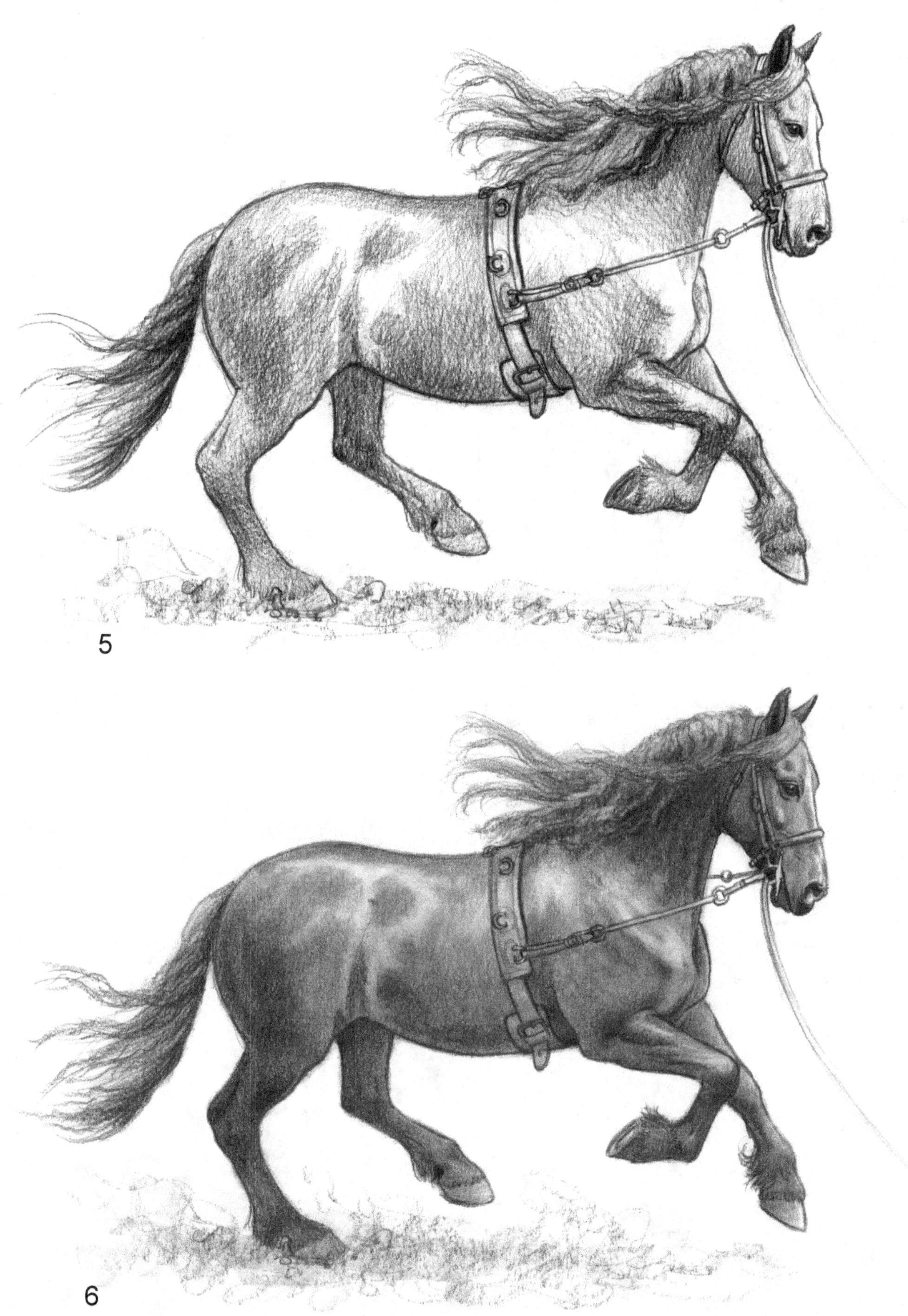

5

6

This one took a long time to slowly build up the darks. I used B and 2B to darken her coat and shadow areas, and I used a blending stump to smooth out the shading. Most of the highlights I made light gray, not white.

NORWEGIAN FJORD Cantering

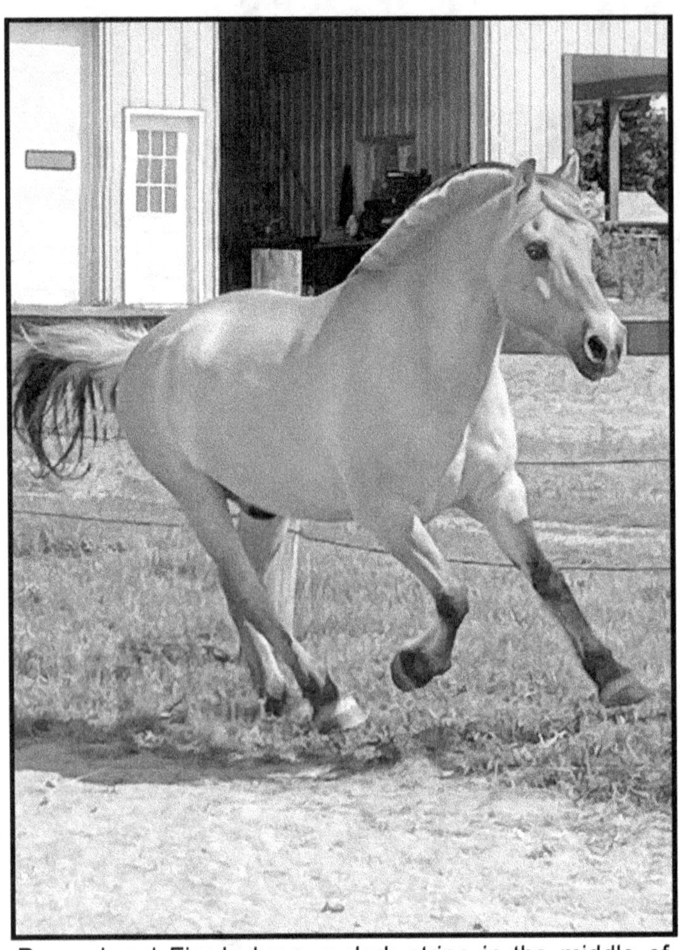

Dun-colored Fjords have a dark stripe in the middle of
their light mane, a two-color forelock and tail. This gelding
also has dark legs and a dark muzzle.

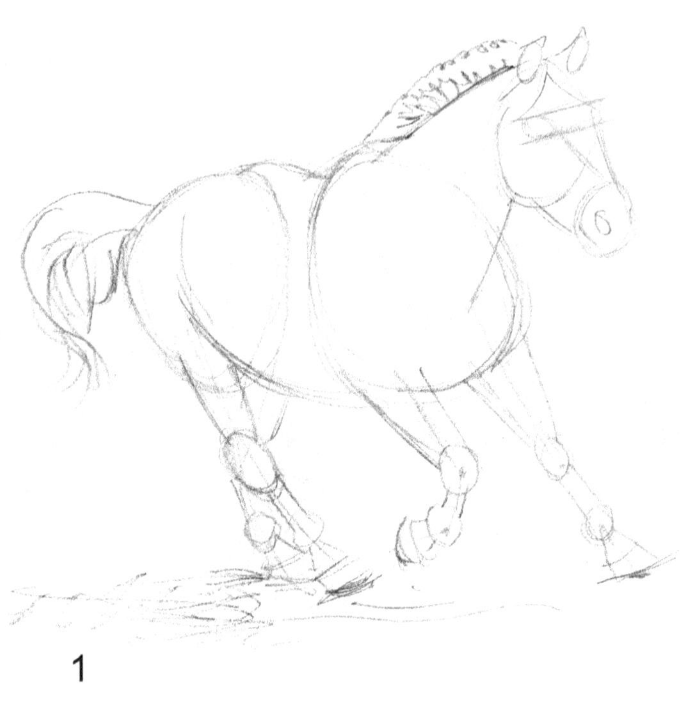

1

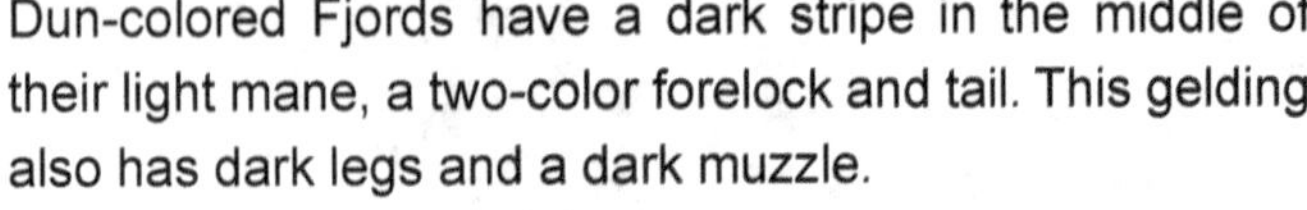

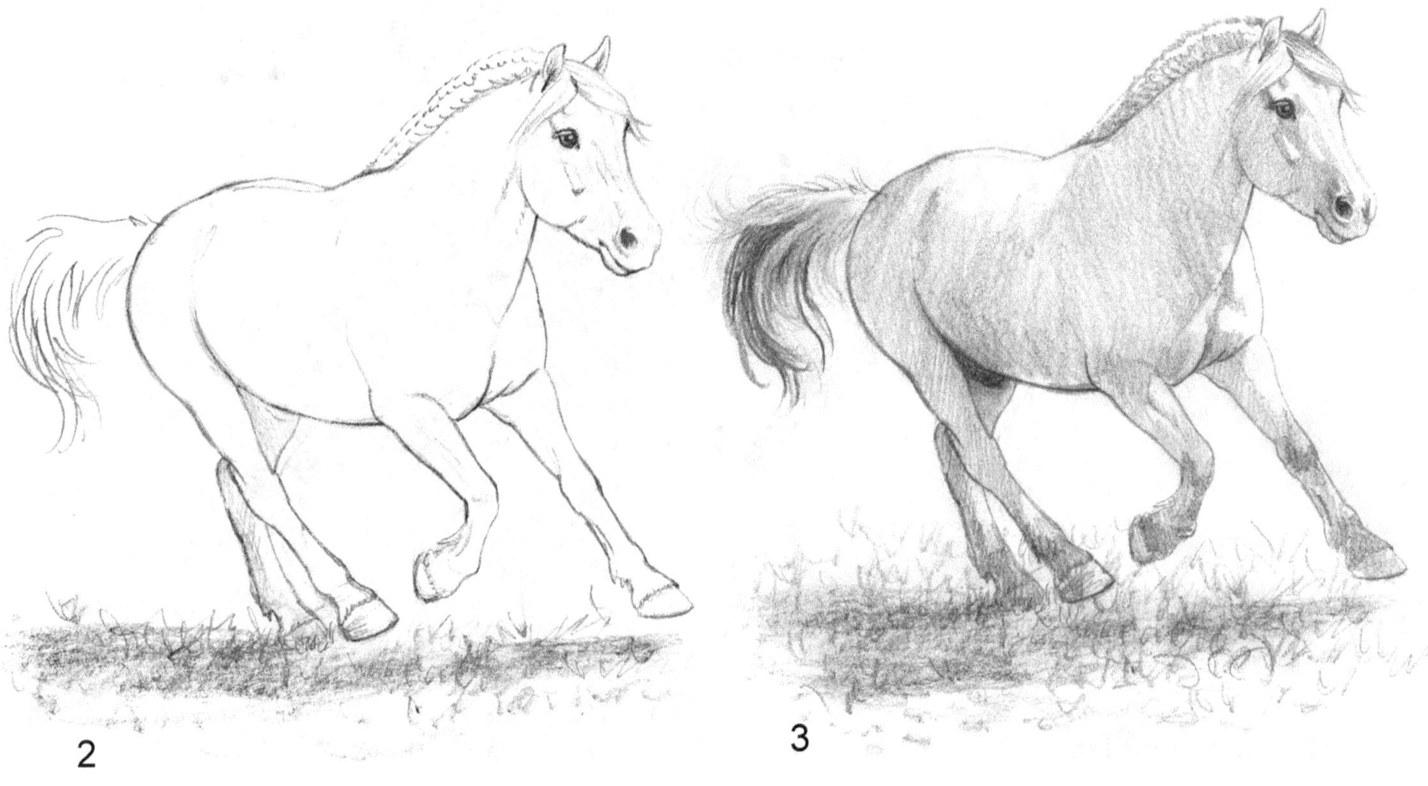

2

3

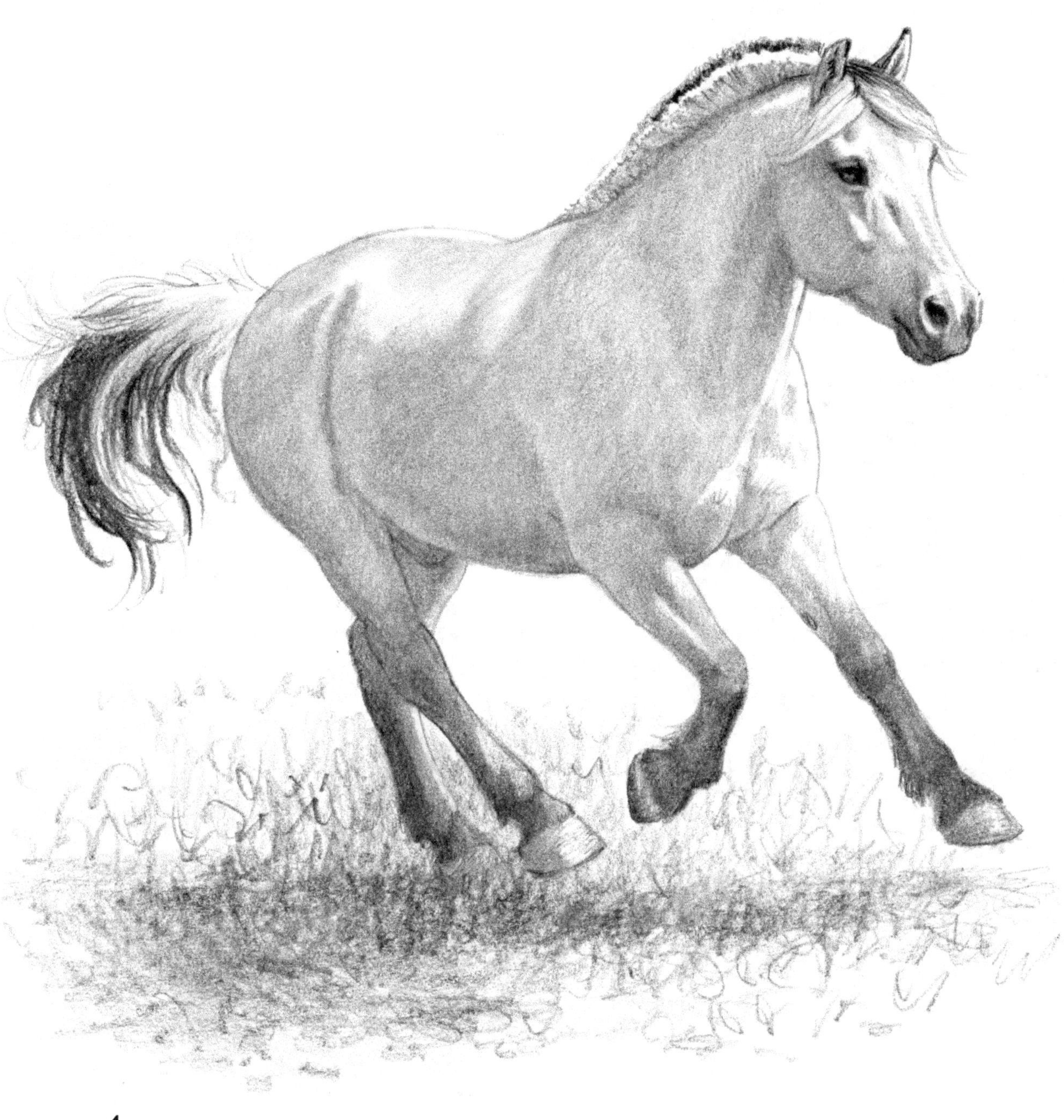

4

This striking boy was fun to draw, with the dramatic front lighting. Make sure not to go too dark on the shadow side of his body, so that his dark legs show up well. Squint to see the values of the photo against the values on your drawing. Note that the top of his tail is light, so pick out some shapes with a 2B, leaving the top lighter, for the lower part of his tail.

THOROUGHBRED FOAL Cantering

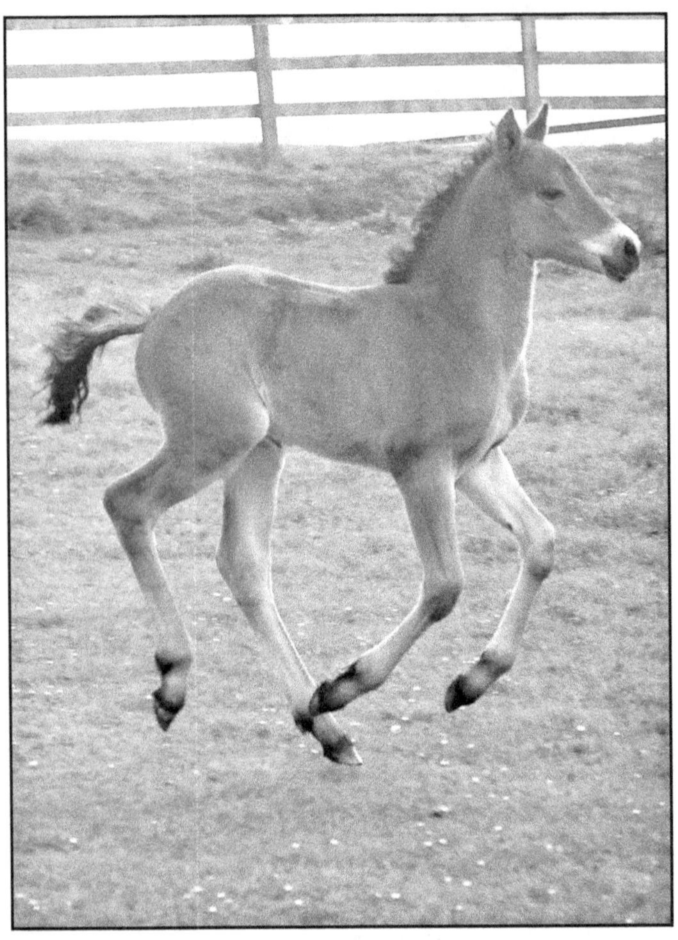

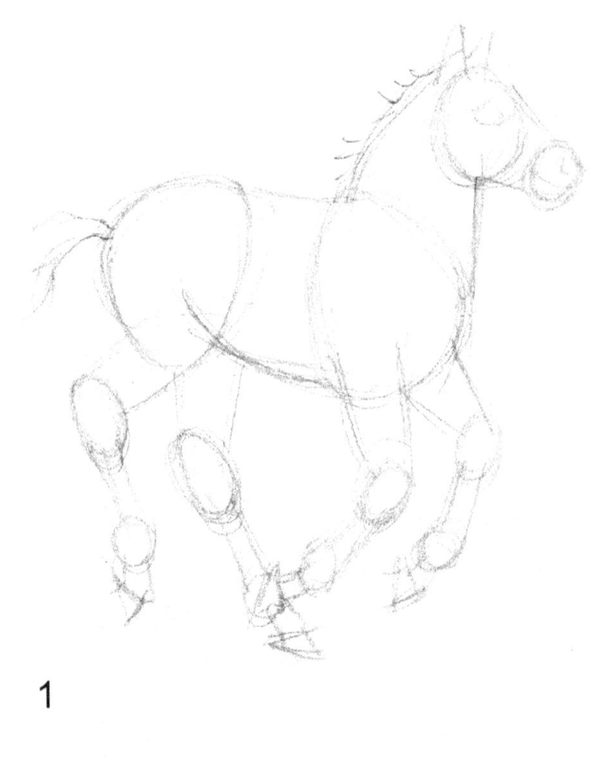

1

In this cantering pose all four feet of the foal are off the ground, like pose #4 on p. 42. Note how different his proportions are from an adult horse. His legs are thin but close to adult size in length.

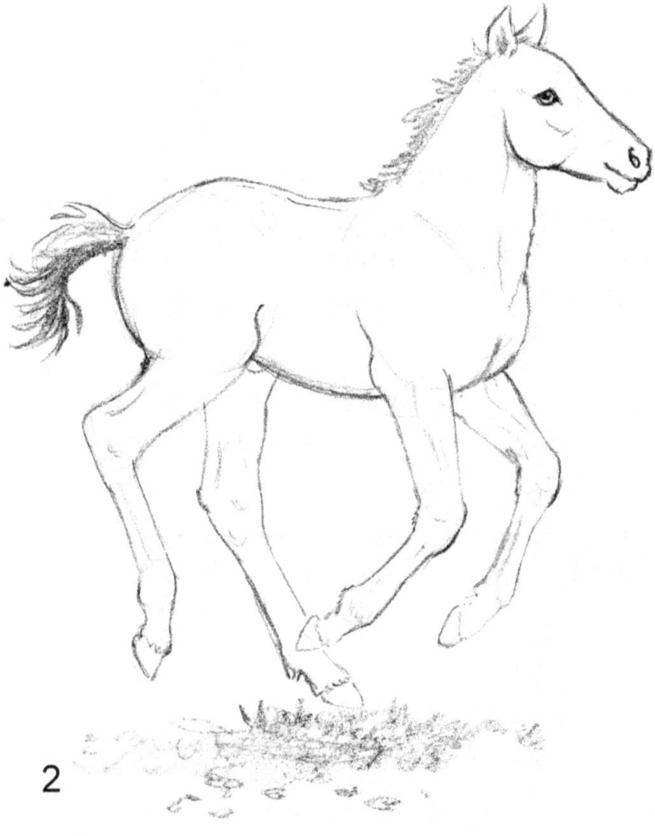

2

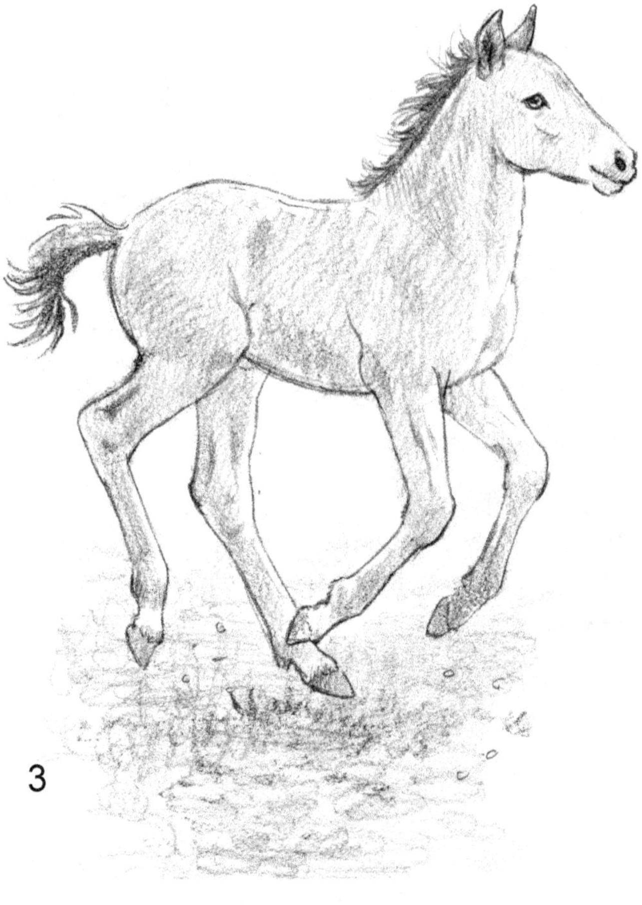

3

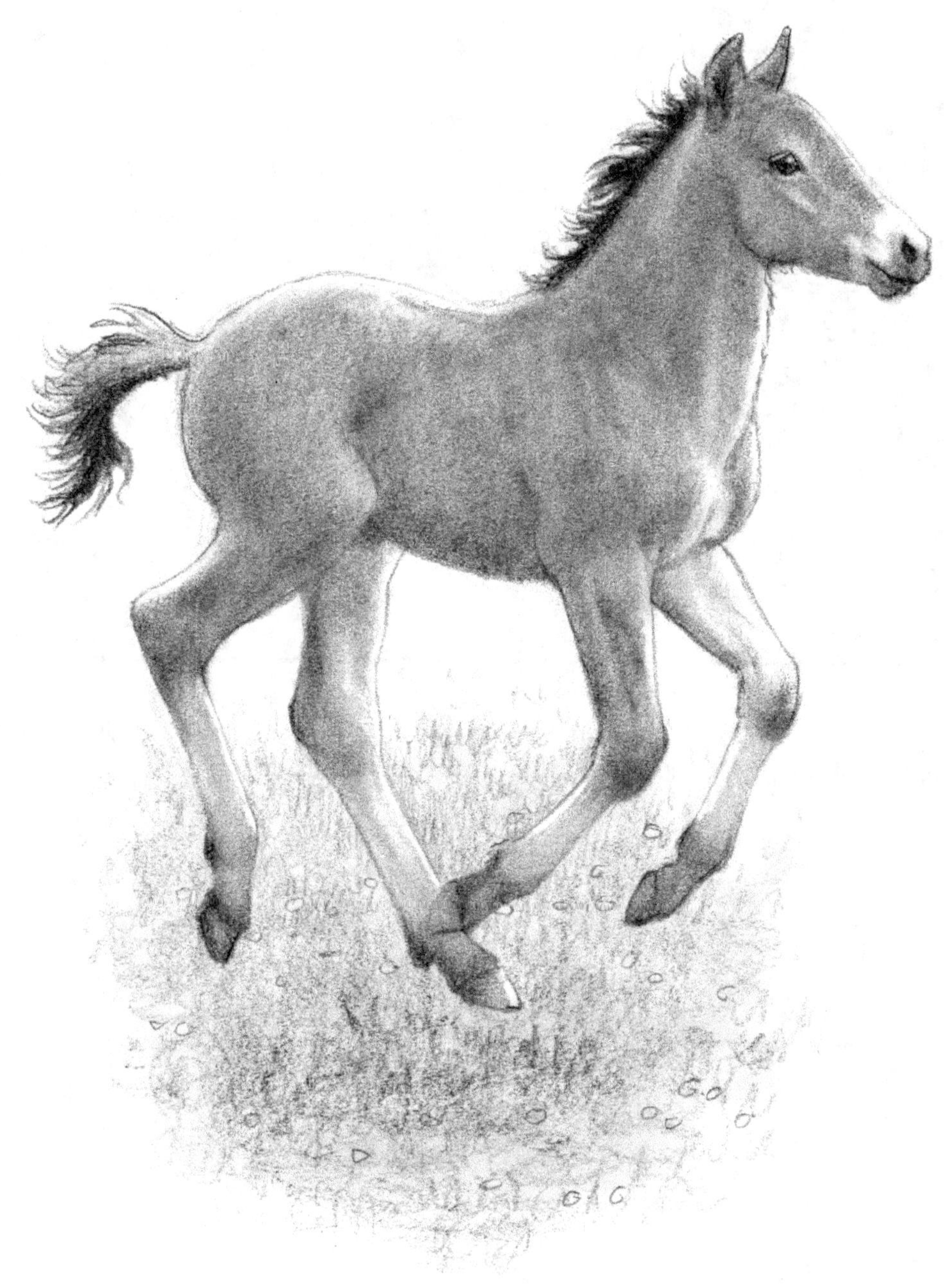

4

This kind of "soft" lighting on an overcast day is for me the most difficult to draw because of all the subtle changes in tone, with no strong difference between light and shadow areas to define the form. I stuck with the HB to build up the body tones, and used a 2B for his mane and tail. Make sure to keep his lower legs lighter than the rest of his body. I did use the blending stump after adding the shading to the body. There is just a little strip of "rim light" from the overcast sky on the right side of his various body parts. I erased this "rim light," leaving a delicate outline against the white of the paper.

MORGAN-PERCHERON CROSS Jumping

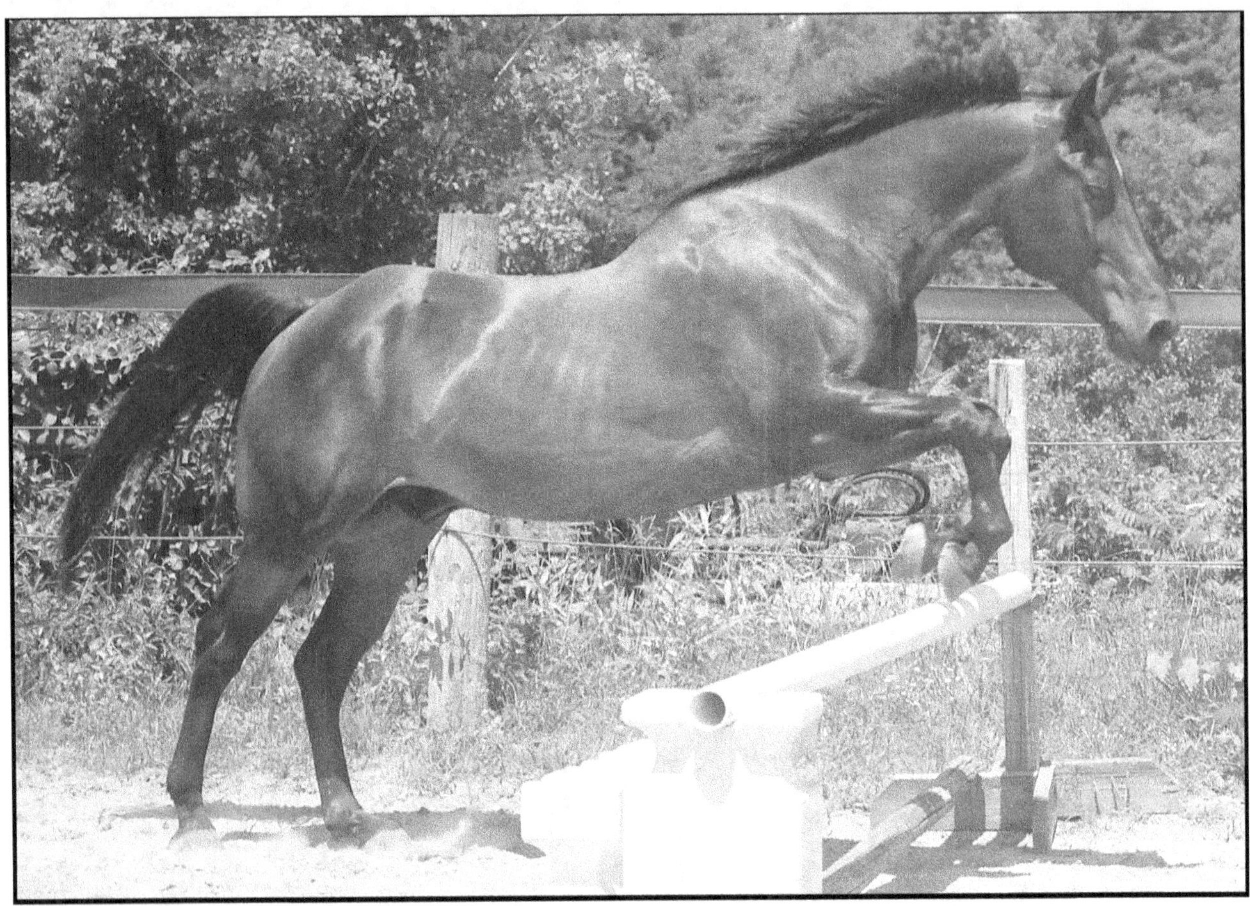

This horse is a dark bay color, with a dark brown body, black legs, mane and tail. He is perhaps the shiniest horse I have ever seen! In this pose, he is pushing off the ground with his hind legs. I have included the jump in my drawing, but you can leave it out if you prefer. I did leave out the extra white block on the left.

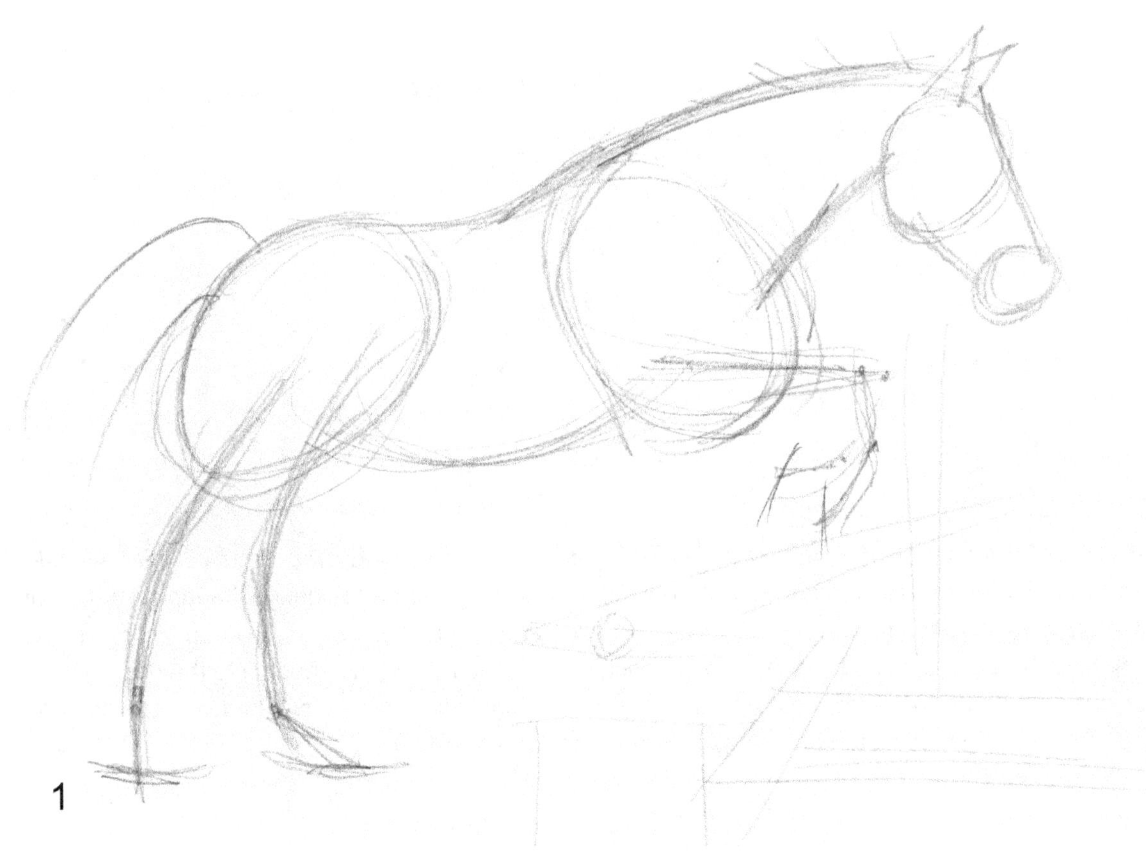

1

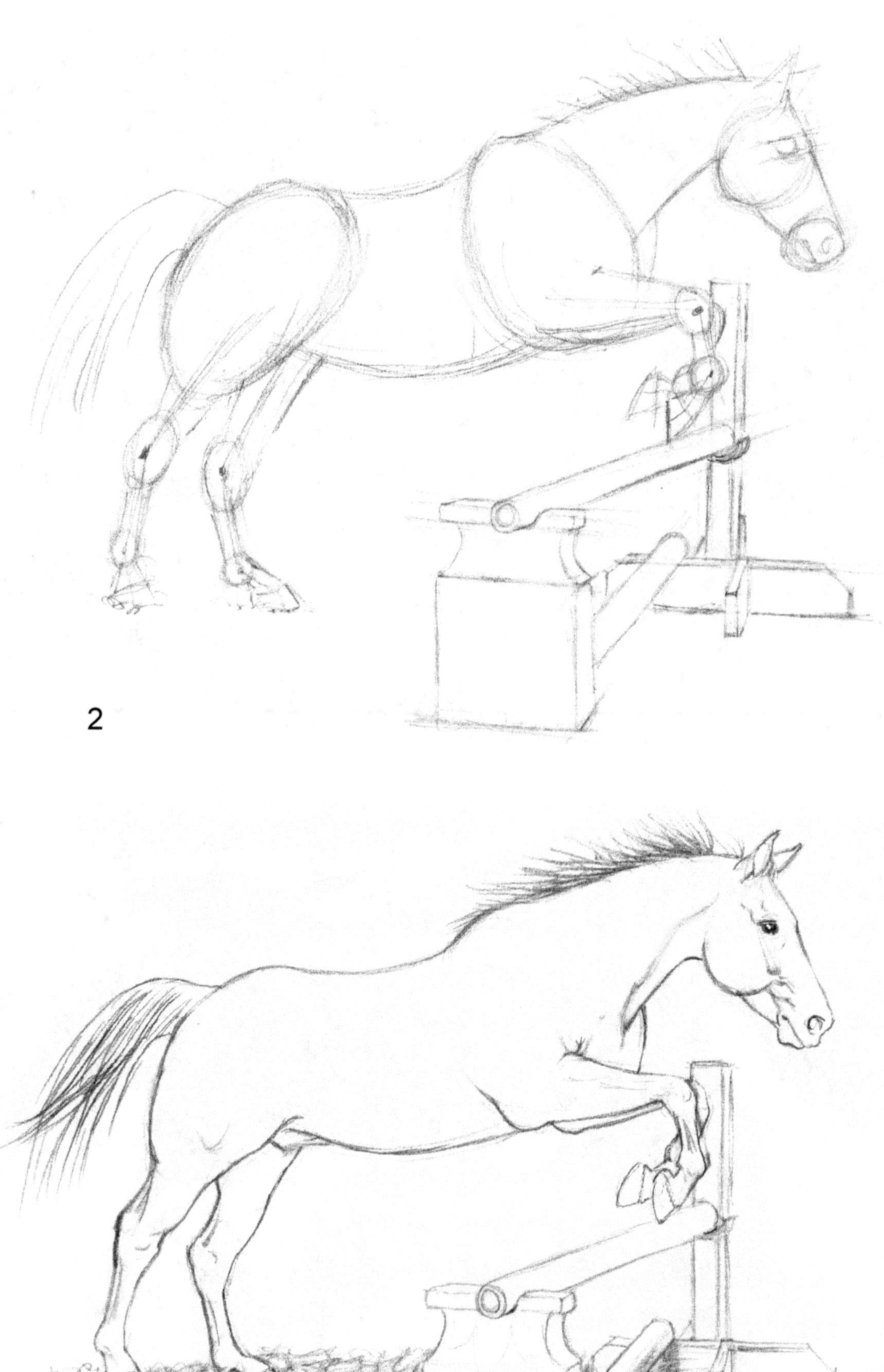

2

3

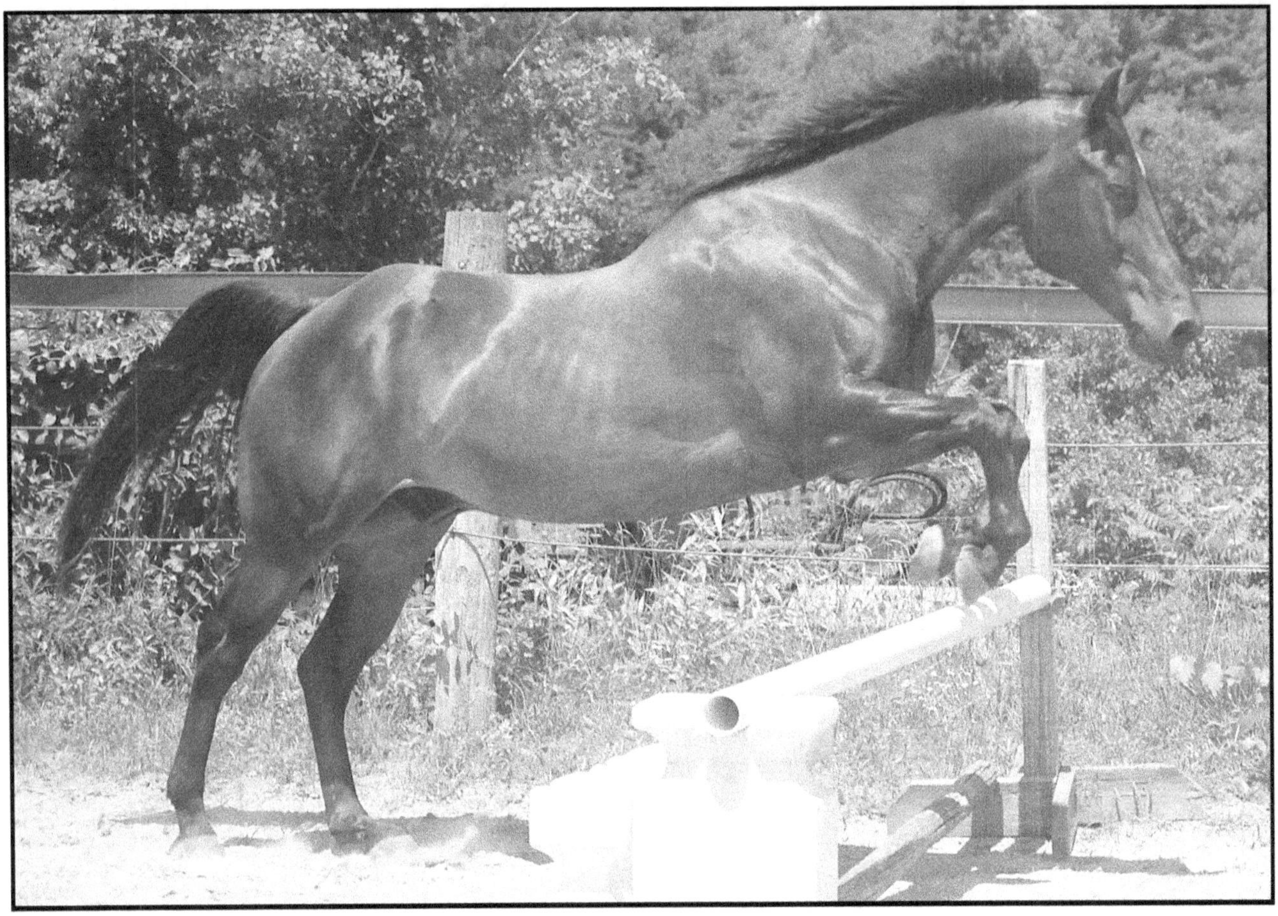

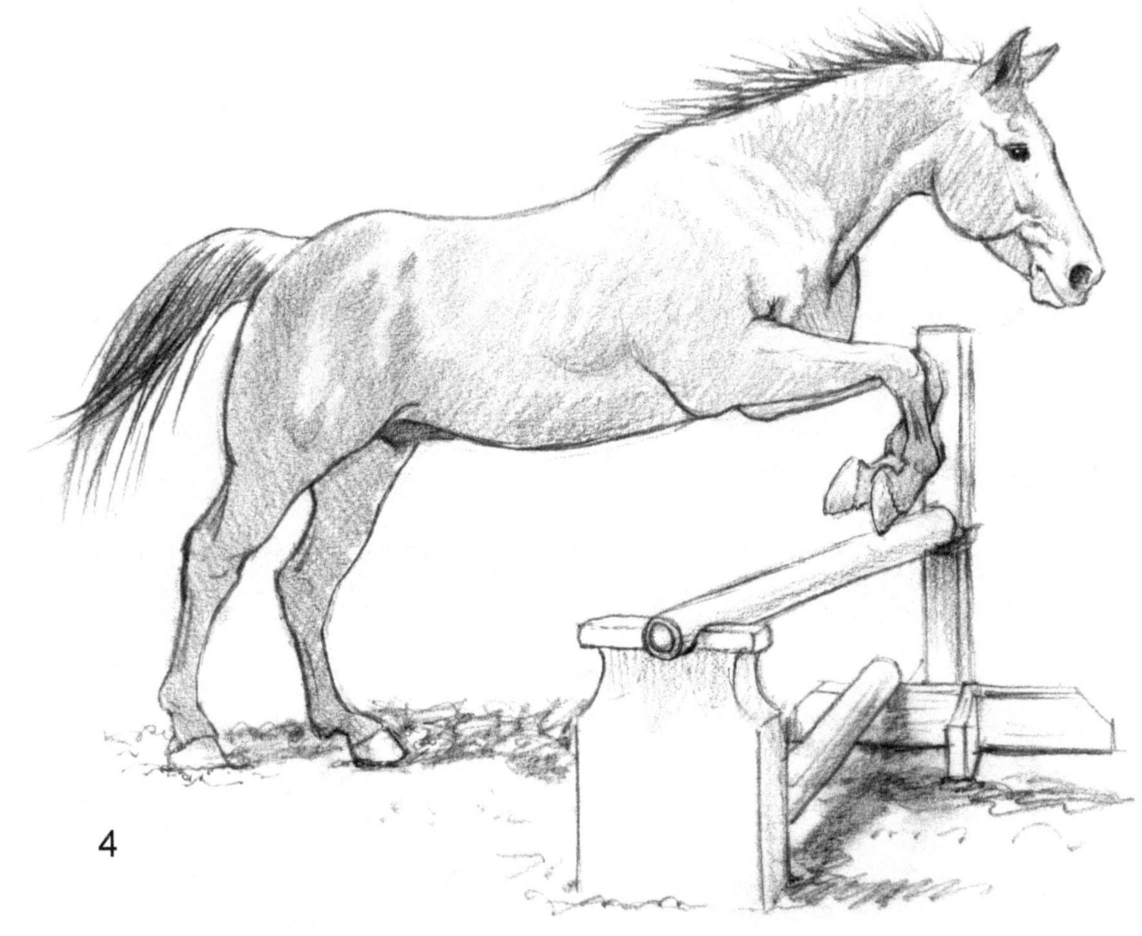

4

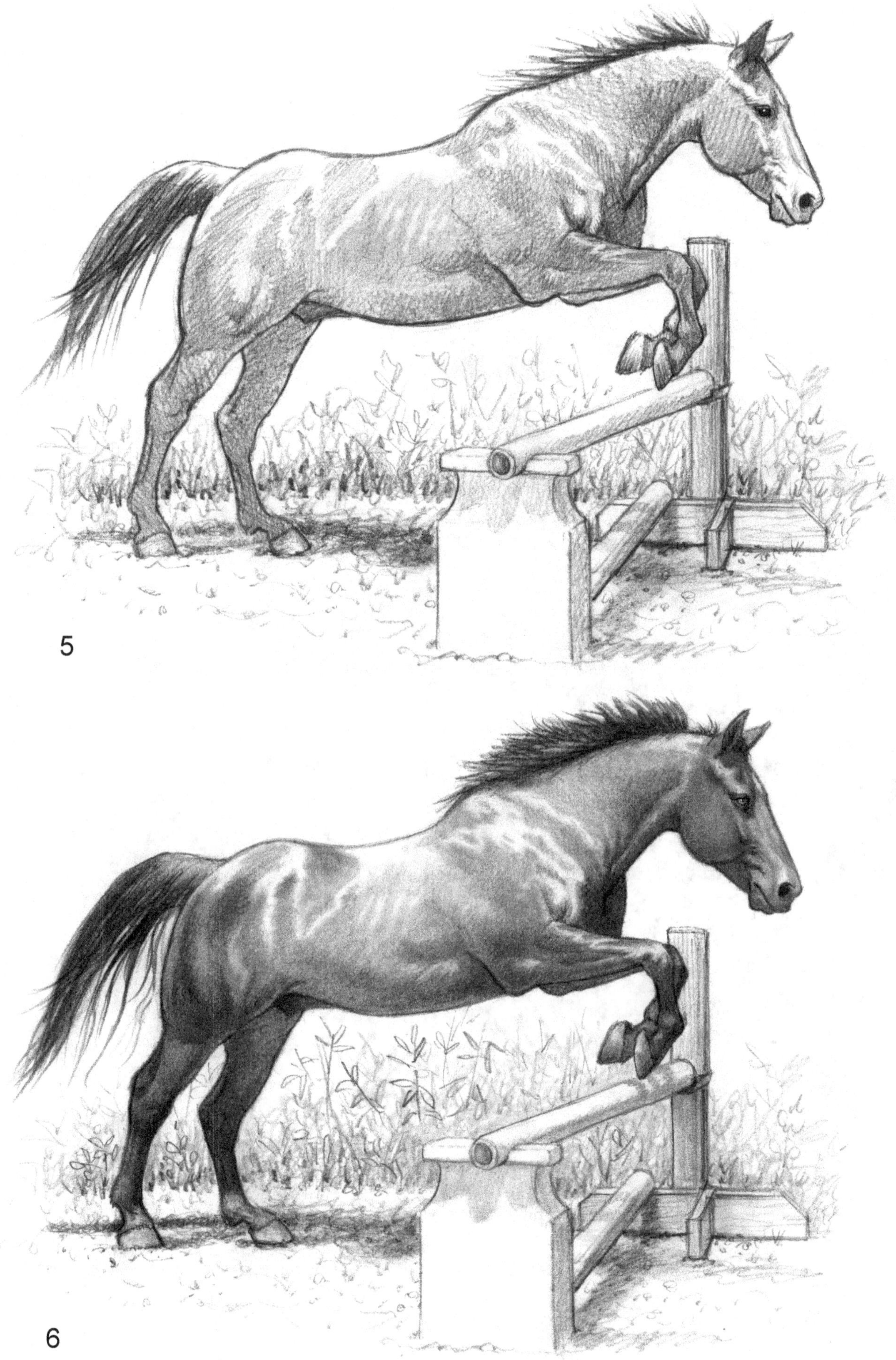

5

6

I decided to "pull out" the highlights on his body with my kneaded eraser, for a dramatic look. I added reflected light in his eye so it could be seen better. And for this pose I added a little extra background in addition to the jump.

PAINT HORSE Rearing

Advanced Lesson: Colored Pencil on Toned Paper

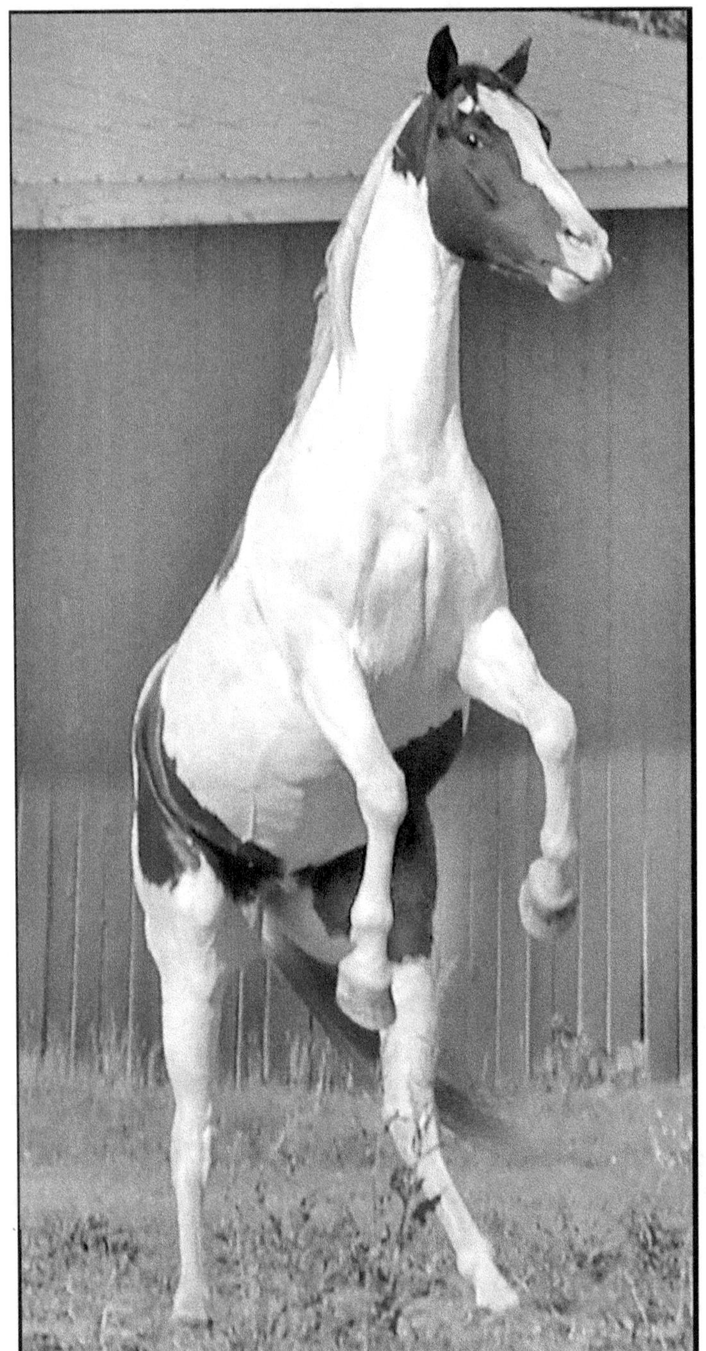

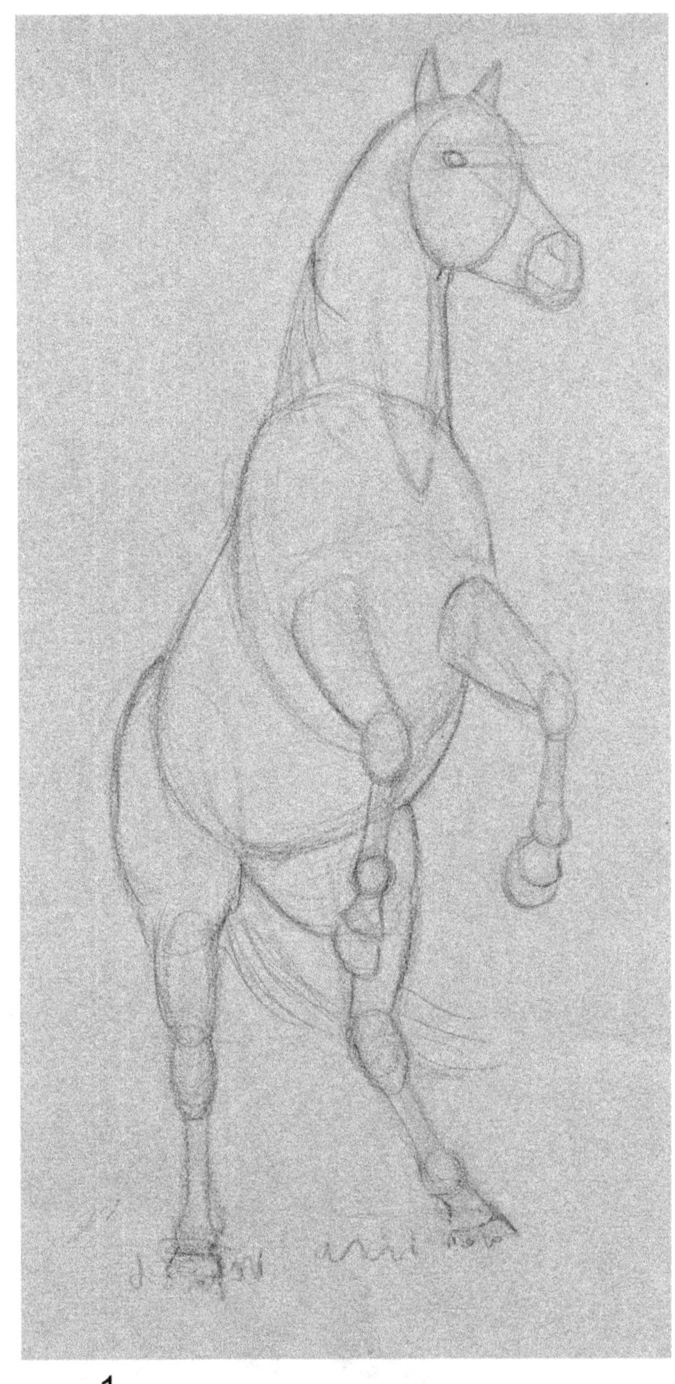

1

I used a black Col-erase Prismacolor colored pencil, and a white Prismacolor colored pencil, on gray toned charcoal paper for this drawing. You can also use a charcoal pencil and a white charcoal pencil.

1. Follow the basic steps for graphite pencil on p. 27 for a 3/4 view, drawing the egg-shaped oval of his chest/front end first. Construct the rest of his body with simple shapes first, like you have done in the other lessons.

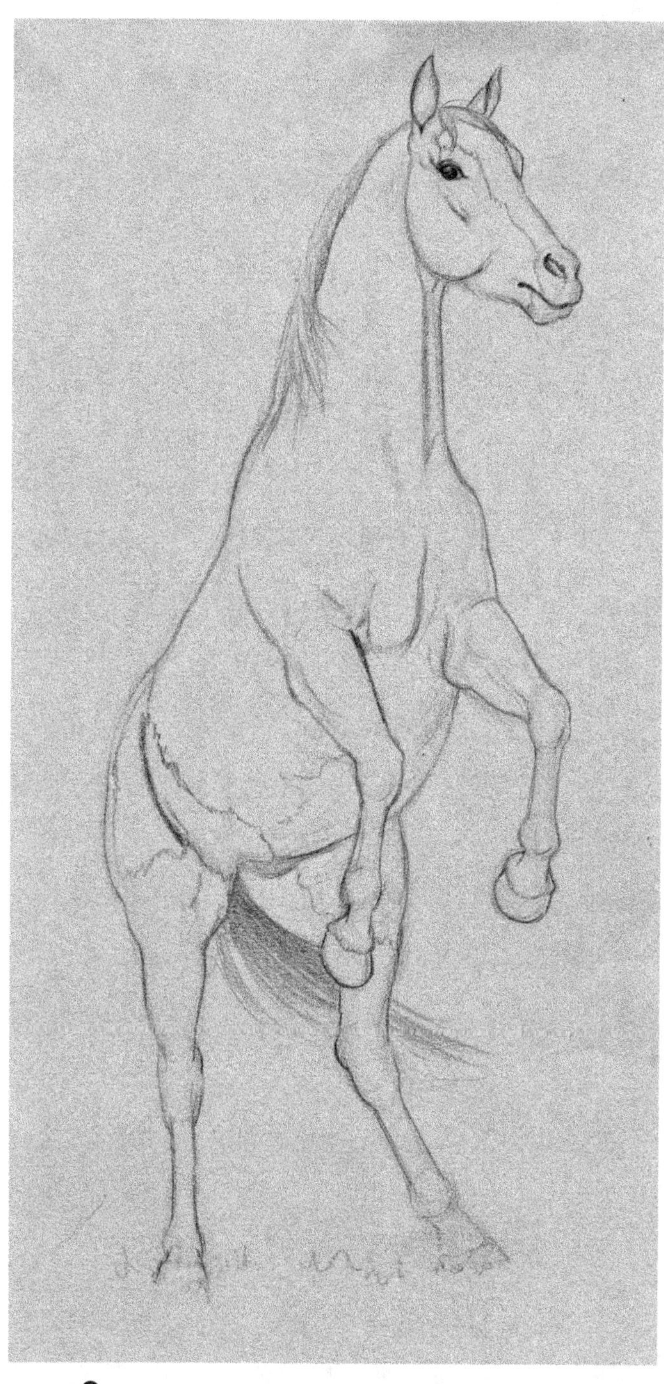

2

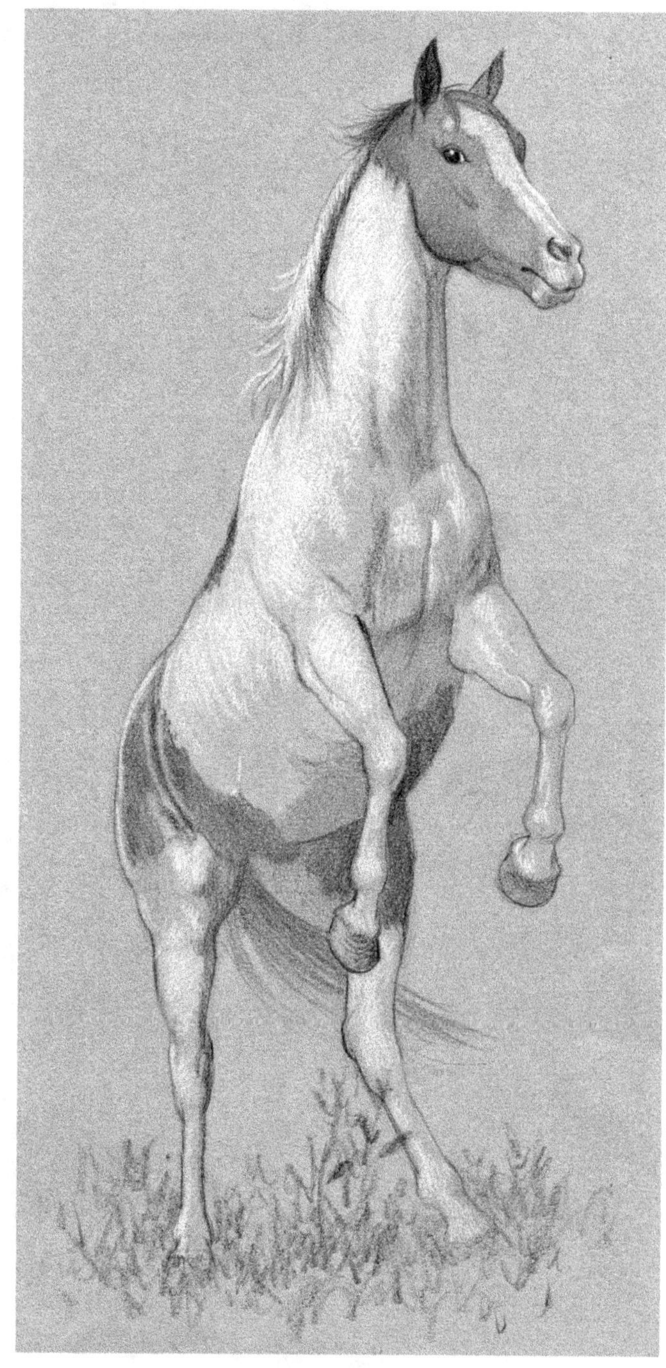

3

2. Study the photo and refine the outline to match what you see. Erase your first block-in lines as you go. Indicate his white blaze and the edges of the paint pattern on his coat.

3. I erased most of the black lines for his mane, and drew them in white, leaving just a few, and leaving the gray paper for some of the mane shadow. In general, I avoid mixing white and black lines. The white pencil and the gray of the paper are all you need for the white side of his body in the light. I decided to add a bit of black mane near his head, to add a little interest. I added the white spark in his eye and the white of his eye on the right. With your white pencil, start to build up the light areas where his coat is white, following the direction the fur is growing. The gray paper becomes the half-tone/shadow of the white coat. Add a bit of grass under him. Start shading with black pencil on the black areas of his coat, and add the sweep of his tail.

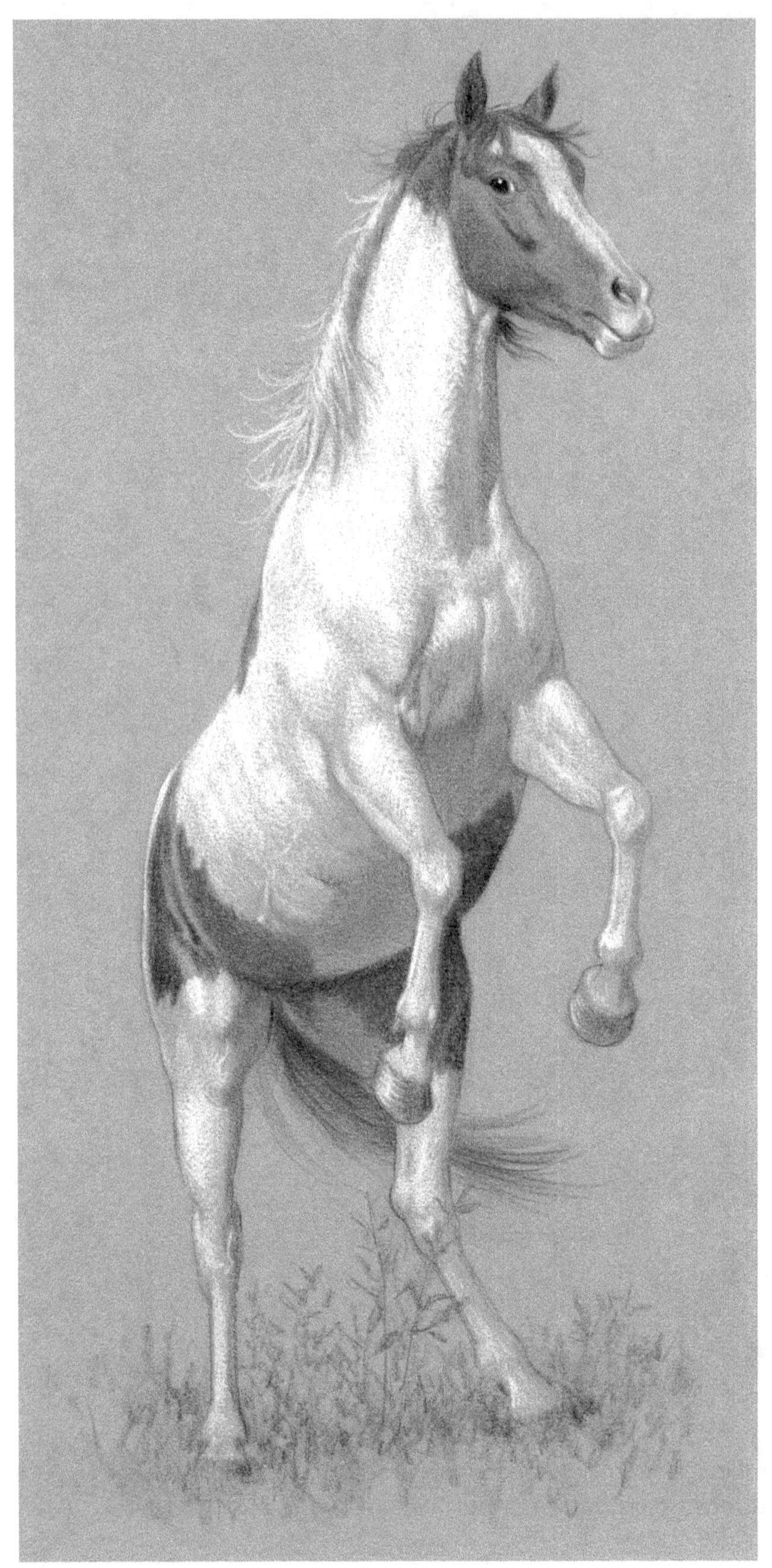

4

4. Build up the white coat carefully with tiny strokes of a sharp white pencil. Don't bear down too hard or the pencil will break. The more you go over and over an area, the whiter it will get. When the tip is worn down, bear down harder where you want pure white. Be patient! I like the look of some of the gray still showing through, so it looks like soft fur. Build up the black areas with the black pencil, and darken the cast shadow area of the white fur with a bit more black. Leave the gray paper untouched for the hightlights on the black part of his body.

BONUS SECTION

Enjoy drawing the ten bonus photos of mares and foals for this Special Edition of DRAWING HORSES. Apply the basic steps you have learned in the previous lessons, finding the simple shapes underlying the form. And later, if you draw from your own photos of horses, or ones you find for free use on the web, I hope this method will help you with any horse you'd like to draw.

As you improve and learn what horses look like from different angles, and how they move, you can start inventing your own poses and simple drawings. However, to get a realistic likeness of an individual horse, I do still find it necessary to have a good photo reference, to capture the horse's unique personality. Like people, no two horses look exactly alike.

I hope you have enjoyed this book, and that you've found the ideas, tips, and methods that I use helpful as you practice and develop your own style and way of drawing horses. Have fun!

—Ruth Sanderson

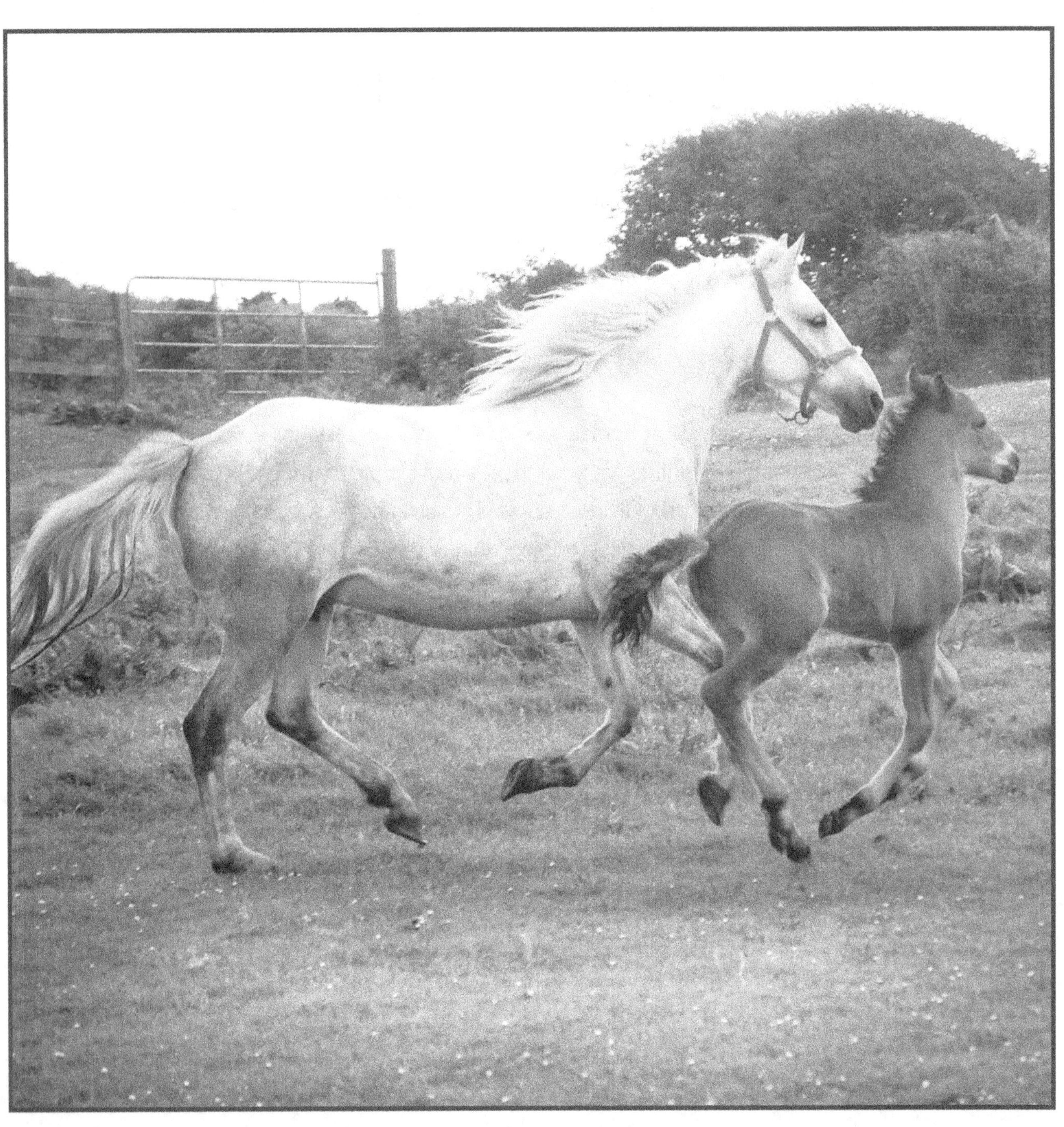

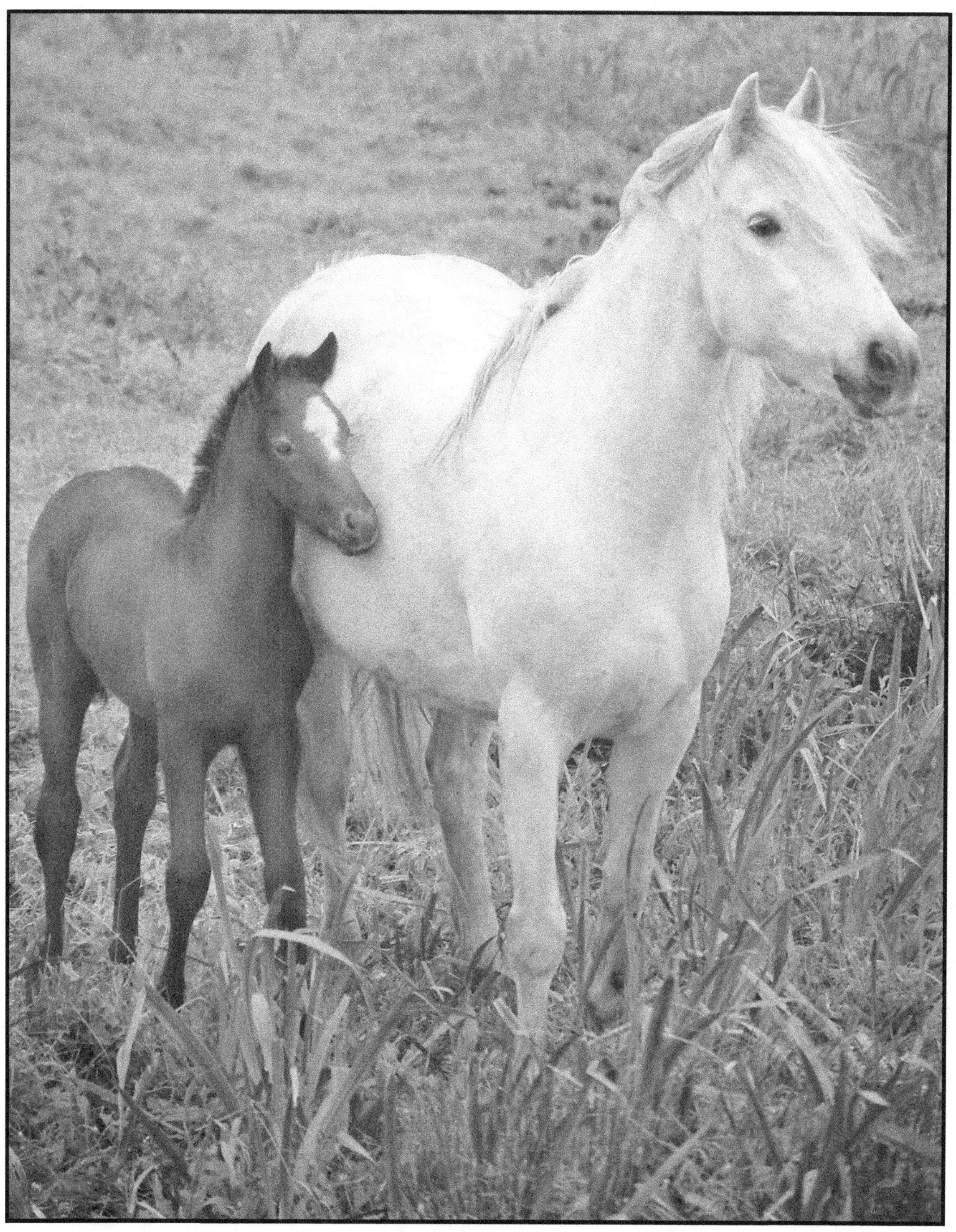

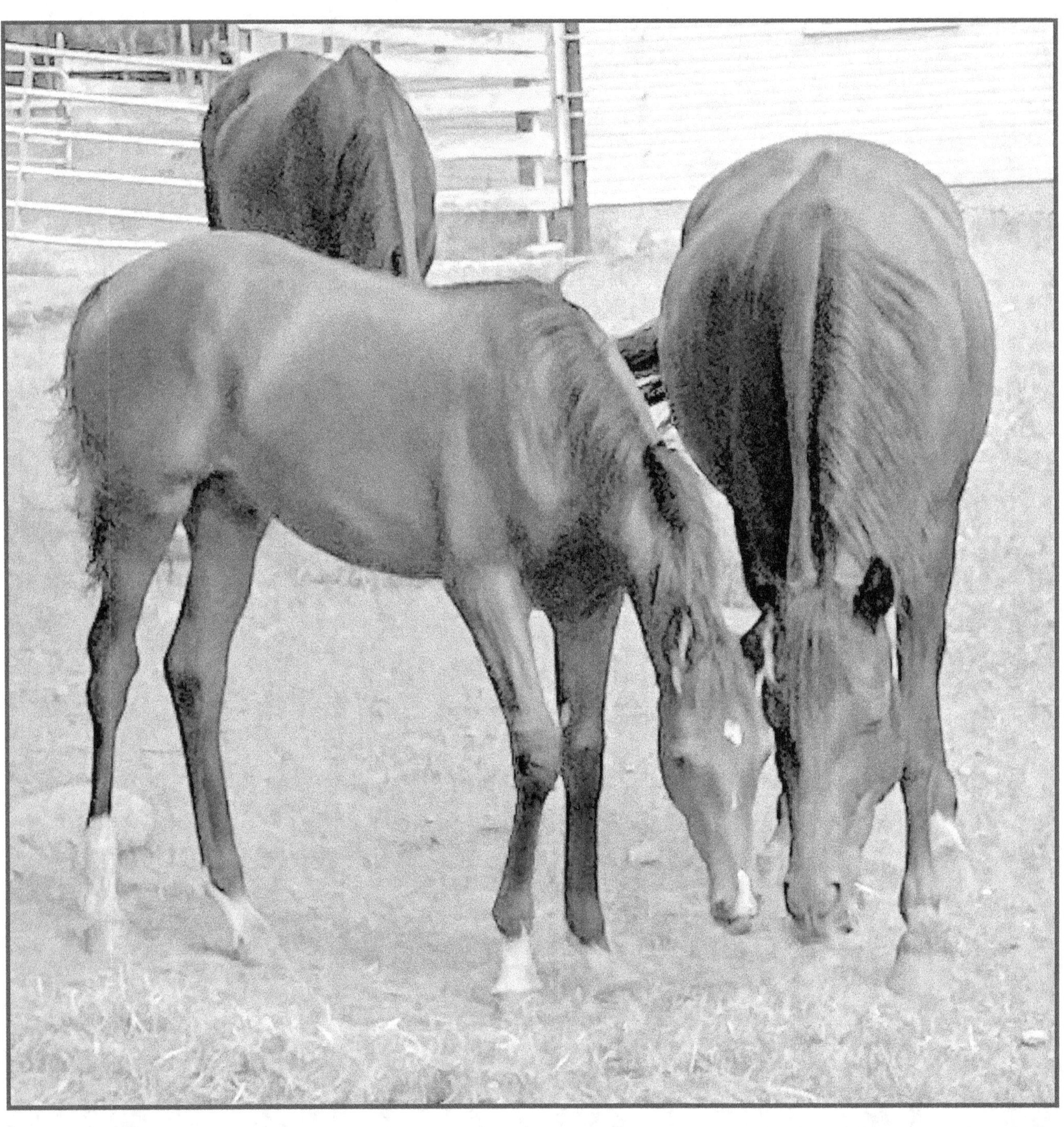

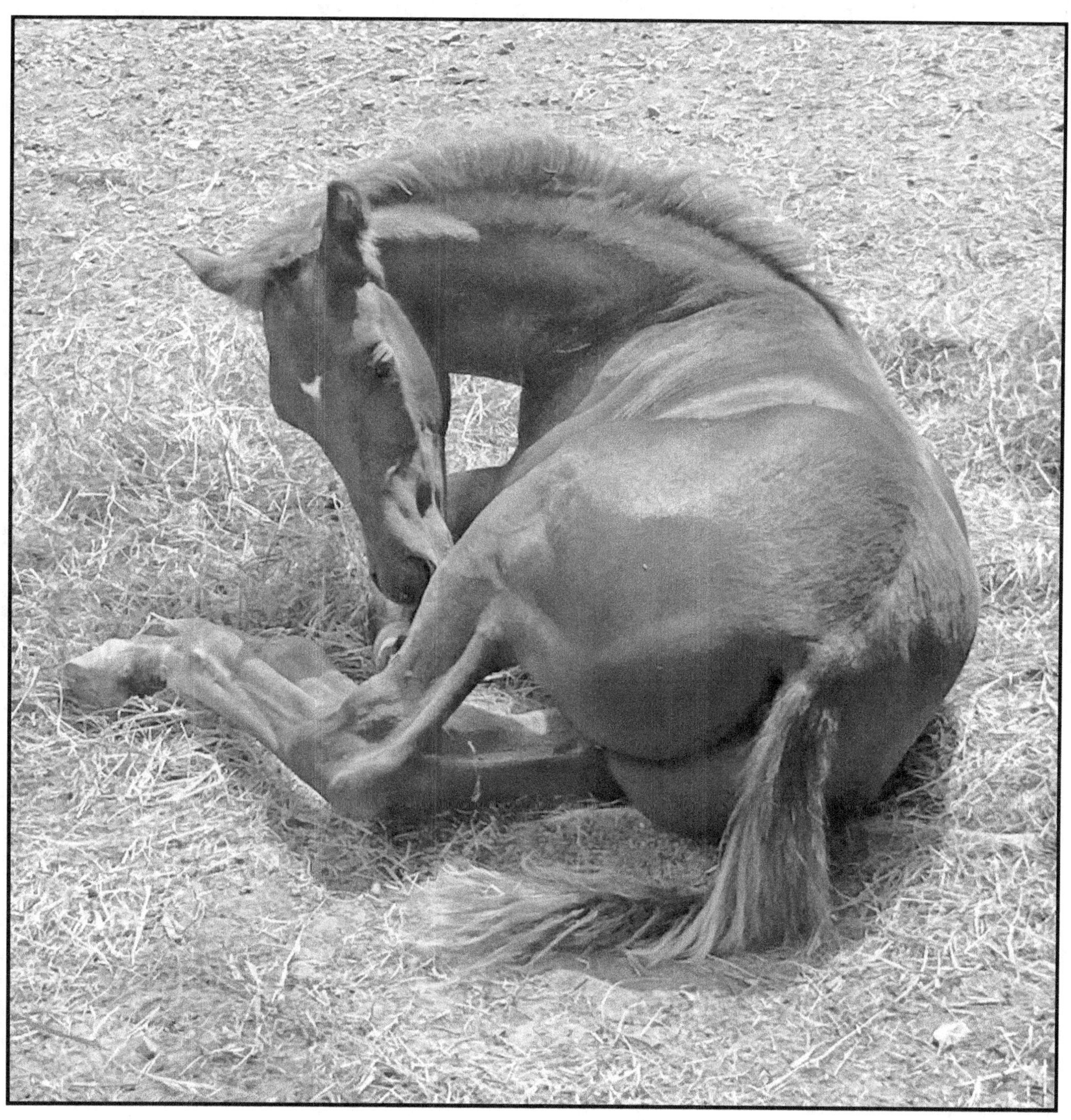

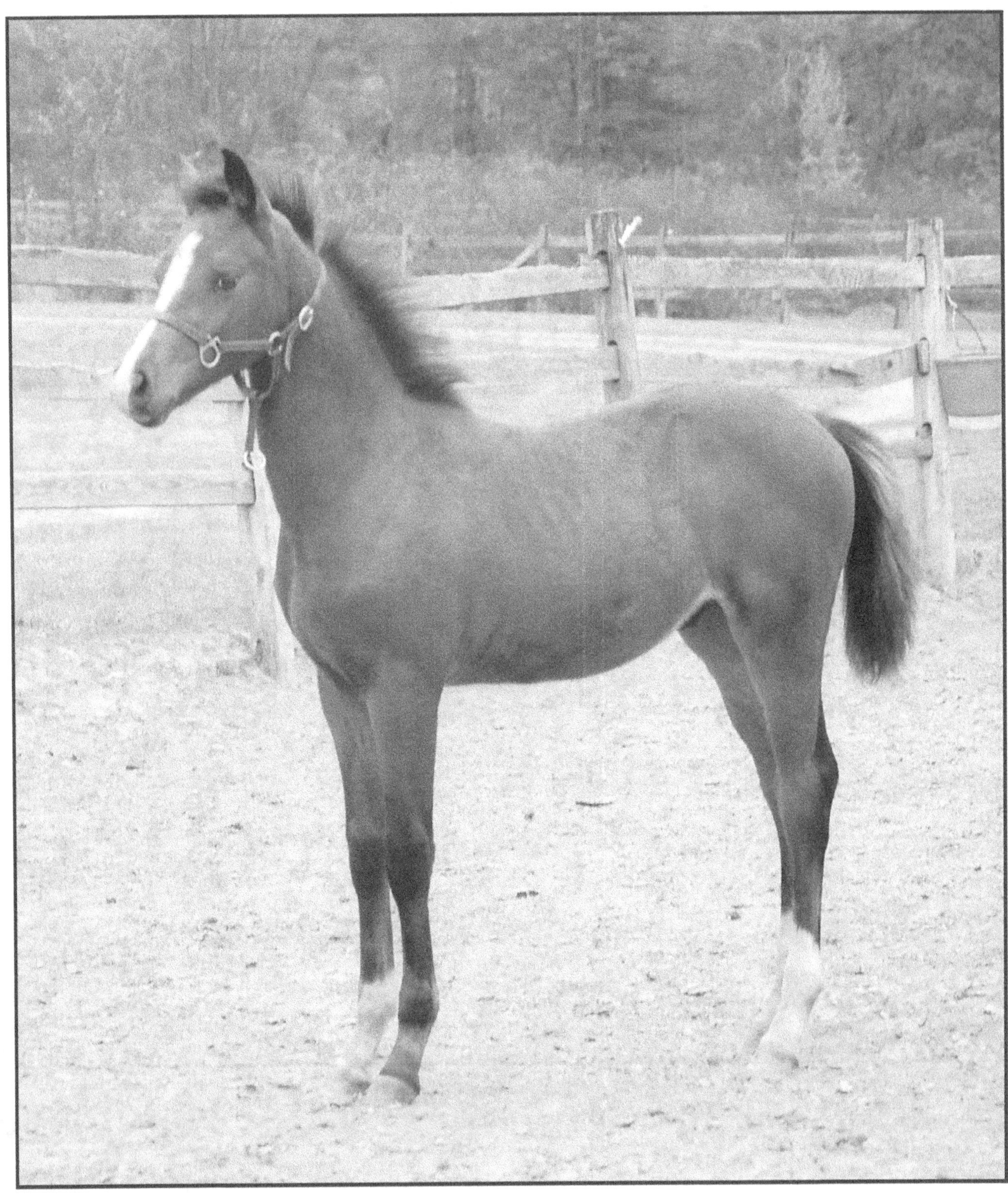

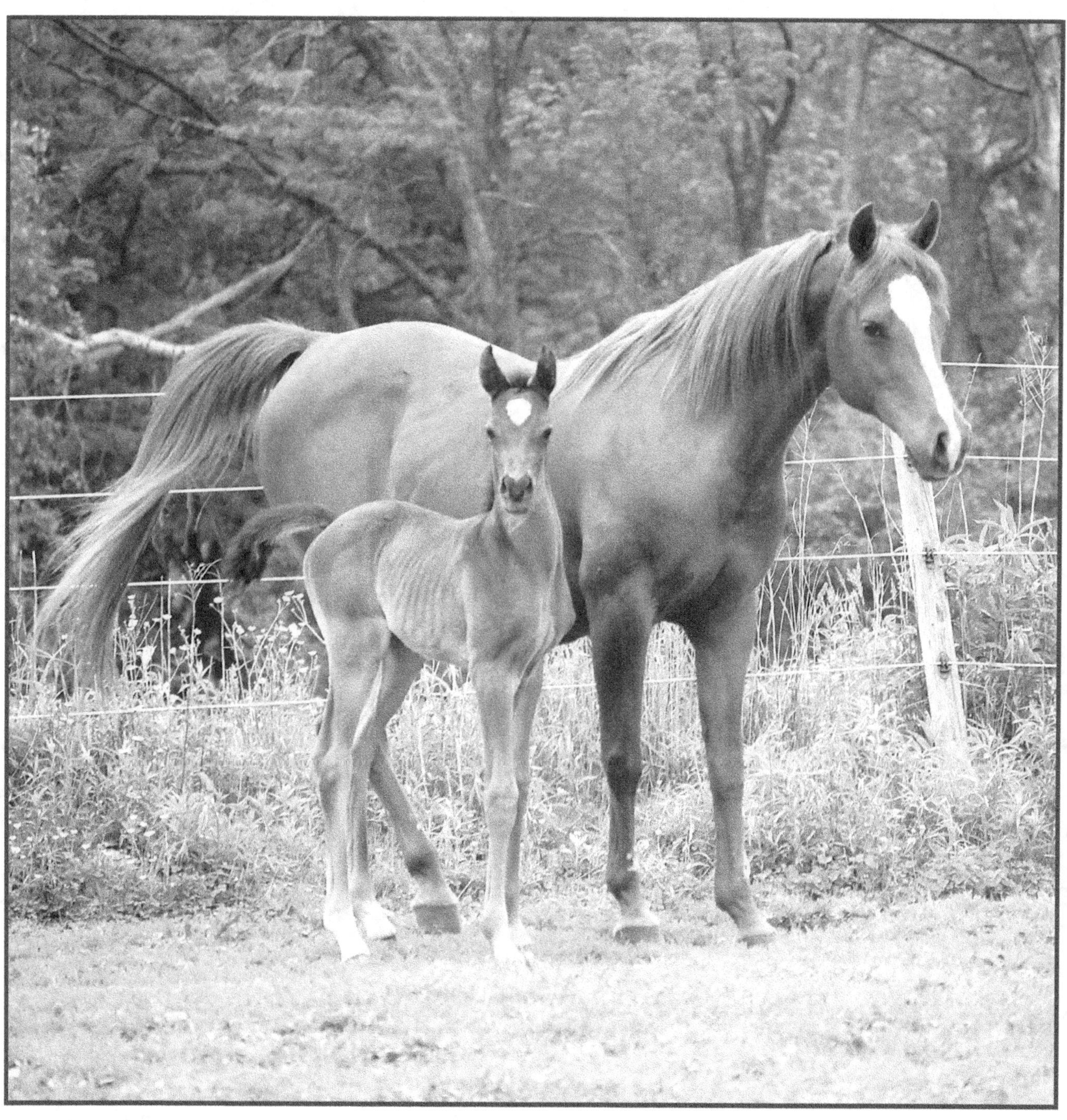

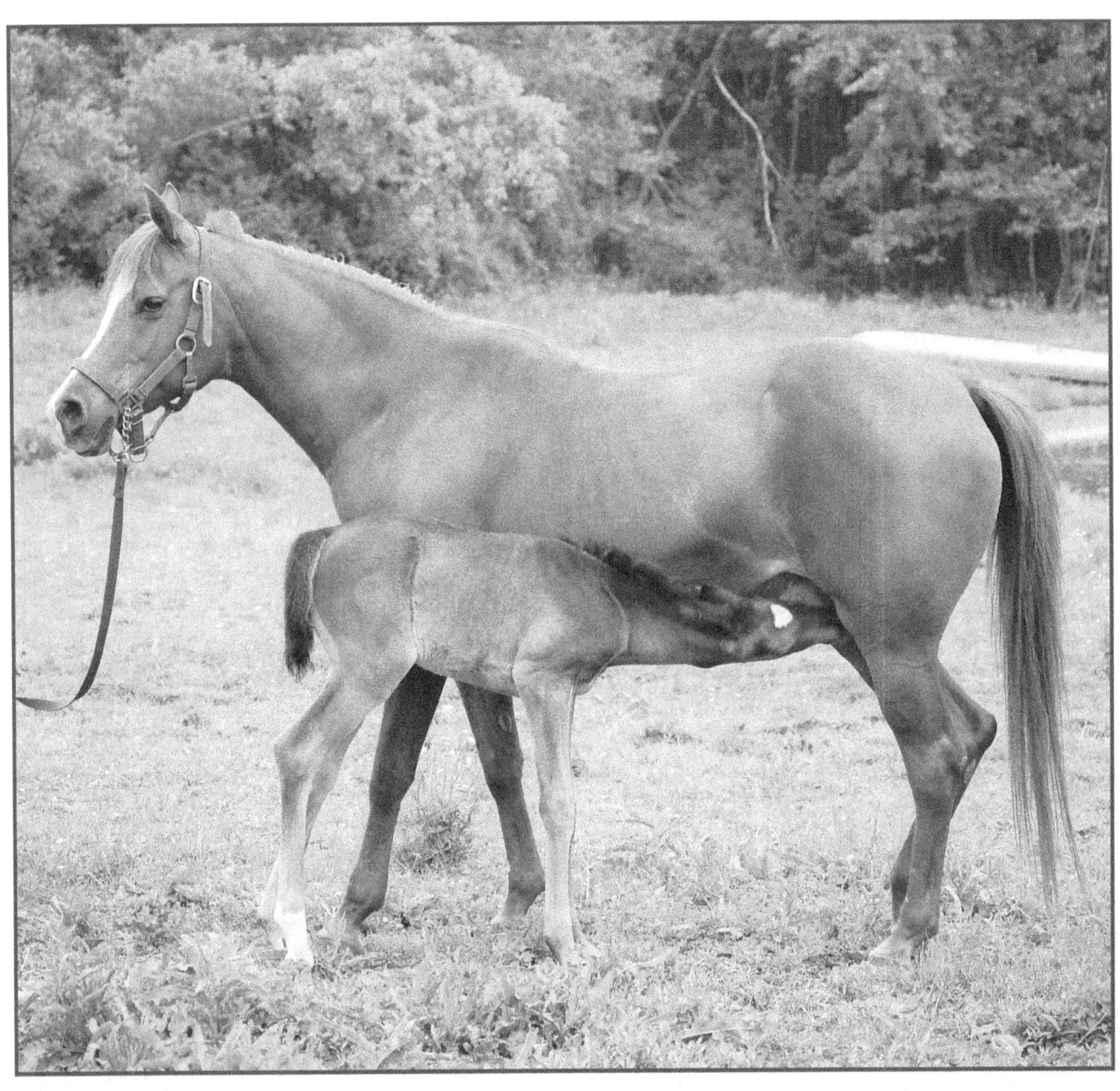

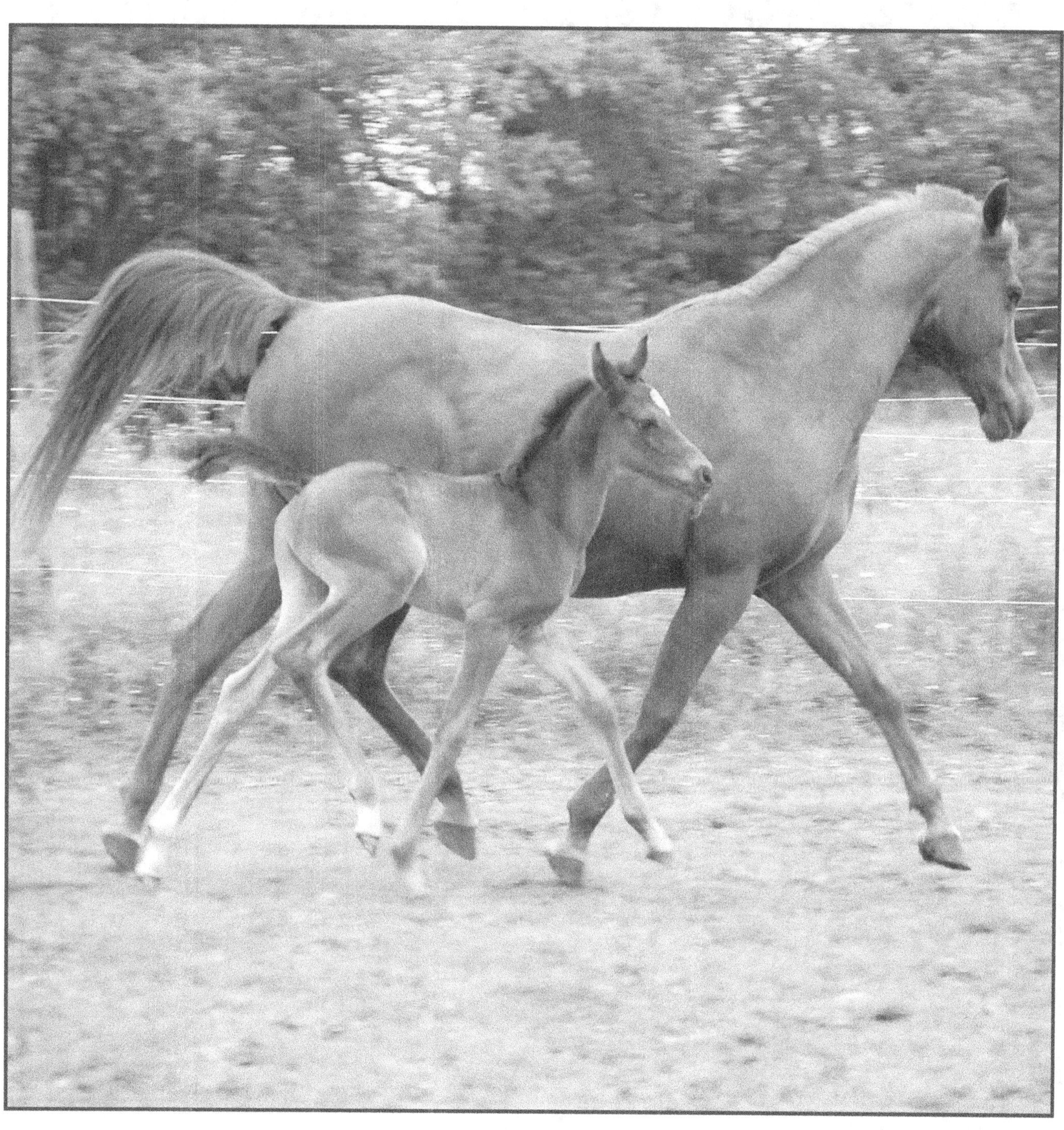

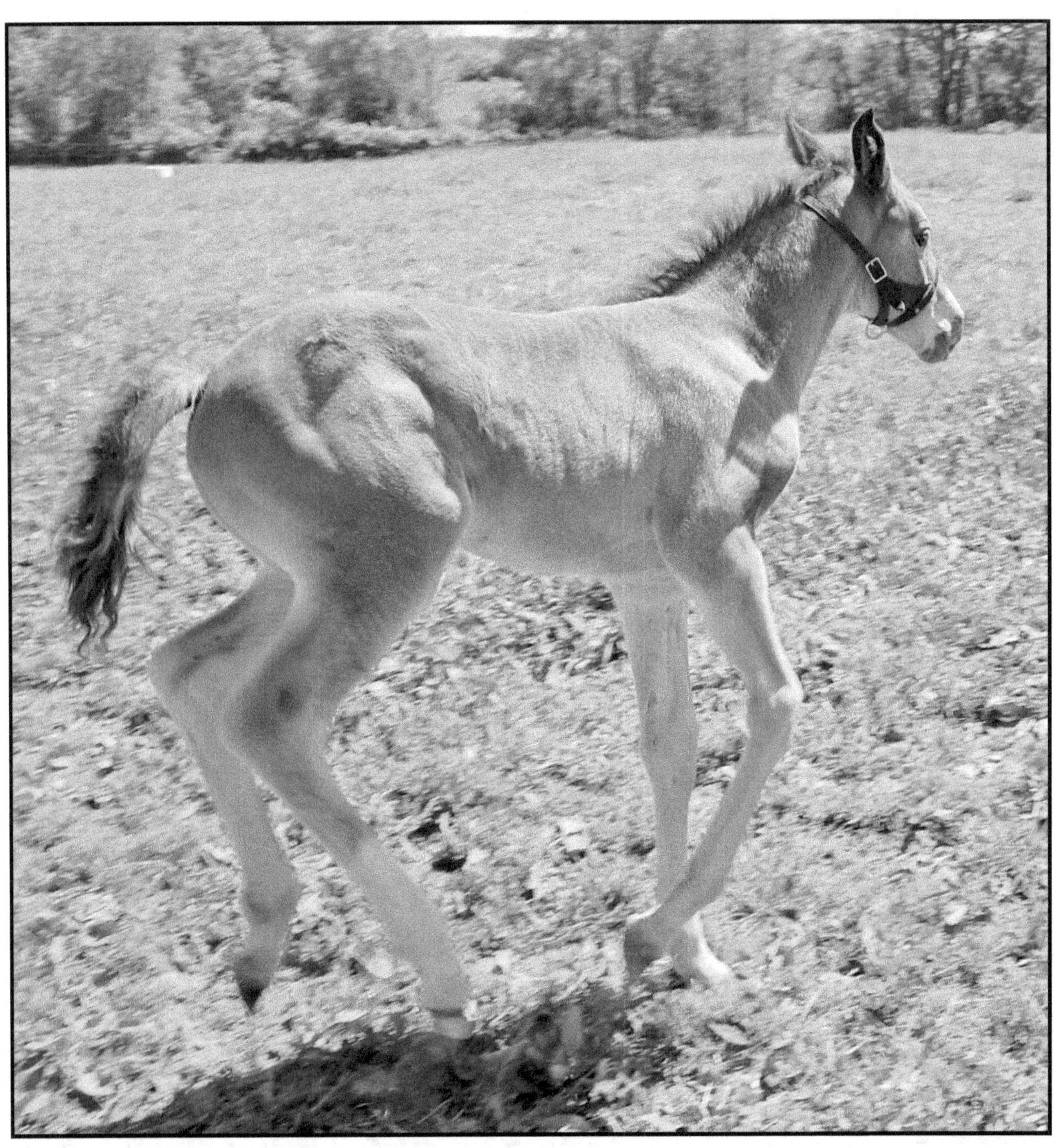

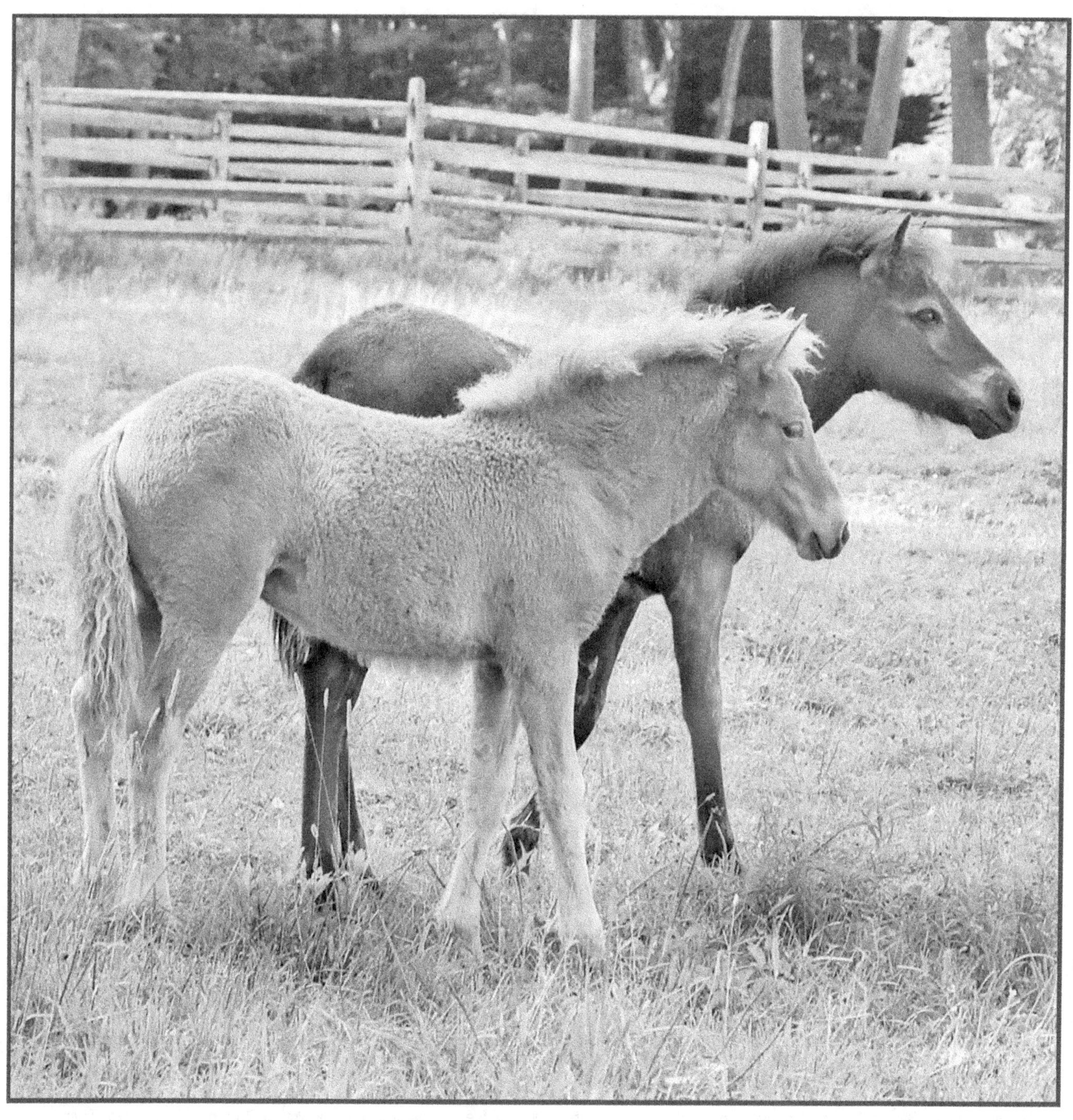

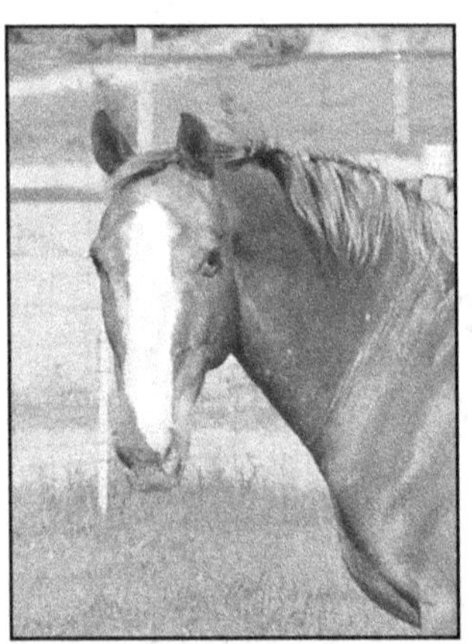 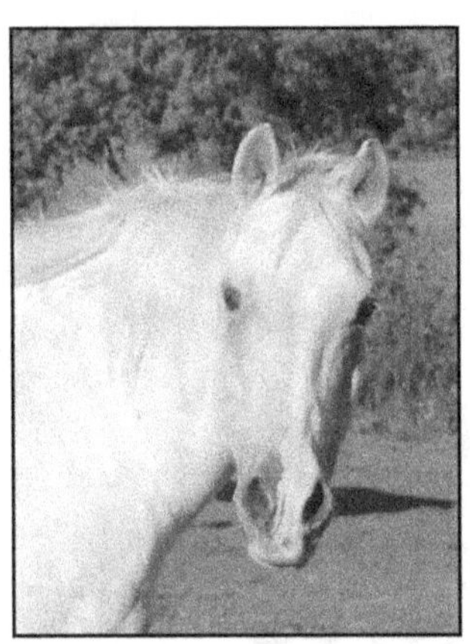

This book is dedicated to the memory of our horses, Thor and Shadow

ABOUT THE ARTIST

The Black Stallion series books by Walter Farley were among Ruth Sanderson's favorite stories growing up. She loved drawing horses and fairytales, and she went to art school to become an illustrator. Early in her career Ruth was thrilled to be chosen to illustrate the first paperback covers of her beloved *Black Stallion* series. She has retold and illustrated many fairytales, including *The Golden Mare, The Firebird, and the Magic Ring*, and in recent years she illustrated the *Horse Diaries* series of chapter books for Random House, five of which were written by her daughter Whitney. The book *Golden Sun* is an Appaloosa story inspired by Whitney's horse Thor.

This book on drawing horses was inspired by Ruth's love of drawing horses, and her picture book *A Storm of Horses: The Biography of Artist Rosa Bonheur. A Storm of Horses* (ages 6-12) will be available to order in March 2022 from any local bookstore, Amazon, or from the publisher, Interlink Publishing: www.interlinkbooks.com.

To learn more about the artist, visit: www.ruthsanderson.com or goldenwoodstudio.com

email ruth @ruthsanderson.com with questions about usage.

www.ingramcontent.com/pod-product-compliance
Lightning Source LLC
Chambersburg PA
CBHW080459030726
47592CB00011B/3177